OFF THE BEATEN

Alaba

FOURTH EDITION

Off the Beaten Path®

by Gay N. Martin

The Globe Pequot Press

Guilford, Connecticut

This one's for my mother,
Edith Sorrells Newsom, who's a great traveler
and who accompanied me on many of the excursions
described in this book

Cover and text design by Laura Augustine
Cover photo by Index Stock
Maps created by Equator.Graphics © The Globe Pequot Press
Text illustrations by Carol Drong

Library of Congress Cataloging-in-Publication Data.

Martin, Gay N.
      Alabama : off the beaten path: / Gay N. Martin. —4th ed.
         p. cm. —(Off the beaten path series)
      Includes index.
      ISBN 0-7627-0530-2
      1. Alabama—Guidebooks. I. Title: Alabama off the beaten path. II. Title. III. Series.
F324.3 .M37   1999
917.6104'63—dc21   99-043940
                                    CIP

Manufactured in the United States of America
Fourth Edition/First Printing

Contents

Introduction v

Northeast Alabama 1

Northwest Alabama 37

Central Alabama 67

Southeast Alabama 103

Southwest Alabama 135

Index.. 173

Introduction

Mention Alabama and associations ranging from cotton fields and kudzu to civilrights and manned space flights begin to surface. America's space program started here with the development of rockets that took men to the moon, and research continues as scientists work on the challenges of Spacelab and interplanetary travel projects that will shape the world's future. The Patriot missiles' performance and the feats of helicopters based at Fort Rucker focused attention on the vital role played by the state during the Persian Gulf War. "Alabama's gone from cotton fields to high tech," says a Huntsville spokesman.

Some consider Alabama almost synonymous with sports and recite exploits of Bear Bryant, Joe Namath, Bo Jackson, Pat Sullivan, John Hannah, Hank Aaron, Joe Louis, Willie Mays, Jesse Owens, LeRoy "Satchel" Paige, Bobby Allison—and the list goes on. Although racing fans throng Talladega's speedway and Birmingham's Alabama Sports Hall of Fame speaks of diversity, visitors soon discover that football reigns supreme here. The first Alabama-Auburn clash dates to February 22, 1893, and loyalty lines continue to divide families, friends, and lovers. The stirring words "Roll Tide" and "War Eagle" enter the typical childhood vocabulary early on.

Unless you agree with Mark Twain that golf is a good walk ruined, you can't pass up the Robert Trent Jones Golf Trail, which will test the skills of all golfers from scratch handicappers to hopeless duffers. Beginning in the mountains and lakes of the Appalachian foothills and continuing southward to the white sands and wetlands of the Gulf Coast, this group of seven PGA tour-quality courses, ranging from thirty-six and fifty-four holes each, provides superb golfing and splendid scenery. From Huntsville's Hampton Cove, Gadsden's Silver Lakes, Birmingham's Oxmoor Valley, and Prattville's Capitol Hill (the newest addition) to Grand National in the Auburn-Opelika area, Highland Oaks at Dothan, Cambrian Ridge at Greenville, and Magnolia Cove near Mobile, travelers can enjoy the exclusive country club experience at affordable prices. To play any or all of these public courses designed by world-famous golf architect Robert Trent Jones, call (800) 949–4444. With one phone call, you can make arrangements for tee times at any of the trail's sites plus lodging reservations in a nearby city.

Other links with the state wax musical. Stars still fall on Alabama, and visitors can dip into a rich musical heritage throughout the state. Depending on your own particular penchant, you may catch a classical music concert at the Birmingham Civic Center or a swinging jazz session during Florence's yearly tribute to the "Father of the Blues," W. C. Handy. The Alabama Music Hall of Fame, near Tuscumbia, features memorabilia of Nat King Cole, Hank Williams, Sonny James, Lionel Richie, the Commodores, Emmylou Harris, Dinah Washington, the Temptations, and many other musicians with Alabama connections.

As a vacation destination, however, Alabama often falls in the proverbial best-kept-secret category. Take a varied and splendid geography, add a moderate climate plus a big serving of Southern hospitality, and you have Alabama, an ideal year-round getaway. From craggy Appalachian bluffs to sugar-sand beaches on the Gulf of Mexico, Alabama's wealth of natural beauty offers a happy (and often uncrowded) vacation choice for everyone.

This book spotlights some of the state's special places—not only major sites such as the United States Space & Rocket Center in Huntsville but also small towns frozen in time and tucked-away treasures occasionally overlooked by the natives. In the state's northern section, Huntsville makes a handy launching pad from which travelers can easily loop both east and west to take in north Alabama's unique attractions. Heading south, the Birmingham area serves as a convenient base from which to branch out into the state's central section. From there one can sweep farther south to Montgomery to see the state capital area and southeastern section, which includes the historic Chattahoochee Trace. This account concludes with the beaches of Gulf Shores and one of the state's most beautiful cities, Mobile. In his book *A Walk Across America,* Peter Jenkins describes being captivated by Mobile, calling it a fantasy city. "Even more than by the psychedelic azaleas," he said, "I was moved by the great-grandfather live-oak trees."

Alabama's surprises start as soon as you cross the border, and the following sneak preview will give you an idea of what to expect. Huntsville, while playing a strategic role in the nation's space program, also preserves its past at EarlyWorks and also Alabama Constitution Village, a living-history museum. Delegates drafted Alabama's first constitution here in 1819, and when you open the gate and walk through the picket fence, you may smell bread baking and see aproned guides dipping beeswax candles or carding cotton—quite a contrast to the future-focused Space & Rocket Center. By the way, if you've harbored a secret yen to taste the astronaut's life but always thought Space Camp was just for kids, you're in for another surprise: The Space & Rocket Center offers programs for all who dare to delve into space technology, from fourth graders to grandparents. You might even participate in a simulated space shuttle mission. If you're not ready for such a challenge, you can still stop by the gift shop and sample some freeze-dried astronaut ice cream.

Heading east gets you to Scottsboro, home of the "First Monday" market, one of the South's oldest and largest "trade days." Also known for its many caves, this area attracts spelunkers from around the world. Russell Cave, located at Jackson County's northeastern tip, could be called Alabama's first welcome center. Some 9,000 years ago bands of Native Americans began occupying the large cave; archaeologists, using carbon dating, have determined it to be the oldest known site of human occupancy in the southeastern United States.

At DeSoto State Park, also in the northeast region, visitors can view Little River Canyon National Preserve, the largest and one of the deepest gorges east of the Mississippi River. Near the charming mountain hamlet of Mentone, Cloudmont Resort features a dude ranch and ski slopes (albeit with Mother Nature getting some assistance from snow machines).

Lakes Guntersville, Wheeler, and Wilson make northern Alabama a haven for water sports enthusiasts. Lake Guntersville State Park hosts Eagle Awareness weekends in January, a good time of the year to spot bald eagles. Many visitors report being surprised by Alabama's state parks, which offer a sampling of some of the state's most spectacular vistas plus a host of recreation options—and at bargain prices.

Speaking of bargains, don't forget your shopping list and credit cards, because you'll get plenty of chances to use them in nearby Boaz, where you can hop aboard a tram and ride from mall to mall. Ranked among America's top outlet centers, the success story of this once-sleepy little town has been reported in publications across the country.

At Cullman, visitors can take a Lilliputian world tour at Ave Maria Grotto, a unique garden filled with more than 125 miniature reproductions of famous buildings. The reproductions were made by a gifted Benedictine monk named Brother Joseph Zoettl.

Another surprise for many visitors is learning that all Alabamians did not back the South during the Civil War. In Winston County an outdoor drama called *The Incident at Looney's Tavern* tells the story of hill-country people who struggled to remain independent during the conflict. In front of the county courthouse at Double Springs stands *Dual Destiny*, the statue of a soldier backed by billowing Confederate and Union flags.

In Blount County you can see three of the state's covered bridges. Master-and-slave team John Godwin and Horace King built a number of Alabama's early bridges. After gaining his freedom, King joined Godwin as a business partner, later erecting a monument in "lasting remembrance of the love and gratitude he felt for his lost friend and former master." The monument can be seen at a Phenix City cemetery.

Each summer visitors can witness the reenactment of a miracle in northwest Alabama at Ivy Green, home of America's courageous Helen Keller.

As Alabama's major metropolis, Birmingham's paths are well trampled. Still, the Magic City offers some not-to-be-missed treats, such as the historic Five Points South area with its boutiques and outdoor eateries. On the somber side, the Birmingham Civil Rights Institute and nearby complex re-creates a journey through the darkness of segregation.

Farther south you'll find Montgomery, a backdrop for sweeping drama since Jefferson Davis telegraphed his "Fire on Fort Sumter" order from here and the Civil War proceeded to rip the country apart. Less than a century later, the Civil Rights Movement gained momentum in this town, paving the way for overdue national reform. Also located here, the Alabama Shakespeare Festival provides top dramatic entertainment.

Don't miss Selma, a quintessential Southern city, but one that preserves its drama-filled past—from Civil War to civil rights. Spring Pilgrimage events include home tours, a reenactment of the Battle of Selma, and a grand ball on Sturdivant Hall's lovely lawn. Selma also stages an annual Tale Tellin' Festival featuring Alabama's first lady of folk legends and ghost stories, Kathryn Tucker Windham (whose intriguing tales you may have heard on National Public Radio broadcasts).

Traveling down to Monroeville, you'll see the courthouse and surrounding square where Truman Capote and Harper Lee, author of *To Kill a Mockingbird,* roamed as childhood friends.

Still farther south, the Gulf Shores and Orange Beach area, with glistening white beaches, sea oats, and sand dunes, lures many visitors. The coastal area also offers historic forts, grand mansions, a multirooted (French, British, and Spanish) heritage, and superb cuisine.

On Mobile Bay's eastern shore, a strange spectacle known as "Jubilee" sometimes surprises visitors. Spurred by unknown forces, shrimp, flounder, crab, and other marine creatures suddenly crowd the shoreline, usually several times a summer. When the cry of "Jubilee!" rings along the beach, people rush to the water's edge to fill containers with fresh seafood.

Alabama's colorful celebrations run the gamut from Mobile's Mardi Gras (which preceded New Orleans's extravaganza), Gulf Shores's National Shrimp Festival, and the Blessing of the Shrimp Fleet at Bayou

LaBatre (home of Forrest Gump's successful shrimping business) to Opp's Rattlesnake Rodeo, Dothan's National Peanut Festival, and Decatur's hot-air balloon gala called the Alabama Jubilee.

When making travel plans, call ahead because dates, rates, and hours of operation change from time to time. Unless otherwise stated, all museums and attractions with admission prices of $5.00 or less per adult will be labeled modest. A restaurant meal (entree without beverage) classified as economical costs less than $8.00; moderate prices range between $8.00 and $19.00; and entrees $20.00 and above are designated expensive. As for accommodations, those that cost less than $75 per day will be described as standard; an overnight price between $75 and $150 is called moderate; and lodging costing more than $150 is designated deluxe.

For travel information, maps, and brochures, stop by one of the eight Alabama Welcome Centers; call (800) ALABAMA; write to Alabama Tourism and Travel, P.O. Box 4927, Montgomery 36103–4927 or visit the Web site at www.touralabama.org. To preview the state parks, log onto www.vten.com. You can make reservations at any Alabama State Park by dialing (800) ALA–PARK. So pack your bags, head for the unforgettable Heart of Dixie, anticipate some surprises, and watch out for falling stars.

Fast Facts about Alabama

Climate Overview

Alabama's climate falls in the temperate range, becoming mostly subtropical near the Gulf Coast. Spring's first flowers appear early, often in February. By April, average statewide temperatures reach the 60s. Summer days often fall in the hot and humid category. Fall brings changing foliage and refreshing cooler weather. Snow is such a rarity in most parts of the state that when the weather person predicts it, everyone gets excited and makes a mad dash to the grocery stores for bread and milk.

Famous Alabamians

Some famous Alabamians include: Helen Keller, Harper Lee, Winston Groom, Fannie Flagg, the country music group Alabama, Hank Williams Sr. and Jr., Rosa Parks, Kenny Stabler, Hank Aaron, Willie Mays, and Tallulah Bankhead.

Newspapers

The state's major newspapers include: *The Huntsville Times, Birmingham News, The Montgomery Advertiser,* and the *Mobile Press Register.* Since printed papers started in the state around 1806, said Bill Keller, executive director of the Alabama Press Association, Alabamians have demonstrated a long-standing appreciation for newspapers. Every county in Alabama produces a newspaper. Current records show twenty-five daily newspapers, printing from five to seven days a week, and ninety-seven weekly papers, publishing from one to three times a week.

General Alabama Trivia

- In 1540 Hernando de Soto traveled through much of what is now Alabama.

- On December 14, 1819, Alabama became the twenty-second state in the Union.

- Alabama seceded from the Union on January 11, 1861, and rejoined on June 25, 1868.

- Montgomery has been home to the state capitol since 1846. Former capitals included St. Stephens, Huntsville, Cahaba, and Tuscaloosa.

- In 1959 the camellia became Alabama's state flower, replacing the goldenrod, which held that honor from 1927.

- The tarpon was designated as Alabama's official saltwater fish in 1955.

- Red iron ore, scientifically known as hematite, is the state mineral.

- Distinguished educator and humanitarian Julia Tutwiler wrote the words for "Alabama," the state song.

- Alabama is comprised of sixty-seven counties.

The prices and rates listed in this guidebook were confirmed at press time. We recommend, however, that you call establishments before traveling to obtain current information.

Maps provided are for reference only and should be used in conjunction with a road map. Distances suggested are approximate.

Space Capital

Traveling through this area of Alabama, with its wooded glens, rugged mountain vistas, and sparkling lakes, is almost like moving through a calendar of splendid landscapes. Keep your camera handy because you'll discover some spectacular vistas.

Entering at the state's northern border, you'll drive through the rolling Tennessee Valley to reach Huntsville, a handy hub whether you're heading east or west to explore north Alabama's numerous attractions.

The birthplace of America's space program, Huntsville also served as an early capital of Alabama and later grew into a cotton mill town. After Dr. Wernher von Braun and his crew of German scientists arrived in the 1950s to pioneer the space program at Redstone Arsenal, Huntsville traded its title as World Watercress Capital for World Space Capital. The decade from 1950 to 1960 saw the population in Rocket City, U.S.A., mushroom from 15,000 to 72,000. Even today, ongoing road construction cannot keep pace with the burgeoning population and traffic.

If you arrive hungry, head for the *Green Bottle Grill* (256–882–0459), located in Westbury Square at 975 Airport Road Southwest. "Here, we call dinner 'supper,'" says Anne Pollard, who, with Rick Paler, established the eatery several years ago. The interior reflects a typical neighborhood French bistro, its subdued color scheme a pleasing backdrop for a collection of photos that Rick made while living in Paris.

As the name suggests, the Green Bottle boasts an extensive wine list. The bread pudding with Tennessee whiskey sauce makes a fitting finale. Moderate prices. Except for major holidays, the Green Bottle opens for lunch Tuesday through Friday from 11:00 A.M. to 2:00 P.M. and supper Monday through Saturday from 6:00 to 10:00 P.M.

A good place to start a local tour is the *Huntsville Depot Transportation Museum* (256–535–6565 or 800–678–1918) at 320 Church Street.

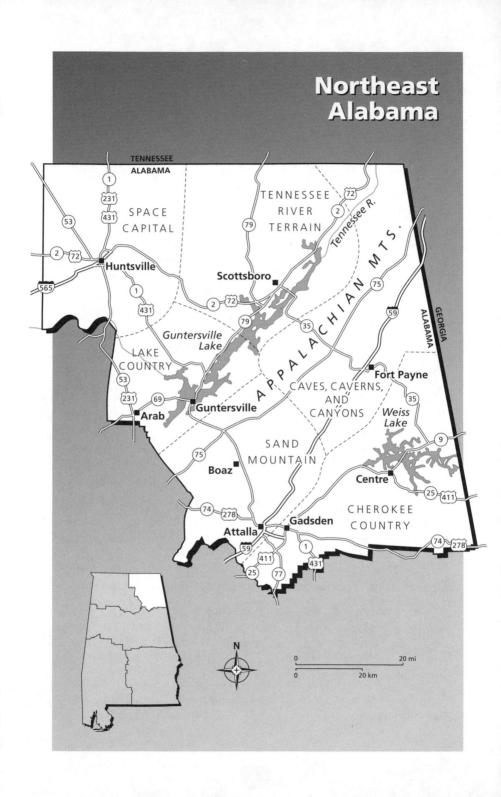

Northeast Alabama

TENNESSEE
ALABAMA

SPACE CAPITAL

TENNESSEE RIVER TERRAIN

Huntsville

Scottsboro

Tennessee R.

A P P A L A C H I A N   M T S.

GEORGIA
ALABAMA

Guntersville Lake

LAKE COUNTRY

Fort Payne

CAVES, CAVERNS, AND CANYONS

Weiss Lake

Arab

Guntersville

SAND MOUNTAIN

Boaz

Centre

CHEROKEE COUNTRY

Attalla   Gadsden

N

0   20 mi
0   20 km

NORTHEAST ALABAMA

GAY'S TOP PICKS IN NORTHEAST ALABAMA

Alabama Constitution Village, Huntsville

Buck's Pocket State Park, Grove Oak

Burritt Museum and Park, Huntsville

DeSoto State Park, Fort Payne

Lake Guntersville State Park, Guntersville

Little River Canyon National Preserve, Fort Payne

Noccalula Falls and Park, Gadsden

Sequoyah Caverns, Valley Head

Town of Mentone

U.S. Space & Rocket Center, Huntsville

Here you can leave your car and hop aboard a reproduction of a 1920 trolley to see the historic downtown area. But first take time to tour the authentically restored depot, a big yellow building where a robotic telegrapher, stationmaster, and engineer welcome visitors and describe railroad life in 1912. During the Civil War the depot served as a prison, and upstairs you'll see some interesting graffiti such as a rather unflattering drawing of Union officer Major Strout and an inscription that reads HAPPY NEW YEARS TO ALL IN THE YEAR OF OUR LORD 1864. The depot's hours are 9:00 A.M. to 5:00 P.M. Monday through Saturday. The museum closes on Sunday and holidays. Admission is charged.

Also on the depot grounds, you'll find locomotives to climb aboard and places to browse, such as the Train and Trolley Shop with railroad memorabilia. The Huntsville Depot Trolley makes half-hour trips through the downtown area all day, stopping at several points along the route, and you can leave the trolley at any attraction to reboard later. The trolley operates Monday through Saturday from 9:00 A.M. to 12:30 P.M. and again from 1:00 to 4:30 P.M. Admission.

The trolley ride takes you past the **Von Braun Civic Center,** a large multipurpose complex, which may well be hosting a concert, sporting event, or play you'd like to take in while in town.

You can also pick up maps and brochures on nearby attractions at the Tourist Information Center located here. Hours are 9:00 A.M. to 5:00 P.M. Monday through Saturday.

Alabama Trivia

With 378 holes, Alabama's Robert Trent Jones Golf Trail is the world's largest golf course construction project.

Your trolley ride continues through Huntsville's *Historic Twickenham District* with more than sixty-five antebellum houses and churches. The conductor's narrative provides some interesting background on various structures along the way. Architectural styles represented include Federal, Greek Revival, Italianate, Palladian, Gothic Revival, and others. For a fine example of Federal architecture, tour the **Weeden House Museum** (256–536–7718) at 300 Gates Avenue. Built in 1819, the home contains period antiques and features the work of Huntsville artist and poet Maria Howard Weeden, who lived here until her death in 1905. Her impressive body of work includes book illustrations, whimsical drawings, fascinating character studies, and portraits. Except for January and February when the museum closes, hours run 1:00 to 4:00 P.M. Tuesday through Sunday. Modest admission.

On the square in downtown Huntsville, stop by **Harrison Brothers Hardware Store** (256–536–3631), located at 124 South Side Square. The store celebrated one hundred years on the Square in 1997. Here you can purchase marbles by the scoop, old-fashioned stick candy, cast-iron cookware, kerosene lamps, seeds, scrub boards, and other merchandise that speaks of yesteryear. Historic Huntsville Foundation volunteers ring up sales on a 1907 cash register. The interior, with pot-bellied stove, ceiling fans, rolling ladders, barrels, tools, and antique safe, looks much as it did in 1879 when the store opened for business. Hours are 9:00 A.M. to 5:00 P.M. weekdays and 10:00 A.M. to 4:00 P.M. Saturday.

Don't miss **Alabama Constitution Village** (256–535–6565 or 800–678–1918) just around the corner. Entering the picket-fence gate at Franklin Street and Gates Avenue takes you back to 1819, when delegates met here to draft Alabama's first constitution. While browsing through Constitution Hall, take a few minutes to watch cabinetmaker Christopher Lang make Windsor chairs and other furniture using nineteenth-century tools and techniques. Afterward, on a tour of the complex, you'll see costumed guides going about their seasonal business of preserving summer's fruits or making candles at hog-killing time.

Don't miss the gift shop, with such unique items as "ugly jugs" once used as containers for harmful substances. Hours are 9:00 A.M. to 5:00 P.M. Monday through Saturday. The village is closed on Sunday and holidays. Admission.

Kids—both young and old—love traveling back in time to the nineteenth century and exploring *Early Works,* a hands-on history museum (256–564–8100 or 800–678–1819) at 404 Madison Street, where new adventures await around every corner. Special exhibits include an amazing 16-foot-tall tale-telling tree, giant-size musical instruments, and a 46-foot keelboat. Youngsters can dress up in vintage clothing and practice tasks that children in the "olden days" performed. Except for major holidays, hours run from 9:00 A.M. to 5:00 P.M. Monday through Saturday. Admission. Special prices are available for combination tours of EarlyWorks with Historic Huntsville Depot and Alabama Constitution Village. Parking is available throughout the downtown area with

Gay's Favorite Annual Events in Northeast Alabama

Art on the Lake, *Guntersville, April;*
(256) 582–3612 or (800) 869–5253

Big Spring Jam Music Festival,
Big Spring International Park,
Huntsville, last full weekend of
September; (256) 551–2359

Christmas on the Rocks, *Noccalula Falls,*
Gadsden, the day after Thanksgiving
through December; (256) 543–3472

Depot Days Festival, *Hartselle,*
September; (256) 773–4370

Eagle Awareness Program,
Lake Guntersville State Park, January;
(256) 571–5440 or (800) 582–6282

Falls Fest, *Noccalula Falls, Gadsden,*
October; (256) 543–3472

Freedom Festival, *Albertville, July Fourth*
weekend; (256) 878 3821

Galaxy of Lights, *Huntsville/Madison*
County Botanical Garden,

Thanksgiving through New Year's Eve;
(256) 830–4447

Harvest Festival, *Boaz, early October;*
(256) 593–8154

Heritage Festival, *Attalla, October;*
(256) 543–3472

Mentone Fall Colorfest, *Mentone,*
October; (256) 845–7225

Panoply, Huntsville's Festival of the
Arts, *Big Spring International Park,*
Huntsville, last full weekend of April;
(256) 519–2787

Riverfest, *Gadsden, May; (256) 543–3472*

St. Williams Seafood Festival,
Guntersville, early September (Labor
Day weekend); (256) 586–9837 or
(256) 582–3612

Stevenson Depot Days, *Stevenson,*
early June; (256) 437–3012 or
(800) 259–5508

handicapped parking on the Gates Avenue side. Learn more about this hands-on facility on the Internet at www.earlyworks.com.

A day of sightseeing requires a hearty breakfast, and you'll find one at **Eunice's Country Kitchen** (256–534–9550), located at 1006 Andrew Jackson Way Northwest. Former governor Fob James declared Eunice's biscuits "the best in Alabama." And humorist, author, and syndicated columnist, the late Lewis Grizzard claimed Eunice serves "the best country ham and homemade biscuits on earth." To reach the restaurant, follow Governor's Drive east until you see California Street. Turn left and stay on California Street, even when it curves, for 1.9 miles. You'll see the restaurant on your right, across the street from Jackson Way Baptist Church. Although Eunice Merrell (better known to her customers as Aunt Eunice) describes her eatery as "just a little greasy spoon," the fame of her homemade biscuits made the *Congressional Record* in a tribute introduced by U.S. Senator Howell Heflin.

You may have to wait a bit for a table or even share one with someone else at this small cafe that does a booming business without advertising.

The menu, posted on the wall, features breakfast fare—ham, bacon, or sausage with biscuits, eggs, and gravy at economical rates. Don't be surprised if another customer refills your coffee mug—it's customary here when pouring yourself a refill to warm up your neighbors' coffee, too. Some people even keep their own favorite brand of preserves or jelly in Eunice's refrigerator, retrieving it when the hot biscuits arrive, but most folks dip into the honey or Sand Mountain sorghum on the tables.

A wooden sign swings over one table, identifying it as the "Liars' Table." During a meal, Eunice often presents customers with an official "Liar's License," permitting them to prevaricate "at any time or place without notice."

Eunice starts serving breakfast at 5:00 A.M. (presumably for early birds such as hunters, anglers, delivery people, and insomniacs) and closes at 11:50 A.M. The restaurant is open every day except Tuesday.

To reach **Monte Sano Mountain,** return to Governor's Drive, turn left on U.S. Highway 431, and continue until you see the Monte Sano sign, where you'll make another left turn. The mountaintop affords sweeping views of Huntsville and the surrounding Tennessee River Valley. **Burritt Museum and Park** (256–536–2882) at 3101 Burritt Drive, just off Monte Sano Boulevard, features 167 wooded acres with walking trails and picnicking facilities. At this living-history site, you'll find a blacksmith shop, smokehouse, church, and some log houses depicting rural life between 1850 and 1900. An X-shaped house, built in 1937 by Dr. William Henry Burritt, serves as the park's focal point. Both a physician and gifted inventor who held twenty patents during his life, Burritt combined Classical and art deco elements when he designed this unusual home.

Inside you'll see archaeological and restoration exhibits, clothing, toys, and displays on Huntsville's history. One room features the paintings of local artist Maria Howard Weeden. Special events include the Fall Sorghum and Harvest Festival and Candlelight Christmas. A modest admission is charged. The museum is open Tuesday through Saturday from 10:00 A.M. to 4:00 P.M. and Sunday noon to 4:00 P.M. March to mid-December. The grounds can be visited daily from 7:00 A.M. to 5:00 P.M. October through March and 7:00 A.M. to 7:00 P.M. April through September.

Dogwood Manor (256–859–3946) at 707 Chase Road makes a lovely base for exploring the Huntsville area. Valerie and Patrick Jones own this restored Federal-style home, set on a sweeping lawn with century-old trees. The home's builder once operated a thriving nursery here and shipped his plants all over the country. Patrick, an attorney, shares history about the home and the Chase community with interested guests.

The couple reserves four charming rooms—appropriately named Dogwood, Magnolia, Azalea, and Rose—for overnight visitors and serves afternoon tea on request. Valerie, a school counselor, prepares gourmet breakfasts, complemented by her own homemade breads and muffins. She often makes apple French toast, crumpets, and English scones. The music you hear may be a recording or perhaps Valerie playing the harp, a birthday present from Patrick. Future plans call for an English garden, gazebo, and outside guest suite. Standard to moderate rates.

Across from Dogwood Manor's driveway stands the *North Alabama Railroad Museum* (256–851–NARM) at 694 Chase Road. The restored green-and-yellow Chase Depot houses a waiting room and agent office filled with exhibits. Home of the Mercury and Chase Railroad and the country's smallest union station, the facility now features a walk-through passenger train and twenty-seven pieces of major railroading stock. Except for major holidays, the museum is open each Wednesday and Saturday from 9:30 A.M. till 2:00 P.M. April through October and offers guided tours and excursion train rides. Children enjoy watching for the concrete animals staged along the track. In addition to regular trips, a Goblin Special and Santa Trail Special are also scheduled. Call for more information on schedules, fares, and reservations, or visit the Internet station at www. suncompsvc.com/narm/ for current happenings.

Tennessee River Terrain

From Huntsville take U.S. Highway 72 east to Scottsboro, home of *"First Monday,"* one of the South's oldest and largest "trade days." This outdoor market might feature anything from cast-iron skillets, church pews, and collie puppies to butter churns, gingham-checked sunbonnets, and pocketknives—all displayed around the Jackson County Courthouse Square. Lasting from morning till dark, the event dates to the mid-1800s, when people met at the courthouse square on the day Circuit Court opened to visit as well as to trade horses, mules, and other livestock. The merry mix of folks who still come to browse, banter, and barter carry on a Southern tradition, and many have honed their trading techniques to a high level of skill. Although this event takes place on the first Monday of every month (plus the Sunday preceding it), the Labor Day weekend typically proves most popular.

If you miss Scottsboro's First Monday, you can console yourself by dipping into a chocolate milk shake, ice-cream soda, or banana split at *Payne's* (256–574–2140), located at 101 East Laurel on the town square's north side. Owned by Shay and Gene Holder, this eatery occupies the site of a former drugstore dating from 1869. The interior, complete with old-fashioned soda fountain, features a black-and-white color scheme with red accents. You can perch on a bar stool, order a fountain Coke that's mixed on the spot and served in a traditional Coca-Cola glass, and munch on a hot dog with red slaw straight from the original drugstore menu. Other options include Payne's popular chicken salad and a variety of sandwiches along with homemade desserts. Hours are 10:00 A.M. to 4:00 P.M. Monday through Saturday (except on Thursday, when closing time is 3:00 P.M.). The eatery is also open 10:00 A.M. to 6:00 P.M. on the Sunday before First Monday.

To learn about the area's history, visit the *Scottsboro-Jackson Heritage Center* (256–259–2122), located on the corner of South Houston and Peachtree Streets. This Greek Revival-style structure, built in 1880-81, houses some interesting exhibits, including Native American artifacts found on land later flooded by TVA and rare photographic displays depicting the early days of Skyline, a unique community north of Scottsboro.

Behind the big house stands the small 1868 Jackson County Courthouse. Nearby, a pioneer village called Sage Town features a collection of authentic log structures that include a cabin, schoolhouse, barn, and blacksmith shop, all filled with vintage items.

The museum offers a wealth of genealogical materials says Judi Weaver, who promotes archaeological awareness in her role as director. The facility focuses on the area's history from the Paleo-Indian era through the 1930s. Special events include heritage festivals and art exhibitions. Hours are 11:00 A.M. to 4:00 P.M. Tuesday through Friday, or by appointment. A modest admission is charged.

If, after a plane trip, you've ever discovered yourself divorced from your bags and wondered about their final destination, it's entirely possible that your lost luggage wound up at Scottsboro's *Unclaimed Baggage Center* (256–259–1525), located at 509 West Willow Street (although your bags may have traveled instead to nearby Unclaimed Baggage Centers in Boaz or Decatur). At this unique outlet you can find such items as cameras, caviar, clothing, hammocks, hair dryers, jewelry, scuba gear, and ski equipment. The ever-changing merchandise from around the world also features baby strollers, books, costume and fine jewelry, briefcases, luggage, personal electronic devices, and high-tech equipment.

"We have to stay on top of technology to know what's coming in here," says a company executive. The diverse inventory of lost, found, and unclaimed items comes from various airlines to be sorted and offered for sale at reduced rates—50 percent or more off retail prices. In this shopping mecca, which now covers more than a city block, you can enjoy a mug of brewed Starbuck's coffee at the facility's in-house cafe, called Cups.

Business boomed here—even before Oprah spread the word on her TV show. The parking lot gets especially crowded on weekends, and car tags reveal shoppers from many states. Recent visitors also came from Ontario, Bavaria, New Zealand, South America, France, and England. Unclaimed Baggage closes on Sunday. The Web site is www.unclaimedbaggage.com.

After sightseeing in the Scottsboro area, you can easily head south on State Route 79 toward Guntersville to take in some Marshall County attractions, or you can continue your loop northwest to Stevenson. *Goose Pond Colony* (256–259–2884 or 800–268–2884), a peninsula surrounded by the Tennessee River, is located 5 miles south of Scottsboro on Route 79 and offers vacation cottages, picnic facilities, camping sites, swimming pool, marina and launching ramp, golf course, and nature/walking trail. Popular with both geese and golfers, the golf course is noted for its beauty and design. Named by *Golf Digest* as one of "The Places to Play," Goose Pond's course also made the top five in a recent PGA opinion poll ranking courses in the Dixie section. For more information click on www.goosepond.org.

Crawdaddy's, Too (256–574–3071), a restaurant on the grounds behind the swimming pool, offers a variety of seafood including Cajun fare. You can dine on the deck with a fine view of the water. Some diners arrive by boat and tie up at the property's private pier. During warm-weather months, the restaurant is open from 5:00 to 10:00 P.M. Wednesday through Friday and for lunch only on Saturday; call for winter hours.

For rates and more information, write Goose Pond Colony at 417 Ed Hembree Drive, Scottsboro 35768.

Before leaving this area, you may want to call the Scottsboro/Jackson County Chamber of Commerce (256–259–5500 or 800–259–5508) or stop by the headquarters at 407 East Willow Street to pick up brochures on various local and area attractions.

Although you might find the tiny town of Pisgah on your road map, you won't find *Gorham's Bluff* (256–451–3435)—yet. Described by its builders as "A New Town in Appalachia," the planned community (inspired by Florida's Seaside) offers travelers some stunning scenery,

Overlook Pavilion at Gorham's Bluff

especially from the Overlook Pavilion, and accommodations at The Lodge. A natural amphitheater on the grounds provides a perfect summer setting for plays, concerts, and other entertainment. The property commands sweeping bluffside views of the Tennessee River. Even the glorious sunsets, which "can send you into rapture," owner/chef Clara McGriff says, don't get taken for granted here. "We call each other—you've got to see this one."

Clara's father, who purchased this property during the 1950s, called it his "thinking place." It remained undeveloped until Clara and her husband, Bill (a CPA still remembered by locals as a basketball star), started exploring their daughter Dawn's idea of creating a brand-new arts-oriented Appalachian town—a walking town with a strong sense of community where residents stop for front-porch chats. With each new home and resident, the McGriffs watch the family vision being translated to reality.

"There is a peace that pervades this place," says Clara, a former English teacher. "We feel it, and guests feel it." The Lodge on Gorham's Bluff gives guests ample opportunity to sample this serenity and beauty. Spacious suites, individually decorated by Clara (who also creates the beautiful floral arrangements and supervises the kitchen); a sound system that pipes soft music into all rooms; double-sided fireplaces; and whirlpool tubs make accommodations even more inviting.

Hiking, biking, bird-watching, rocking, reflecting, reading, and listening to classical music all rank as popular pastimes here. Dawn frequently schedules special events such as the annual Gerhart Chamber Music Festival's Concert under the Stars, seasonal floral seminars, and story-telling and theater festivals. (During my visit a snowman played to a make-believe audience in the amphitheater.)

Sometime during your stay, slip up to the observation deck, replete with chaise, for a panoramic overview. Many visitors want to linger at Gorham's Bluff forever. A quote from the guest book reads: "Forward our mail. We are not leaving."

Meals (enhanced by the property's own fresh herbs) feature traditional Appalachian food—served with flair. "Breakfasts, included in the rates, are huge Southern-style affairs," notes Dawn. Guests can also enjoy candlelight dinners, and a pianist plays old and new favorites on Friday and Saturday evenings and during Sunday lunch. By reservation only, the lodge's thirty-seat dining room offers dinner for the public nightly, and a weekly lunch on Sunday. From Pisgah, located on Jackson County Road 58, signs point the way to Gorham's Bluff. Call for hours and specific directions or write the staff at P.O. Box 160, Pisgah 35765. Lodge rates range from moderate to deluxe. Make reservations for an evening or a weekend. You just may decide to become one of the town's new residents.

Before departing, stop by a shop on the grounds of Gorham's Bluff called *At Home,* which features unique gifts and furnishings for the home and garden—from antique European pine furniture to hand-painted birdhouses, books, pottery, and more. For more background or a map, click on www.thebluff.com or e-mail onthebluff@aol.com.

To reach the *Stevenson Railroad Depot Museum* (256–437–3012), take U.S. Highway 72 and travel northwest. Near Stevenson turn at State Route 117 to go downtown. On Main Street you'll see the museum positioned between two railroad tracks. Look carefully before crossing the tracks because the Iron Horse still whizzes by. This railroad junction played a strategic role during the Civil War, and the museum director showed me an assortment of uniform buttons, coins, and other military items brought in by a resident who had dug them up nearby. The Stevenson Depot also contains displays of Native American artifacts, period costumes, early farm tools, and railroading history information.

Each June the annual Stevenson Depot Days celebration commemorates the city's past with a variety of family activities that might include an ice-cream social, spelling bee, pioneer breakfast, wagon ride to the nearby Civil War fort, square dancing, tour of homes, parade, old-fashioned

Stevenson Railroad Depot Museum

street dance, and fireworks. From January through March the museum is open Monday through Friday from 9:00 A.M. to 5:00 P.M. The facility is also open Saturday from 9:00 A.M. to 5:00 P.M. between April 1 and December 31. Admission is free.

Beside the museum, the Downtown Choo-Choo Restaurant offers country breakfasts and a steam table of lunch items as well as "the real hamburger," made from fresh ground chuck, and an assortment of homemade desserts.

From Stevenson return to U.S. Highway 72 and continue to Bridgeport, in Alabama's northeastern corner.

Caves, Caverns, and Canyons

While exploring this region in June 1540, Spaniard Hernando DeSoto and his crew chose this area for their entry into what is now Alabama. You might like to take a driving tour of Bridgeport, once called Jonesville but renamed in the 1850s for the railroad bridge that spans the Tennessee River.

Drive through Kilpatrick Row Residential District and up bluff-based Battery Hill, the site of several Civil War battles, to see the lovely historic homes of Victorian vintage with turrets, fishscale shingles, and wraparound porches.

In order to reach *Russell Cave National Monument* (256–495–2672), located about 8 miles west of Bridgeport, from U.S. Highway 72 at Bridgeport, follow Jackson County Route 75 west to Jackson County Route 98. Long before DeSoto's visit, the large limestone cave served as an archaic hotel for Native Americans traveling through the area about 9,000 years ago.

The visitors center, in addition to housing a museum that displays weapons, tools, pottery, and other artifacts found in the cave, also offers several audiovisual presentations. After browsing through the museum, you can walk about 250 yards to the cave's big opening at the base of craggy bluffs. A ranger-led tour takes you to the cave, where you can learn about how the occupants fed, clothed, and protected themselves.

One of the century's most significant archaeological finds, the relic-filled cave remained pretty much a secret until 1953 when some members of the Tennessee Archaeological Society discovered the history-rich shelter and alerted Smithsonian Institution officials, who collaborated with the National Geographic Society to conduct extensive excavations here. The National Park Service carried out more excavations in 1962. Their joint research revealed Russell Cave to be one of the longest, most complete, and well-preserved archaeological records in the eastern United States. Radioactive carbon from early campfires placed human arrival between 6500 and 6145 B.C. Remains of animal bones, tools, weapons, and pottery all helped archaeologists fit together portions of this ancient jigsaw puzzle. The evidence implies seasonal occupation, suggesting that various groups of early people wintered in Russell Cave, then moved on to hunt and live off the land during warm-weather months.

Be sure to ask a ranger about a living-history demonstration. I found it fascinating to watch a piece of flint fashioned into an arrowhead in about four minutes with the same simple tools early Native Americans used.

Serious spelunkers who want to see more of the cave's 7 miles of mapped passageways can obtain a free permit and equipment list from the park superintendent. Proper equipment is essential because the cave's untamed interior contains no lights or trails, and normal conditions require crawling through difficult passages and wading in water up to 4 feet deep. The cave's temperature averages about 56 degrees.

Except for Thanksgiving, Christmas, and New Year's Day, you can visit Russell Cave seven days a week. During daylight savings time hours are 8:00 A.M. to 5:00 P.M.; otherwise the closing time is 4:30 P.M., and there's no admission charge. For more information or to make arrangements for a permit for wild caving prior to your visit, call (256) 495–2672, or write to park personnel at 3729 County Road 98, Bridgeport 35740. Explore the cave on the Internet by clicking on www.nps.gov/ruca.

A cave adventure of a different sort awaits at *Sequoyah Caverns* (256–635–0024 or 800–843–5098), located about 6 miles north of Valley Head. Returning to Stevenson, you can follow State Route 117 south to reach the caverns, well marked by signs. Travelers arriving on I–59 can take either the Hammondville-Valley Head exit or the Sulphur Springs-Ider exit to the caverns, located a few hundred yards off the interstate between these two exits.

The caverns take their name from Sequoyah (also spelled Sequoya or Sequoia), who moved to this part of Alabama as a young man. California's giant trees and Sequoia National Park were also named in honor of this Cherokee chief, who developed an alphabet for his people after being intrigued by the white man's "talking leaf." As a result the Cherokee people learned to read and write in a matter of months and soon started publishing books and newspapers in their native language.

You'll enter the caverns through the Cherokee Cooking Room, so called because of the salt troughs, cooking implements, pottery, and blackened walls found here. Wending your way through this magical world of spectacular stalactites and stalagmites in gorgeous colorations is like traveling through a giant kaleidoscope. The many reflecting pools known as "looking-glass lakes" allow you to study remote features on the multilevel ceiling that rises as high as a twelve-story building in certain portions of the caverns. A guided tour takes about an hour, and the temperature remains a constant 60 degrees. Admission. From March through November the caverns are open daily from 8:30 A.M. to 5:00 P.M.; however, they are open only on Saturday and Sunday from December through February.

In *Valley Head,* only a few miles south of the caverns, you'll find *Woodhaven* (256–635–6438), a bed-and-breakfast owned by Judith and Kaare Lollik-Andersen. Located on Lowry Road and fronted by a wooden fence, the 1902 three-story white house features a wraparound porch with an inviting swing and white wicker furniture. A creek runs through the pastures of the forty-acre farm, making it a pleasant place to explore, hike, jog, or bike. Children especially enjoy helping feed the animals.

While living in south Florida, Judith and Kaare started searching out a location for a bed-and-breakfast inn because they enjoyed staying in such facilities in Europe. They wanted mountains, trees, water, and a gentle climate, "but one with seasons." Their search brought them to this part of Alabama, where the geography reminded Kaare of his native Norway, with the nearby Tennessee River a substitute for the sea.

For early risers, Judith serves a pre-breakfast snack of Danish or muffins with coffee and juice. Later comes the real thing with fresh fruit, croissants or English muffins, oatmeal or cereal, and one of the house specialties: eggs (provided by the farm's own chickens) with bacon or a Norwegian dish of herring and eggs with caviar on toast. You can also expect afternoon tea and evening snacks. Standard rates. For reservations and specific directions, call or write to Woodhaven, 390 Lowry Road, Valley Head 35989.

One block off State Route 117 in the center of Valley Head stands **Winston Place** (256–635–6381 or 888–4–WINSTON), a white-columned antebellum mansion owned by Leslie and Jim Bunch. Located 2 miles from Mentone, the property features a panoramic view of Lookout Mountain. Two levels of encircling porches with ferns, white wicker rocking chairs, and a nanny swing invite guests to relax and savor the setting. Built by William Overton Winston from Virginia, the circa 1831 home boasts a rich history. During the Civil War, Union officers occupied the home, and 30,000 soldiers camped on its grounds before leaving to fight at Chickamauga. Leslie, who shares anecdotes about her family home and its fascinating background, has amassed a collection of books and articles detailing Winston Place's role in history.

Previously selected as a Northeast Alabama Designer Showcase Home, Winston Place contains lovely period antiques and lends itself well to entertaining, just as its builder intended. Original outbuildings include servants quarters, a slanted-wall corncrib, and a smoke-house with hand-painted murals depicting the area's history.

While immersing yourself in the home's ambience, take time to see the tucked-away media room with Jim's football awards—trophies, plaques, and photos. A former Alabama football All-American (whose mastery of the game took him to three Sugar Bowls and a Liberty Bowl), Jim played under legendary coach Bear Bryant.

The couple offers five elegant suites for guests and a sumptuous breakfast, served in the dining room. Rates range from moderate to deluxe. Visit Winston Place's home in cyberspace at www.virtualcities. com/ons/al/n/aln1602.htm.

From Valley Head it's a short but scenic drive up to **Mentone**, a charming hamlet perched on the brow of Lookout Mountain at the intersection of State Highway 117 and DeKalb County Route 89. Once a fashionable summer resort town that flourished through the Gay Nineties, Mentone attracted visitors from all over the country with its cool mountain temperatures, especially appealing in the days before air-conditioning.

Shops, rustic and quaint, line the single main street, but the large, rambling **Mentone Springs Hotel** (256–634–4040) remains the town's focal point. The three-story structure with turrets, dormers, porches, and steep-sloped roof captured my imagination the first time I saw it three decades ago. Open for bed-and-breakfast guests, the building also houses a restaurant called **Caldwell's**, named for the doctor who built the hotel in 1884. Owners Claudia and Dave Wassom, who moved here from northern California, offer ten rooms for guests and a big breakfast. Rates are standard to moderate.

Strange As It Sounds

*B*uck's Pocket State Park (256–659–2000), a secluded expanse of rugged nature that spills into three counties—DeKalb, Jackson, and Marshall—is rich in botanical beauty and local lore. Covering more than 2,000 acres of craggy canyon scenery on the western side of Sand Mountain, the park is located near Grove Oak.

For a magnificent overview of the entire canyon, head first to Point Rock, the park's highest area and a wonderful place for picnicking and hiking. According to local legend, early Native Americans took advantage of the area's geography to help them acquire their food supply by driving deer over the edge at Point Rock right into the "pocket." Both spring, with its plentiful supply of wildflowers, and fall make great times to visit.

To reach the headquarters and campground, you'll descend from Point Rock about 800 feet via a curving road to the canyon's base. The bottom line on the park's wooden sign says: HAVEN FOR DEFEATED POLITICIANS. Buck's Pocket acquired its reputation as a refuge for election losers after "Big Jim" Folsom, a former Alabama governor, lost a senate bid and announced his intention to go to Buck's Pocket, get his thoughts together, and "lick his wounds." He invited other defeated candidates to join him at this favorite retreat.

In addition to trails for hiking and rocks for climbing, recreation options include swimming and fishing at South Sauty Creek. Also, nearby Morgan's Cove offers a fishing pier and boat launching ramps. Rappelers and rock climbers should first stop by headquarters for a permit, good for a year. Write to Buck's Pocket at 393 County Road 174, Grove Oak 35975. For reservations you can call (800) ALAPARK. For a guided tour call (256) 571–5445.

The name *Mentone* translates into "musical mountain spring," appropriate because the hotel's grounds once boasted two springs—Mineral Springs and Beauty Springs—which were reputed to possess "strengthening and curative properties." The hotel's early guests enjoyed nature walks, croquet, billiards, boating, and other genteel pursuits.

Although you can't join a picnicking party with a basket lunch packed by the hotel and you won't be summoned to meals by a dinner bell, you can explore the town's shops. Some of them close or limit their hours in winter, so it's best to check ahead. Also, you might inquire about the dates of upcoming festivals because Mentone stages special events throughout the year.

The downtown **Log Cabin Deli** (256–634–4560), originally a Native American trading post, serves sandwiches, salads, plate lunches, and dinner entrees with home-cooked vegetables and desserts. The eatery, where you'll find a cozy fire when temperatures drop, is open Tuesday through Sunday from 11:00 A.M. to 7:00 P.M. Nearby **Dessie's Kountry Chef** (256–634–4232), closed on Tuesday, serves evening fare along with short orders and home-style lunches.

While browsing for antiques and collectibles, stop by **The Hitching Post,** a complex housing several interesting shops including the antiques-filled **Crow's Nest;** the **Village Boutique,** with "art to wear" handwoven apparel; and **Country Corner,** featuring handmade quilts, needlework, and rugs.

At the **Gourdie Shop** (256–634–4767) you'll see Sharon Barron's unique and whimsical creations made from locally grown gourds, each signed and dated by the artist. Except for January, the shop is open Wednesday through Sunday from 10:00 A.M. to 4:00 P.M. (till 5:00 P.M. in summer) and also carries collectibles and antiques.

Across the road from the old hotel is **St. Joseph's on the Mountain.** Be sure to notice the log structure, dating to 1826, that serves as the central portion of this unusual church. North of the church on the mountain's brow, you'll find **Eagle's Nest,** a massive rock formation overlooking Valley Head.

After exploring the village, take a drive along the area's meandering roads. You'll see strategically placed destination markers nailed to trees and posts at junctions—these are quite helpful because the mountain terrain can prove confusing to newcomers.

Tucked away at 651 County Road 644 stands **Raven Haven** (256–634–4310), a bed-and-breakfast perched atop Lookout Mountain.

Owners Eleanor and Tony Teverino welcome travelers to share their ten acres of nature and theme rooms: Queen Anne, Nautical, Casablanca, and Little Room on the Prairie—each with private bath.

"Two things that drew us here were the beauty of the place and the people," said Eleanor, who was born in Northern Ireland. "When I came to Mentone, it was very much like going back home." The Teverinos hosted recent guests from Ireland, who compared some of Mentone's narrow boulder-flanked curves to "driving on the roads right back at home."

Eleanor whisks warm and wonderful pastries from her oven and prepares a delightful breakfast daily, complete with homemade jams. Served buffet style, the menu always features a main dish, fruit, and vegetable to get your day off to a good healthy start. From Scotch eggs to fried green tomatoes to sticky buns, each morning's choices offer plenty of variety. Afterward, you can trek through the woods and admire the wildflowers along the property's 1/4-mile walking trail. Moderate rates. For more information on this hideaway, pay a Web visit to www.virtualcities.com/ons/al/n/alnc502.htm.

While driving through the area, you'll pass a number of summer camps for youngsters. In fact the boyhood days spent at one such camp called Cloudmont inspired local landowner Jack Jones to pursue his unlikely dream of creating a ski resort in Alabama. After buying Cloudmont in 1947, he started developing the property as a resort and opened "the southernmost ski resort in the country" in 1970. *Cloudmont Ski and Golf Resort* (256–634–4344), about 3 miles from Mentone on DeKalb County Route 89, is marked by a large roadside sign on the left. To reach the information center, take a left onto County Route 614 for half a mile or so. Besides skiing (and yes, Mother Nature does get help from snow machines), this unique family enterprise offers golfing, hiking, fishing, and swimming for guests. Jack's son Gary and his instructors have taught thousands of people to ski. Winter season at Cloudmont usually begins around mid-December and extends through March 15. It's a good idea to call ahead and check on slope conditions. Better yet, log onto www.cloudmont.com for schedules, rates, and information on current activities, which include golfing, horseback riding, and more at both Cloudmont and *Shady Grove Dude Ranch.* You can write the resort at P.O. Box 435, Mentone 35984.

Before leaving the Mentone area, make dinner reservations at *The Cliffs* (256–634–3040). You'll find the restaurant, owned by Sherri and Brent Black, at 15861 County Route 89. Notice the handsome rock walls—both exterior and interior—that Sherri designed and constructed.

Start with a sourdough bread bowl of French onion soup and continue with an entree featuring Sherri's homemade pasta. Or you may prefer pork medallions, filet mignon, or fiesta shrimp with corn, black beans, and spices. Hours are 5:00 to 8:30 P.M. Tuesday through Thursday and 5:00 to 9:30 P.M. on Friday and Saturday. Moderate prices.

Cragsmere Manna Restaurant (256–634–4677), located about a ½ mile beyond the resort in one of the area's oldest houses, offers a "country gourmet" dinner on Friday and Saturday from 5:00 to 9:00 P.M.

While in this area, don't miss the *Sallie Howard Memorial Chapel,* located 6.7 miles from downtown Mentone and adjacent to DeSoto State Park. A 20-foot-tall boulder serves as the rear wall of the small church, and stones from Little River form the pulpit. Visitors often attend worship services held here each Sunday at 10:00 A.M.

To more fully explore this area's magnificent terrain, consider headquartering at *DeSoto State Park* (256–845–0051 or 800–568–8840), about 7 miles from Mentone. You'll find almost 5,000 acres of breathtaking beauty and glimpses of unspoiled nature at every turn. The gorgeous scenery around here makes it hard to concentrate on driving, but if you don't, you might bash into one of the big weathered boulders that partially jut into the road.

The park extends about 40 miles along Little River, a unique waterway that runs its complete course on top of a mountain. Resort facilities include a stone lodge with large restaurant, chalets, cabins, nature trails, playgrounds, a store, and picnic areas. Miles of hiking trails, bordered by Queen Anne's lace, blackberry vines, honeysuckle, and black-eyed Susans, beckon you to explore the terrain. The park's new handicapped-accessible boardwalk attracts families and features a covered pavilion and waterfall view. Don't miss spectacular *DeSoto Falls* (about 7 miles northeast of the park's Information Center), where water rushes over a dam to crash more than 100 feet before continuing its journey. Park superintendent Talmadge Butler has twice traveled to Washington, D.C., to accept awards for park preservation and beautification.

About 10 miles away in the park's southern section, you'll find the beginning of *Little River Canyon National Preserve,* the largest and one of the deepest chasms east of the Mississippi River. Stretching about 16 miles, the canyon drops to depths of some 700 feet. Skirting the western rim, a canyon road offers breathtaking views of rugged bluffs, waterfalls, and the rushing river.

Don't miss Fort Payne, the stomping ground of award-collecting country music group ALABAMA and home to the redbrick *Fort Payne Opera House* (256–845–3137 or 256–845–0419) at 510 North Gault Avenue. The building, which dates to 1889, has served as a vaudeville playhouse, a theater for silent movies, and an upholstery shop. The opera house is listed on the National Register of Historic Places and the National Register of Nineteenth Century Theatres in America. Be sure to notice the murals, painted by artists Jeff Wright and John T. Hill Jr., which depict the history of DeKalb County. Restored in 1969, the opera house now opens for special events and performances. Tours can be arranged by appointment.

Alabama Trivia

Alabama ranks twelfth in the nation for attracting retirees, and eighth in the nation for attracting military retirees.

The building on the opera house's north side will house a new Hosiery Museum, scheduled to open in the near future. Featured exhibits will focus on the hosiery industry and its history.

Nearby, the Fort Payne Depot at Fifth Street Northeast houses the *Fort Payne Depot Museum* (256–845–5714). Completed in 1891, the handsome Romanesque depot of pink sandstone served as a passenger station until 1970. The museum's permanent collection includes artwork, early farm equipment, pottery, glassware, and a restored caboose containing railroad memorabilia. You'll also see beaded moccasins, Iroquois baskets made of birch bark trimmed with porcupine quills, and Mayan and pre-Columbian artifacts dating from A.D. 400 to 800. An area resident willed to the museum her Cherokee, Hopi, Pueblo, Apache, and Seminole artifacts. Be sure to notice the collection of dioramas that were once part of a traveling medicine show and an unusual bed that belonged to local resident Granny Dollar, whose lifetime spanned more than a century. The museum is open 10:00 A.M. to 4:00 P.M. on Monday, Wednesday, and Friday. Sunday hours are 2:00 to 4:00 P.M. Admission is free, but donations are welcome.

Before leaving the "Sock Capital of the World," stop by *Big Mill Antique Mall* (256–845–3380) and browse among yesteryear's treasures. Located at 151 Eighth Street Northeast, this 1889 structure, once home to Fort Payne's first hosiery mill, now houses antiques, collectibles, reproductions, and a deli. Mall hours are 10:00 A.M. to 4:00 P.M. Monday through Saturday and 1:00 to 4:00 P.M. on Sunday. The deli is open Monday through Friday.

For information on accommodations at the Davis House Loft Apartments located across the street, inquire at the mall's front desk. Once part of the old mill complex and later a cabinet shop, the structure features beautifully restored suites and apartments with interesting architectural features. Some of the thirty-six units are reserved for short-term use.

While traveling through *Collinsville,* you might want to consider spending some time at Trade Day, an event that draws some 30,000 or so bargain hunters and browsers every Saturday. Spread over sixty-five acres near Collinsville on U.S. Highway 11 South, this weekly occasion has had a country carnival flavor since it first cranked up in 1950. Vendors start setting up their wares at the crack of dawn and stay until early afternoon. "We offer today's collectibles at yesterday's prices," says owner Charles Cook. Sightseers can munch on snacks such as boiled peanuts and corn dogs while surveying displays of wares from antiques and crafts to fresh vegetables and houseplants. Swans, ducks, rabbits, geese, goats, peacocks, hunting dogs, game cocks, and exotic pets often find new owners here. Parking costs 50 cents, but admission is free. For more information call (256) 524–2536 or (888) 524–2436.

Cherokee Country

From Collinsville it's just a short jaunt to Leesburg and *the secret Bed & Breakfast Lodge* (256–523–3825). Located at 2356 Highway 68 West on a mountaintop overlooking Weiss Lake, the lodge boasts a view that won't stop. "Last summer our guests saw Fourth-of-July fireworks in three cities from our rooftop pool," says Diann Cruickshank, who with husband Carl owns this property perched on the eastern brow of Lookout Mountain.

The view, the sunsets and sunrises, the llama and deer (which guests can feed), plus a miniature deer and wallaby make the secret a special place. Carl cooks a delicious country breakfast, which Diann serves on a 10-foot wide round table topped by a lazy susan. You'll see a collection of porcelain dolls made by Diann's mother and a showcase containing Carl's interesting memorabilia. Bring your camera and prepare for surprises galore here because Diann delights in acquiring the unusual. (Not to divulge any secrets, but one surprise may leave you feeling a bit like Goldilocks.) For each guest room and the Sugar Shack—a cottage on the grounds— Diann compiled a booklet of her engaging anecdotes along with recommended local attractions and restaurants. Movie buffs will find a video library containing more than 200 titles. Moderate rates. Visit the secret Bed & Breakfast Lodge via the Web at www.bbonline.com/al/thesecret or send a message by e-mail to secret@peop.tds.net.

Cherokee County, home of *Weiss Lake,* offers beautiful scenery. Add a chunk of Little River Canyon to this 30,200-acre lake bordered by 447 miles of shoreline, and you've got plenty of recreational options. Famous for its fine fishing, the Crappie Capital of the World also offers ample opportunities for catching bass and catfish. The water attracts large populations of wintering birds such as seagulls, wild ducks, and cranes.

While exploring Cherokee County's many scenic spots, don't overlook *Cornwall Furnace Park,* about 3 miles east of Cedar Bluff. To reach the park, take State Route 9 east and turn left on Cherokee County Route 92. Then make another left onto a gravel road and follow the signs. A flight of steps leads down a steep bank (covered by lilies in spring) to the picturesque stone stack that stands about 5 feet tall— all that remains of a structure built to supply crude iron to be transformed into Confederate arms. General Sherman's forces destroyed the furnace works during the Civil War.

The well-kept grounds offer attractive picnicking facilities and a short nature trail. The park, which opens at daylight and closes at sundown, can be visited year-round. Running water is available, but there are no bathroom facilities. Admission is free.

Afterward, take State Route 9 to Centre, about 6 miles away. Next to the courthouse stands the *Cherokee County Historical Museum* (256–927–7835), located at 101 East Main Street. This museum, formerly a department store, houses historical objects and memorabilia that characterize the area's past. You'll see a Pennsylvania Amish town buggy. Other exhibits include Bob Hope's first typewriter, Grand Ole Opry memorabilia, wagons, housewares, antique telephones, Civil War relics, early appliances, Native American artifacts, a printing press, a telephone switchboard, a doll collection, and a bale of cotton. The basement contains a blacksmith shop as well as old farm equipment such as plows, mowing machines, cotton planters, and tractors. Visitors sometimes see a quilting session in progress. Modest admission. The museum is open from 9:30 A.M. to 4:00 P.M. on Tuesday and from 8:30 A.M. to 4:00 P.M. Wednesday through Saturday.

Don't leave Centre without stopping by *Muffins 50's Cafe* (256–927–CAFE), on U.S. Highway 411 at the town's eastern edge. Owners Judy (nicknamed Muffin) and Bob Caldwell invite you to join them in getting "lost in the fifties." You'll see a gleaming black 1957 Cadillac parked inside the restaurant, with posters of James Dean, Marilyn Monroe, and other stars of that decade displayed in the background. Diners can also enjoy Muffins' extensive collection of autographed celebrity photos.

Try the smothered chicken, a house specialty consisting of a marinated chicken breast charbroiled and topped with cheese, fresh sautéed bell pepper, and onions. The staff uses choice meats and serves superb steaks.

Bob gets quite a few rock-climbing customers and meets people from all over the world who come to scale Lookout Mountain. Prices are economical to moderate, and the cafe is open daily from 10:30 A.M. to 8:30 P.M. on Sunday, till 9:00 P.M. Monday through Thursday, and till 10:00 P.M. on Friday and Saturday. Take time to browse through the fifties gift shop before leaving.

Continue toward Gadsden, situated in Lookout Mountain's foothills. *Turkeytown,* named for Chief Little Turkey during the late 1700s, is a tiny community on the Coosa River's banks near Gadsden that once served as the capital of the Cherokee nation.

Although long known as one of the state's leading industrial centers with abundant deposits of iron, manganese, coal, and limestone, Gadsden is gaining recognition for its rich Cherokee legacy. The Turkeytown Association of the Cherokee, a nonprofit organization, works to preserve and promote the region's Native American heritage with such projects as a *Cherokee Pow Wow and Green Corn Festival.* Held in September at the Turkeytown Ceremonial Grounds, this annual celebration features Native American arts and crafts, food, music, dances, and displays of tepees, jewelry, and pottery.

Downtown at Gadsden's Broad Street entrance to the Coosa River Bridge stands the statue of Emma Sansom, who, at age sixteen, helped Confederate troops find a place to ford Black Creek after Union forces crossed and burned the local bridge.

While in Gadsden, stop by the *Center for Cultural Arts* (256–543–2787) on the corner of Fifth and Broad Streets. The complex, with a bold gold-and-black exterior in a Mondrian-like design, offers plays, concerts, lectures, classes, and art exhibits. To see the current art shows, take the escalator to the second floor. Before returning downstairs, be sure to notice the model railroad layout depicting Gadsden during the 1940s and 1950s with trains traveling past miniature reproductions of more than a hundred historical structures including the Gulf States Steel complex. Modest admission. Call for information on current exhibits and hours or visit the Web site at www.culturalarts.com.

Adjacent to the Center for Cultural Arts, the historic Kyle Building now houses the new *Imagination Place Children's Museum.* Youngsters can play in a kid-size city complete with Grandma's House, a bank, grocery store, doctor's office, fire station, and other interesting sites. Visitors can observe a 10-foot tornado, a desert-making machine, and traveling exhibits.

At **Noccalula Falls and Park** (256–549–4663), situated on Lookout Mountain Parkway (and easily reached from I–59), the bronze statue of a legendary Cherokee princess stands ready to leap to her destiny in a rushing stream 90 feet below. Legend says Noccalula loved a brave of her own tribe and chose to die rather than marry the wealthier suitor selected by her father.

Explore the park's botanical gardens, especially attractive in spring with masses of azaleas in bloom. You can either walk through the park or take a mini-train ride to see the Pioneer Homestead, a village of authentic log structures including a barn, blacksmith shop, gristmill, school, and cabins moved here from various sites in Appalachia. Also here you'll find the restored Gilliland-Reese Covered Bridge.

Nearby are campgrounds, hiking trails, picnic tables, play areas, and a pool. Except for the evening light show during the annual Christmas on the Rocks, which takes place from the day after Thanksgiving through New Year's Eve, the park closes from November through February. Otherwise, the facility opens daily from 9:00 A.M. to sundown. Although the park is free, a modest admission fee is charged to see the Pioneer

And the Winner Is . . .

*L*ocal caterer Nancy Gross used her culinary expertise to create the following summer-fresh dish that took first prize at the Tomato Jubilee, a festival held at nearby Horse Pens 40. Nancy suggests pairing the recipe with sandwiches or soup.

Fresh Tomato Mango Slaw

One head each of red and green cabbage, finely shredded

Three mangoes—2¹/₂ peeled and diced with remaining ¹/₂ reserved to chop on the pit as garnish

Three beefsteak tomatoes, thinly sliced

Dressing and marinade:

¹/₃ cup Japanese rice vinegar

¹/₃ cup olive oil

3 tablespoons sesame seed oil

¹/₂ teaspoon sugar

2 tablespoons cilantro leaves, finely chopped

salt and freshly ground pepper to taste

In a medium bowl, whisk the dressing ingredients. Fold mango cubes into shredded cabbage and toss with dressing, reserving ¹/₃ of dressing to drizzle over sliced tomatoes. Arrange the tomatoes around the cubed mango half and serve.

Homestead and Botanical Gardens. The campground number is (256) 543–7412.

If you're in the area on a weekend, you may want to schedule a jaunt to **Mountain Top Flea Market,** which opens every Sunday at 5:00 A.M. year-round. You'll find this all-day market, recently listed by *Good Housekeeping* as the top flea market in the United States, about 6 miles west of Attalla on U.S. Highway 278. For more information call Janie Terrell at (800) 535-2286.

To reach Boaz, located on Sand Mountain, take U.S. Highway 431 north from Attalla.

Sand Mountain

A foothill of the Appalachians, Sand Mountain covers an area about 25 miles wide by 75 miles long. Atop this plateau you'll find **Boaz Shopper's Paradise**—so many stores, so little time. Ranked among America's top outlet centers, Boaz attracts people from across the country. Shoppers can browse through more than 145 stores and specialty shops in the town's outlet centers. For discount coupons and maps, make your first stop the Official Outlet Information office on Billy Dyar Boulevard and check the Closeout House for the week's best bargains.

Approximately 70,000 people descend on Boaz, population 7,500, for the annual Harvest Festival, an event in which sunbonneted ladies in long gingham frocks stroll about carrying pokes (sacks) filled with their purchases and men turn out in overalls and straw hats. The weekend celebration features an antique car show, musical entertainment, and some 200 booths brimming with handcrafted items ranging from birdhouses, cornshuck dolls, and crazy quilts to paintings, leather items, and furniture. Music runs the gamut from bluegrass, country, and gospel to jazz. For more information on the outlets or the festival, contact the Boaz Chamber of Commerce, P.O. Box 563, Boaz 35957, or call (205) 593–8154 or (800) 746–7262.

During your shopping spree, you might enjoy browsing among items from yesteryear at **Adams' Antiques** (256–593–0406) at 10310 Highway 168. Hours are 10:00 A.M. to 5:00 P.M. Tuesday through Saturday and 1:30 to 5:00 P.M. Sunday.

When you're ready for a shopping break, visit nearby **Snead State Community College Museum.** Snead's origins go back to 1898, when it opened as a seminary, making it the oldest school in the state's junior college system. In the Norton Building, you'll find a museum with outstanding exhibits of minerals, rocks, and fossils collected and donated by Preston Watts, an engineer and Snead Seminary graduate. In addition to the museum's natural science section with its several hands-on displays, you'll see a gospel music section featuring a vintage music printing press, recordings, hymnals dating to the 1880s, photos of gospel groups, and Sacred Harp singing memorabilia. Brought to America by the Pilgrims and Puritans, Sacred Harp singing (a

Angels in Arab

*O*ne spring day, a friend and I drove to Guntersville for an art exhibit and lunch. Walking into Covington's, we saw two angels, dressed in flowing white tunics with gold accessories— which included halos. One wore gold combat boots.

We soon found out the B-Team Angels, Paula Joslin and Kay Jennings, came from **Somewhere in Time,** then a gift shop in nearby Arab. They were "on a quest to earn their wings by spreading happiness." Wafting a wand in our direction, the angels then glided outside, where traffic screeched to a halt.

A year later I met the B-Team Angels in Albertville and learned their league had grown and their happiness ministry had expanded. Each month, for example, they surprise a local resident with an Earth Angel award, honoring people who bring happiness to others, often without recognition. On Valentine's Day the angelic band entertained at area nursing homes. They charge nothing for their programs of songs, skits, puppet shows, and birthday parties.

"We feel that sharing love with others is what life's all about," writes Kay, in her introduction to The B-Team Angels' Quest, a book filled with Paula's whimsical photo-collages featuring 700 Arab residents. (A professional artist, Paula works in all mediums and has won numerous awards in juried shows.) Proceeds from the book sales help defray costs incurred for this ministry—gifts, certificates, photography, costumes, transportation, etc.

Angelic agendas left little time for a retail shop, so Somewhere in Time (the B-Team's headquarters) now houses Paula's art studio, Kay's puppet theater, and Kay's husband's "junk/antiques shop."

Arab resident Ralph Hammond (also Alabama Poet Laureate emeritus) describes the angels as a "wonderful group of girls, who have added a luster to Arab." The angels want to broaden their mission beyond Alabama's borders and have launched some new chapters. So if you see an angel flitting about Arab, you know why: She's out to brighten someone's day—maybe yours. If you need to speak to a B-Team Angel, call the art studio (256–586–TIME), located at 119 First Street Northwest.

unique musical form using shaped notes to represent certain sounds) all but disappeared in most areas of the country but still survives in the South.

During school sessions the museum is open on Tuesday and Wednesday 8:00 A.M. to 3:00 P.M. and on Thursday from 8:00 A.M. to 2:00 P.M., or by appointment. For more information call (256) 593–5120.

If you can't finish all your shopping in one day (and many people can't), *Boaz Bed and Breakfast* (256–593–8031) at 200 Thomas Avenue offers a variety of accommodations. Co-owners Faye Markham and her daughter, Margaret Casey, converted the historic Whitman-Hunt house into a haven for travelers. Built in 1924 for cotton broker Edward Fenns Whitman, the Craftsman-style two-story brick structure features a clay tile roof. In 1999 the Boaz Altrusa Club sponsored the home as a Decorator Show House.

Faye, a former teacher, knows that shopping takes lots of stamina, so she provides her guests with a good hearty breakfast. Her usual Sand Mountain-style breakfast features pan-fried boneless chicken breasts with gravy, hot biscuits, grits, and fresh fruits. On Sunday she serves ham and waffles. Rates range from standard to moderate.

Afterward, continue about 5 miles north to *Albertville,* the "Heart of Sand Mountain." Albertville's *Freedom Festival,* chosen five times by the Southeast Tourism Society as one of July's Top Twenty Events, attracts a large Independence Day crowd.

For a look at some of the city's lovely historic homes, drive along East Main Street off U.S. Highway 431. At the street's end stands the 1891 *Albertville Depot,* which is listed on the National Register of Historic Places. The depot now houses a senior citizens center.

Albertville acquired its title as Fire Hydrant Capital of the World because the local Mueller Company turns liquefied steel into dome-topped fire hydrants and ships them to countries near and far. In front of the chamber of commerce building, you'll see a special nickel-plated version that marks Mueller's one-millionth locally manufactured fire hydrant.

For a sampling of some of the town's interesting stores, follow Sand Mountain Drive to the *Little Village Shop* (256–878–6400) in Eastwood Plaza. Located at 109 Sand Mountain Drive, the shop offers unique gifts, housewares, china, and Waterford crystal. Hours are 10:00 A.M. to 5:00 P.M. Monday through Saturday, except Wednesday, when the shop closes.

At 113 Sand Mountain Drive, you'll find *Whitten's* (256–878–3901), a clothing store that features upscale town and country fashions for women and men. Hours are 9:00 A.M. to 5:00 P.M. Monday through Saturday. The shop closes on Thursday afternoon. Next door at 115 Sand Mountain Drive, *Traditions Gift Shop* (256–891–2903) stocks an array of collectibles and decorator pieces ranging from crystal, brass, and china to chaise lounges, upholstered in your choice of pattern and favorite color. The shop is open Monday through Saturday from 9:00 A.M. to 5:00 P.M.

When visiting a new place, some travelers like to search out a restaurant where the locals eat. Here it's *The Food Basket* (256–878–1261), located just off U.S. Highway 431 at 715 Sampson Circle. The Daniel family has been feeding folks in Albertville since 1959.

Noted for its country ham and homemade biscuits, the restaurant draws a big breakfast crowd. Lunch specialties include Sand Mountain fried chicken and home-style fresh vegetables. Dinners feature steaks and seafood. The restaurant's original salad dressing and sweet rolls, served at dinner, prove perennial favorites. Economical to moderate. Hours are 5:00 A.M. to 3:00 P.M. Sunday through Wednesday and 5:00 A.M. to 9:00 P.M. Thursday through Saturday.

Traveling along Baltimore Avenue, you may notice identical two-story brick homes that date to the late 1920s and were built by business partners. The *Twin House* (256–878–7499) at 705 Baltimore Avenue makes a great base for sightseeing, outlet shopping, and golfing. Owners Jane and Vernon Rucks "talked for years about opening a bed-and-breakfast." On a visit from their Kentucky home to see family members in Guntersville, they launched a search and "found the perfect house in Albertville." Previously selected as a Northeast Alabama Decorator Showcase Home, the Twin House features four charming rooms for guests. Preview the home at www.bbonline.com/al/twinhouse.

Parents of four grown children, Jane (a former first grade teacher) and Vernon (a hospital administrator) have entertained extensively and enjoy company. They offer full packages for golfers, noting their location puts them about halfway between two of the Robert Trent Jones courses. Vernon, a single-digit handicapper, admits he "might be persuaded to conduct guest tours to area golf courses and throw some steaks on the grill afterward." Navaho fry bread, mastered during the couple's missionary days in northern Arizona, might appear on the menu, too. Breakfast specialties include sourdough pancakes and waffles, crepes, quiche, and eggs LeRoy (Vernon's version of eggs Benedict). Rates range from standard to moderate.

To learn more about Alabama's rural heritage, stop by the *Albertville Public Library,* at 200 Jackson Street, and buy a copy of *The Good Ole Days* by Jesse Culp—broadcaster, author, speaker, syndicated columnist, and former newspaper editor. In his "living-history" book, Mr. Culp discusses such topics as blue back spellers, log rollings, settin' hens, funeral home fans, and cow pasture baseball; and his gift for reminiscing brings back a bit of yesteryear.

Take time to drive along some of Marshall County's rural roads. Along the way you'll notice fertile rolling farmland and chicken houses. Broilers, eggs, and turkeys produced on the state's individual farms add up to a billion-dollar poultry industry. In broiler production, Alabama ranks second in the nation.

Lake Country

While in the area, consider headquartering at *Lake Guntersville State Park* (256–571–5440 or 800–ALA–PARK), located just off State Route 227. Perched on Appalachian bluffs about 6 miles northeast of Guntersville, the park lodge offers panoramic views and 34.3 miles of hiking trails. You can roam almost 6,000 acres of woodland— much of it undisturbed—and follow paths once used by the Cherokee.

Park naturalist Linda Reynolds gives guided hiking tours on request, pointing out local flora and fauna. Deer often dash across the road in front of cars and roam the lodge's grounds. In addition to hiking, park activities include camping, canoeing, fishing, and boating. The park hosts Eagle Awareness weekends throughout January. Birders, binoculars in hand, can watch bald eagles soar from their roosts by dawn's early light and return at dusk. In between the apple cider opener and the closing banquet, you can sandwich a host of activities to expand your knowledge of raptors and your circle of friends. For a brochure on Eagle Awareness for next January, contact the lodge or the Nature Center at Lake Guntersville State Park Lodge, 190 Campground Road, Guntersville 35976, or call (256) 571–5445 or (256) 571–5444.

Resort facilities include a restaurant, a lounge, motel rooms, chalets, and campsites ranging from primitive to fully equipped and modern (that is, complete with utility hookups, tables, grills, bathhouses, hot showers, play areas, and a camp store). You'll also find tennis courts, a championship eighteen-hole golf course, a heliport, and 7 miles of scenic drives.

Continue to nearby *Lake Guntersville,* a Tennessee Valley Authority creation where sailboats and fishing vessels dot shining expanses of open water. "The most striking thing about Guntersville," says local newspaper editor Sam Harvey, "is that it's a country town with a lake all around it. Of the five approaches to Guntersville, four take you across water." With 69,100 acres of water, Guntersville bills itself as a vacationer's paradise. Truly a haven for water-sports enthusiasts, the area offers boating, swimming, skiing, and fishing. The Bass Anglers Sportsman Society calls Lake Guntersville "one of the finest sport fishing lakes in America," and the Alabama Bassmasters stage invitational tournaments here.

Drive through the downtown area and stop by Lake Guntersville Chamber of Commerce and Welcome Center, which is in a house with a beckoning front porch at 200 Gunter Avenue near the big river bridge. Here you can pick up brochures on area attractions and inquire about current happenings. For instance, the local theater group The Whole Backstage mounts a mix of productions throughout the year, so check on possible performances during your visit.

Continue into town, looking upward at 280 Gunter Avenue to see *The Spanish House* (256–582–3861), perched just above eye level. This unique structure of vanilla stucco, topped with a roof of terra-cotta tile, dates to 1928 and houses fine antique china, crystal, and furniture. The owners specialize in American Victorian furnishings.

Sandra Campbell, an optician and former soprano with the Mobile and Meridian symphonies, and her sister Rosemary Little, a Huntsville artist, inherited the home and antiques business. Sandra's husband, Grady, a trombonist who played with Bob Hope and many of the big bands, helps with gardening. Before leaving be sure to see the adjacent terraced garden with fish pond. This property also affords a fine view of Lake Guntersville. (When I stopped by, Sandra's brother-in-law had

Strange As It Sounds

*I*f a boat outing fits into your travel schedule, try to catch the evening exodus of bats from Hambrick Cave. Some 350,000 American gray bats, a protected species, consider this cave home from late April to mid-October (although the females migrate the first of August). You'll probably join a bevy of other boaters, clustered around the water-level cave mouth at the base of a bluff, all waiting for the sunset performance as a cloud of bats swoops overhead on their nocturnal foraging flight. Going downriver toward Guntersville Dam, look for a cave (marked by a small overhead sign) on your right. Flashlights are prohibited. (For more information on this and other area bat caves, call the Wheeler Wildlife Refuge at 256–350–6639.)

just landed a thirty-pound catfish, affirming the area's reputation as an angler's paradise.)

Up the hill, *Lake Guntersville Bed and Breakfast* (256–505–0133) at 2204 Scott Street offers suites with private entrances and more lovely water views from its two levels of wraparound porches. While living in Fairfield, Connecticut, former Guntersville resident Carol Dravis dreamed of returning. She got to do just that when an unexpected opportunity came along to purchase the handsome circa 1910 white brick home.

Carol picks up guests who arrive by boat and serves a bountiful breakfast—on the veranda when weather permits. Breakfast might feature her special European pancakes, beautiful and puffy with various toppings, or a sausage-and-cheese strata. Accompaniments include fruit, muffins, pastries, and biscuits. Based on individual interests, Carol recommends local activities and provides directions to nearby walking trails and other scenic spots. In the foyer you'll see a selection of matted prints featuring the work of artist Betty Morris Hamilton.

Carol offers several special-occasion packages such as Eagle Awareness, Valentine, Anniversary, Birthday, Pamper Yourself, etc. One guest wrote, "How wonderful to have found such a thoughtful, talented hostess! Your charming B&B has been true lagniappe [a lower Alabama expression meaning something extra special], and we've discovered again the great delight of porch-sitting. Thank you for a lovely and delicious visit." Visit Lake Guntersville B&B's Web site at www.bbonline.com/al/lakeguntersville/. Standard to moderate rates.

Don't miss nearby *Fant's Department Store* at 355 Gunter Avenue. Still locally known as Hammer's, the rambling structure with original wooden floors offers a bargain basement and surprises galore. (You'll enjoy browsing through Hammer stores in Albertville and Boaz, too.)

Go around the corner to the *Basket Case* (256–582–8454) at 2310 Taylor Street for a selection of unique gifts. Owner Debbie Newman creates gift baskets filled with items of your choice from bath products to gourmet foods such as jellies, sauces, candies, and coffees. You'll also find silver jewelry, frames, pewter trays and bowls, lamps, and other home accessories. Hours run 10:00 A.M. to 5:00 P.M. Tuesday through Saturday.

Step inside the Guntersville Post Office to see the mural that depicts DeSoto's arrival in the area. Located at the north end of the lobby, the large canvas with life-size figures of Native Americans, costumed Spanish, and spirited horses, can be seen at any time.

Covington's (256–582–5377) makes a great stop for lunch. Housed in The Glover at 524 Gunter Avenue, the eatery offers tasty homemade soups, salads, sandwiches, and desserts. Try the Downtowne Delight with chicken or tuna salad, a home-baked muffin, pimento cheese on rye, and a choice of veggies or pasta salad. Economical prices. Hours run 11:00 A.M. to 2:00 P.M. Monday through Friday, and closing is 2:30 P.M. during summer.

Your sightseeing excursion may take you past the **Guntersville Museum and Cultural Center** (256–571–7597) at the corner of O'Brig and Debow Streets. The former Parish Hall of the Episcopal Church of the Epiphany now houses an art gallery and archives, with collections of documents, photos, and other items relating to the town's early days. You'll find a Tennessee Valley Authority Room, a River Room, and an Indian Room with displays of Native American projectile points and other artifacts. Hours are 10:00 A.M. to 4:00 P.M. Tuesday through Friday and 1:00 to 4:00 P.M. on Saturday and Sunday. Admission is free.

For some fresh steamed seafood prepared with Cajun flair, stop by **Crawmama's Seafood Shop** (256–582–0484), housed in a structure that owner Charlotte Harrison describes as "a chicken house with a rusty tin roof." The eatery offers take-out meals or easygoing dinners on the premises, located at 5000 Webb Villa just off U.S. Highway 431. You can watch Cajun crawfish, corn, and potatoes cook in a big pot while you wait. Call for seasonal hours. Moderate prices.

Other local events include Guntersville's two-day **Art on the Lake Show,** held each April, and the **Gerhart Chamber Music Festival.** The latter offers world-class entertainment with renowned musicians performing traditional and contemporary classical chamber repertoires in a series of concerts held at locations throughout Marshall County. For more information or to see a current art exhibit, stop by the Mountain Valley Arts Council (MVAC) office at 300 Gunter Avenue, or call (256) 582–1454.

On the Saturday before Labor Day, **St. William's Seafood Festival** features more than 5,000 pounds of fresh shrimp, oysters, crab, flounder, and other fish imported from coastal waters. Parish members prepare the seafood, which includes making about 400 gallons of gumbo.

For some good old-fashioned fun and a mess of "poke salat," take State Route 69 to Arab during the first weekend in May. When the Arab Liars' Club (the self-appointed title for a group of local men who meet daily for coffee at L Rancho Cafe) came up with the idea of the **Poke Salat**

Festival, they probably did not expect it to become an annual affair with everything from street dances and craft shows to beauty contests and drama productions.

You can spend the night at *Stamps Inn* (256–586–7038), located at 102 First Avenue Northeast. Restored with period antiques, this two-story home dates to 1936. Owners Tiny Bruce and Cynthia Hollingsworth reserve six rooms for guests and offer a nightly turn-down service. "Breakfast can be healthy or hearty," says Tiny. Standard rates.

About 3 blocks away on Arad Thompson Road, you'll find an inviting city park with historical structures, a 2-mile walking trail, a pool, and ball fields.

Arab is also home to a dozen antiques stores, which you may want to explore, and a tearoom when you're ready for a shopping break. Notice the *Farmer's Exchange,* a weather-beaten structure that now houses a garden center. Then head toward Huntsville to launch an exploration of Alabama's northwestern region.

PLACES TO STAY IN NORTHEAST ALABAMA

ALBERTVILLE
Jameson Inn
315 Martling Road
(256) 891–2600

Twin House Bed and Breakfast
705 Baltimore Avenue
(256) 878–7499

ARAB
Stamps Inn
102 First Avenue Northeast
(256) 586–7038

ATTALLA
Econo Lodge
507 Cherry Street
(256) 538–9925 or
(800) 424–4777

BOAZ
Best Western
751 U.S. Highway 431
(256) 593–8410 or
(800) 528–1234

Boaz Bed and Breakfast
200 Thomas Avenue
(256) 593–8031

Key West Inn
10535 Alabama
Highway 168
(256) 593–0800 or
(800) 833–0555

FORT PAYNE
DeSoto State Park
265 County Road 951
(256) 845–0051 or
(800) 568–8840

GADSDEN
Hampton Inn
129 River Road
(256) 546–2337 or
(800) HAMPTON

Holiday Inn Express
801 Cleveland Avenue
(256) 538–7861 or
(800) HOLIDAY

GUNTERSVILLE
Holiday Inn Resort Hotel
2140 Gunter Avenue
(256) 582–2220 or
(800) 579–KING

Lake Guntersville Bed and Breakfast
2204 Scott Street
(256) 505–0133

Lake Guntersville
State Park Lodge
7966 Alabama
Highway 227
(256) 571–5400 or
(800) ALA–PARK

HUNTSVILLE
Bevill Conference Center and Hotel
550 Sparkman Drive
(256) 721–9428 or
(888) 721–9428

Courtyard by Marriott
4804 University Drive
(256) 837–1400 or
(800) 321–2211

Dogwood Manor
707 Chase Road
(256) 859–3946

Hampton Inn
4815 University Drive
(256) 830–9400 or
(800) HAMPTON

Huntsville Hilton
401 Williams Avenue
(256) 533–1400 or
(800) HILTONS

Huntsville Marriott
#5 Tranquility Base
(256) 830–2222 or
(800) 228–9290

LEESBURG
the secret Bed and Break-
fast Lodge
2356 Highway 68 West

MENTONE
Mentone Springs Hotel
One Hotel Square
State Highway 117
(256) 634–4040

Mountain Laurel Inn
624 Road 949
(256) 634–4673 or
(800) 889–4244

Raven Haven
651 County Road 644
(256) 634–4310

Valhalla Luxury Cottages
Off County Road 626
(256) 634–4006

PISGAH
The Lodge at Gorham's
Bluff
P.O. Box 160
(256) 451–3435

SCOTTSBORO
Goose Pond Colony
417 Ed Hembree Drive
(256) 259–2884

Hampton Inn
46 Micah Way, Highway 72
(256) 259–4300 or
(800) 426–7860

Jameson Inn
208 Micah Way, Highway 72
(256) 574–6666 or
(800) 526–3766

TONEY
Church House Inn
2017 Grimwood Road
(256) 828–5192

VALLEY HEAD
Winston Place
1 block off State Route 117
(256) 635–6381 or
(888) 4–WINSTON

Woodhaven
390 Lowry Road
(256) 635–6438

**PLACES TO EAT IN
NORTHEAST ALABAMA**

ALBERTVILLE
Catfish Cabin
8524 U.S. Highway 431
(256) 878–8170

The Food Basket
715 Sampson Circle
(256) 878–1261

Giovanni's Pizza Italian
Restaurant
711 Miller Street
(256) 878–7881

BOAZ
The Mill Street Deli
10749 Alabama
Highway 168
(256) 593–7677

Ryan's Family Steak House
568 U.S. Highway 431
(256) 593–1436

CENTRE
Muffins '50s Cafe
U.S. Highway 411
Centre
(256) 927–CAFE

Tony's Steak Barn
804 Alexis Road
(256) 927–2844

FORT PAYNE
Little River Cafe
Fischer Crossroads on
Lookout Mountain Parkway
(256) 997–0707

GADSDEN
The Choice
531 Broad Street
(256) 546–8513

Miss Jean's Cajun
Connection Restaurant
906 Forrest Avenue
(256) 547–8555

The Olde Warehouse
315 South Second Street
(256) 547–5548

Top O' the River
1606 Rainbow Drive
(256) 547–9817

GUNTERSVILLE
Covington's
524 Gunter Avenue
(256) 582–5377

Crawmama's
5002 Webb Villa
(256) 582–0484

El Camino Real
14274 U.S. Highway 431
(256) 571–9089

KC's Coyote Cafe
410 Old Town Street
(256) 582–1675

Neena's Lakeside Grille
Inside the Holiday Inn
2140 Gunter Avenue
(256) 505–0550

Willie J's
7004 Val Monte Drive
(256) 582–2245

HUNTSVILLE
Bubba's
109 Washington Street
(256) 534–3133

Cafe Berlin
505 Airport Road Southwest
(256) 880–9920

Clementine's
525 Madison Street
Southeast
(256) 533–4438

Eunice's Country Kitchen
1006 Andrew Jackson Way
Northwest
(256) 534–9550

Green Bottle Grill
975 Airport Road Southwest
(256) 882–0459

Green Hills Grille
5100 Sanderson Road
(256) 837–8282

Landry's Seafood House
5101 Governor's
House Drive
(256) 864–0000

Ol' Heidelberg
6125 University Drive
(256) 922–0556

MENTONE
Caldwell's
Mentone Springs Hotel
(256) 634–4040

Cragsmere Manna
Restaurant
17871 DeKalb County Road
89
(256) 634–4677 or
(256) 845–2209

Dessie's Kountry Chef
(256) 634–4232

Log Cabin Restaurant
and Deli
6080 State Highway 117
(256) 634–4560

PISGAH
The Lodge at Gorham's Bluff
P.O. Box 160
(256) 451–3435

SCOTTSBORO
Crawdaddy's, Too
Goose Pond Colony
417 Ed Hembree Drive
(256) 574–3071

Liberty Restaurant
907 East Willow Street
(256) 574–3455

The Lite Side
145 East Laurel Street
(256) 574–3362

Payne's
101 East Laurel Street
(256) 574–2140

Triple R Bar-B-Q
2940 Veterans Drive
(256) 574–1520

STEVENSON
Downtown Choo-Choo
Restaurant
Main Street
(256) 437–8736

Friday's
507 Second Street
(256) 437–8201

MAINSTREAM ATTRACTIONS
WORTH SEEING IN
NORTHEAST ALABAMA

Alabama Fan Club
and Museum,
201 Glen Avenue,
Fort Payne; (256) 845–1646.
This museum showcases the
band's musical achieve-
ments, which are many: The
group has garnered numer-
ous awards, gold albums,
and plaques for such
releases as "My Home's in
Alabama," "Mountain
Music," and "Fallin' Again."
Fans can purchase souvenirs
ranging from T-shirts and
jackets to photographs and
mugs—and of course
albums. The museum fea-
tures individual sections on
band members Randy
Owen, Teddy Gentry, Jeff
Cook, and Mark Herndon.
For a little background and
a Web tour, visit www.wild-
country.com.

Huntsville Museum
of Art, 300 Church Street
South, Huntsville;
(256) 535–4350. Save time
for browsing through the
new $7.5 million home of

the Huntsville Museum of Art, with twice as much gallery space as its former quarters in the Von Braun Civic Center. This beautiful building stands in Big Spring International Park, the heart of the city, and offers a wide range of exhibitions, art classes, and educational programs. You'll see an outstanding permanent collection with works by Picasso, Matisse, Toulouse–Lautrec, Goya, and other renowned artists as well as exhibits on loan from major institutions.

U.S. Space and Rocket Museum, Huntsville; (205) 837–3400. Located at Tranquility Base on Huntsville's western side, you may feel like a character out of a science fiction movie as you wander through a world of rockets, spaceships, shuttles, nose cones, and lunar landing vehicles. Other interesting artifacts include a moon rock, Apollo 16's command module, the overpowering Saturn V moon rocket, and a SR–71 Blackbird reconnaissance plane. Don't miss the featured film presentation at the Spacedome Theater, or, for a unique adventure, sign up for Space Camp. For some background and a look at current offerings, log onto www.ussrc.com. You'll find Space Camp dates, rates, registration information, and everything else you need to know for blasting off at www.spacecamp.com.

For More Information about Northeast Alabama

Alabama Mountain Lakes Association
25062 North Street P.O. Box 1075
Mooresville 35649
(256) 350–3500 or (800) 648–5381
Web site: www.almlakes.org
e–mail: info@almtlakes. org
This organization covers sixteen north Alabama counties that are home to some one hundred attractions in a 100–mile radius.

DeKalb County Tourist Association
P.O. Box 681165 Fort Payne 35968
(256) 845–3957
Web site: www.hsv.tis.net/; dekbtour/
e–mail: pattyt@ mindsrping. com

Gadsden/Etowah Tourism Board, Inc.
#90 Walnut Street, Amphitheatre Annex (35901)
P.O. Box 8267; Gadsden
35902–8267 (256) 549–8267
Web site: www.cybrtyme. com/tourism
e–mail: tourism@cybrtyme. com

Huntsville/Madison County Convention
& Visitors Bureau
von Braun Civic Center
700 Monroe Street Huntsville 35801
(256) 551–2230 or (800) SPACE–4–U
Web site: www.huntsville. org
e–mail: info@ huntsville. org

Marshall County
Convention & Visitors Bureau
200 Gunter Avenue P.O. Box 711
Guntersville 35976
(256) 582–7015 or (800) 582–6282
Web site: www.marshallcountycvb.com
e–mail: mccvb@mindspring.com

Scottsboro–Jackson County Chamber of Commerce
407 East Willow Street P.O. Box 973
Scottsboro 35768
(256) 259–5500 or (800) 259–5508
Web site: www.sjcchamber.org
e–mail: sjcc@hiwaay.net

Northwest Alabama

Tennessee Valley

Mooresville, just east of I–65 at exit 2 on I–565 between Huntsville and Decatur, makes a good place to start a tour of Alabama's northwest region. For information on local and area attractions, call the Alabama Mountain Lakes Tourist Association's office at (800) 648–5381.

To best see Mooresville, a town that dates to 1818 (it's one year older than the state itself), plan to take a walking tour. Not only does everybody know everybody in this community of some twenty families, everybody knows everybody's dog. Don't be surprised if Ruby, Brute, Max (or their descendants), and other local canines choose to accompany you on your stroll through town. Listed on the National Register of Historic Places, this charming village occupies an area of one-quarter square mile and can easily be covered in half an hour. Cedar trees and

Turning Back the Clock to Mark Twain's Time

*I*f you saw the Disney production Tom and Huck, *you visited the well-preserved village of Mooresville via video. Jonathan Taylor Thomas (of TV's* Home Improvement *fame) and Brad Renfro (*The Client*) starred in this remake of a Mark Twain classic.*

"The moment I saw Mooresville, I knew this was the perfect setting for Tom Sawyer," said the film's production manager, Ross Fanger, after searching for a town that fit the 1876 era of Mark Twain's novel.

For the movie, Mooresville's paved streets became dirt-covered lanes, and a Hollywood facade of nineteenth-century stores sprang up. Film crews shot some scenes along the Tennessee River and inside Cathedral Caverns (soon to be reopened to the public as a state park) in Marshall County. The caverns served as a backdrop for the novel's account of Tom and his girlfriend Becky Thatcher's lost-in-a-cave adventure.

If you missed the movie, don't despair—the film is available as a home video, and you can still visit Mooresville.

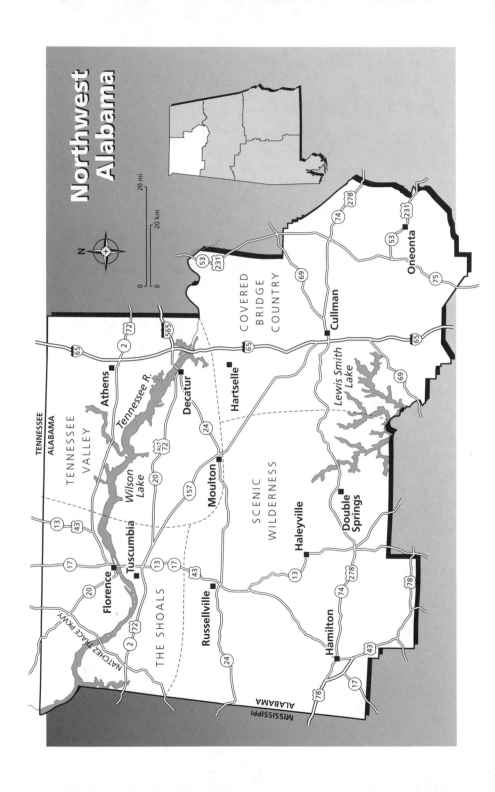

Northwest Alabama

20 mi
20 km

N

TENNESSEE
ALABAMA

TENNESSEE VALLEY

Tennessee R.

Athens

Decatur

Hartselle

COVERED BRIDGE COUNTRY

Cullman

Oneonta

Wilson Lake

Moulton

Lewis Smith Lake

SCENIC WILDERNESS

Haleyville

Double Springs

Tuscumbia

THE SHOALS

Florence

NATCHEZ TRACE PKWY.

Russellville

Hamilton

MISSISSIPPI
ALABAMA

65 · 72 · 2 · 565 · 65 · 53 · 231 · 69 · 74 · 278 · 231 · 53 · 75 · 65 · 13 · 43 · 17 · 20 · ALT 72 · 20 · 157 · 24 · 69 · 13 · 17 · 43 · 74 · 278 · 78 · 43 · 78 · 17

GAY'S TOP PICKS IN NORTHWEST ALABAMA

Alabama Music Hall of Fame, Tuscumbia

Ave Maria Grotto, Cullman

Bankhead National Forest, Double Springs

Blount County Covered Bridges, Oneonta

Dismals Canyon, Phil Campbell

General Joe Wheeler Plantation Home, Hillsboro

Indian Mound and Museum, Florence

Ivy Green, Tuscumbia

Natural Bridge, Natural Bridge

wild hydrangeas make lovely accents as you wend your way through the town. Strolling along streets lined by picket fences and fine old shade trees, you'll see a variety of vintage structures including lovely old Federal-style homes.

On Lauderdale Street you'll pass a brick church that dates to 1839 and contains its original pews. Although regular worship services no longer take place here, the historic structure is sometimes used for weddings and funerals. Notice the herringbone pattern of the brick walkway in front of the church. Mooresville's postmistress, Barbara Coker, using many of her lunch hours, excavated through grass and layers of dirt to expose the original brickwork.

Be sure to stop by the tiny post office on the corner of Lauderdale and High Streets. Built around 1840, this small weathered poplar building, with tin roof, pegged joints, and square head nails, contains the town's forty-eight original post boxes (first installed at the nearby Stagecoach Inn and Tavern).

The Stagecoach Inn, built sometime before 1825, once sold "supper for two bits." Across the street from the inn stands a small cottage, an example of Downing Gothic architecture. Dating to about 1890, the home was built and owned by Uncle Zack Simmons, a Black carpenter, and his wife, Aunt Mandy. Former Mooresville mayor Kathleen Lovvorn says that Aunt Mandy, famous for her jellies and pickles, often handed out homemade treats to the village youngsters.

The *Hurn-Thach-Boozer-McNiell House,* built around 1825 and located near the end of Market Street, once housed a tailor shop, where Andrew Johnson, who later became president, studied drafting and construction techniques under the supervision of Joseph Sloss (who specialized in making Prince Albert coats for gentlemen).

After departing Mooresville you may want to travel north to *Athens,* Limestone County's seat. Start your local tour by visiting the downtown courthouse square with its surrounding stores and stately old churches. Founded in 1818, Athens barely missed being the state's oldest incorporated town. (Nearby Mooresville won the race by only three days.) To see some of the town's antebellum and Victorian homes—many of which are identified by historic markers—drive along Pryor, Jefferson, and Clinton Streets.

Aunt Mandy and Uncle Zack Simmons Cottage

You may want to stop by the *Houston Memorial Library and Museum* (256–233–8770). Located at 101 North Houston Street, this house dates to 1835 and served as the home of George S. Houston (a former Alabama governor and United States senator) from 1845 to 1879. Exhibits include family portraits, period furniture, Native American artifacts, Civil War relics, and various items relating to local history. Each April, the library sponsors the Houston Street Fair featuring Civil War reenactments, blacksmithing demonstrations, clogging, an old-time auction, and plenty of good food. Hours are 10:00 A.M. to 5:00 P.M. Monday through Friday and 9:00 A.M. to noon Saturday.

For a toe-tapping good time, plan to take in the *Tennessee Valley Old Time Fiddlers Convention* held at Athens State College each October. Visitors converge on campus for two days of outdoor competitions featuring harmonica, banjo, fiddle, mandolin, dulcimer, and guitar playing and buck dancing sessions. For more information on local attractions and events, call (256) 232–2600.

Beaty Street takes you to Athens State College, Alabama's oldest institution of higher learning. While on this street, be sure to notice the Beaty-Mason House built in 1826, now the college president's home. Located at 302 North Beaty Street, the lovely 1840s Greek Revival *Founder's Hall* houses school offices, a library, and a chapel. This building's original portion escaped being burned by the Yankees when a letter allegedly written by President Lincoln appeared in the nick of time. On the second floor, the Altar of the New Testament features fine wood carvings in tulip poplar. Founder's Hall may be visited Monday through Friday from 8:00 A.M. to 4:30 P.M. Admission is free.

Before leaving Athens, plan to tour *Pleasant Hill,* locally known as the Donnell House. The circa 1845 T-shaped home, which contains some period furnishings, is located at 601 South Clinton Street on the Middle School campus. A chinked log cabin kitchen with working fireplace stands nearby. Historian Faye Axford offers an in-depth look at notable area homes in *The Lure and Lore of Limestone County,* which she coauthored with Chris Edwards. The book is available here, and proceeds from the sales go toward the Donnell House's continuing restoration. The home is open from 2:00 to 4:00 P.M. on Monday, Wednesday, and Friday, or by appointment. For more information call (256) 232–0743, (256) 232–5471, or (256) 233–0898.

After exploring Athens, head south to Decatur for another dose of history along with wildlife. Founded on the banks of the Tennessee River and originally called Rhodes Ferry, Decatur acquired its current name in 1820. At that time Congress and President James Monroe decided to honor Comm. Stephen Decatur by naming a town after him. A daring naval hero who commanded a three-ship squadron during the War of 1812, Decatur once proposed the following toast: "Our country: In her intercourse with foreign nations may she always be in the right; but our country, right or wrong."

You can see mallards along with blue buntings, herons, owls, woodpeckers, bald eagles, and other birds on exhibit at *Cook's Natural Science Museum* (256–350–9347), located at 412 Thirteenth Street Southeast. Hands-on exhibits and changing displays present the world of nature—from insects and seashells to reptiles and rocks. The privately owned museum features displays of iridescent butterflies and a mounted, life-size black bear dripping with honey. Chester, Percy, Steve, Corny, and other live snakes help visitors learn to distinguish between the poisonous and harmless members of their species. Hours are 9:00 A.M. to noon and 1:00 to 5:00 P.M. Monday through Saturday and 2:00 to 5:00 P.M. Sunday. Admission is free.

Nearby at 1715 Sixth Avenue Southeast, the folks who work at *Big Bob Gibson's* (256–350–6969) say they cook "the best barbecue in town." A Decatur tradition since 1925, the restaurant serves real hickory-smoked pit-barbecued pork, beef, and chicken. Barbecued potatoes (baked and topped with meat) also prove popular menu items. You can grab a bite here or get an order to go. Hours are "can to can't" (10:00 A.M. to 8:30 P.M.) seven days a week, excluding Thanksgiving and Christmas days. Economical prices.

Stop by Decatur's Visitor Information Center at 719 Sixth Avenue Southeast for a pamphlet called *A Walking Tour of Historic Decatur,* which notes many of the city's late nineteenth-century homes that can be seen in the Old Decatur and New Albany historic districts. Call (256) 350–2028 or (800) 524–6181 for more information on local attractions.

Head to the city's northern section to tour the handsome *Old State Bank* (256–350–5060), established during Andrew Jackson's presidency. Located at 925 Bank Street Northeast, Alabama's oldest bank building now serves as a museum. Upstairs you'll see the head cashier's spacious living quarters, furnished in the 1830s style.

During the Civil War this classic style structure served as a hospital for both Union and Confederate soldiers. The bank's thick vault possibly became a shielded surgery chamber during the heat of battle. Outside, the large limestone columns, quarried at a local plantation, still retain traces of Civil War graffiti along with battle scars from musket fire. The bank was among Decatur's few buildings to survive the Civil War. Bank tours are free, and the building is open Monday through Friday from 9:30 A.M. to noon and 1:30 to 4:30 P.M. or by appointment.

Nearby at 901 Railroad Street Northwest, you'll find the *Dancy-Polk House* (256–353–3579), where owners Jan and Jeff Lea offer bed-and-breakfast accommodations. Listed on the National Register of Historic Places, this large home also withstood the Civil War's ravage and has done duty as a boarding house and hotel. The 1829 house contains a Civil War Museum on the main floor, and the Leas, who travel all over the South participating in Civil War reenactments, offer tours by appointment for a small donation. Standard rates.

To sample a good mix of shops featuring antiques, clothing, toys, and gifts, take a stroll down Bank Street. At 722 Bank Street Northeast, you'll see *Nebrig-Howell House Antiques* (256–351–1655). Owner Pam Howell carries an inventory of fine French and English pieces. For a memorable dining experience, step across the street to *Simp McGhee's* (256–353–6284), at 725 Bank Street Northeast. Named for a colorful early-twentieth-century riverboat captain, this pub-style eatery offers Simp's stuffed Gulf flounder as well as many pasta, poultry, and beef entrees. Chef Dean Moore directs culinary activities and offers seafood specialties. Lunch is served from 11:00 A.M. till 1:30 P.M. Monday

Gay's Favorite Annual Events in Northwest Alabama

*Alabama Jubilee Hot-Air Balloon
Classic,* Point Mallard Park, Decatur,
Memorial Day weekend;
(256) 350–2028 or (800) 524–6181

Alabama Renaissance Faire,
Florence, fourth weekend in October;
(256) 766–3234

Bloomin' Festival at St. Bernard,
Cullman, mid-April; (256) 734–0454

Covered Bridge Festival, Oneonta, fourth
weekend of October; (205) 274–2153

Helen Keller Festival, Tuscumbia, late
June; (256) 383–4066

Oktoberfest, Cullman, early October;
(256) 734 0454

September Skirmish, Point Mallard
Park, Decatur, Labor Day weekend;
(256) 350–2028 or (800) 524–6181

Southern Wildlife Festival, Decatur,
October; (255) 350–2028 or
(800) 524–6181

The Spirit of America Festival,
Point Mallard Park, Decatur, July 4;
(256) 350–2028 or (800) 524–6181

W. C. Handy Festival, Florence, early
August; (256) 766–7642

Waterloo Heritage Days,
Waterloo, Memorial Day weekend;
(256) 740–1141

through Friday. Dinner hours are Monday to Thursday from 5:30 to 9:00 P.M. and Friday and Saturday from 5:30 until 9:30 P.M.

Standing in Decatur's New Albany downtown area at 115 Johnston Street Southeast, you'll see the *Old Cotaco Opera House.* Often called the Old Masonic Building, the big brick structure dates to 1890. Although you won't see a touring vaudeville act here today, you'll find the complex offers other enticing treats. For instance, hungry travelers can visit *Curry's on Johnston Street* (256–350–6715), located on the building's lower level, for lunch or pick-up items. The eatery serves homemade soups, sandwiches, casseroles, fresh bread, and desserts. Hours are 8:00 A.M. to 5:30 P.M. Monday through Friday and 11:00 A.M. to 2:00 P.M. Saturday. Dinner hours run from 6:00 to 10:00 P.M. Thursday through Saturday. Upstairs in the *Carriage House* (256–355–4349), owned by Marella and Jim Adams, you'll find upscale women's fashions and a bridal department along with unique accessories and gift items. Hours are 9:30 A.M. to 5:30 P.M. Monday through Friday and 10:00 A.M. to 5:00 P.M. Saturday.

Heading along to 402 Johnston Street Southeast, you'll see *Shelley's Iron Gate* (256–350–6795) in a lovely butter-colored brick house with green awnings and shutters. The restaurant, a pleasant place to enjoy lunch in a tearoom atmosphere, serves a scrumptious strawberry pretzel salad. Other favorites include Miss Daisy's beef casserole and poulet de Normandie, consisting of baked chicken and dressing in a cheese-mushroom sauce. Prices range from economical to moderate. Hours are 11:00 A.M. to 2:00 P.M. Monday through Saturday.

To visit one of *The 100 Best Small Towns in America* (selected by Norman Crampton for his nationwide guide), head south for **Hartselle,** now a mecca for antiques shoppers. (For a list of the other ninety-nine towns, you'll have to buy the book.) Make your first stop the historic Depot Building, which houses the Hartselle Area Chamber of Commerce (256–773–4370 or 800–294–0692). On one wall you'll see a WPA mural painted in 1937 that illustrates the major role cotton played in the area's early economy. While here collect a map and guide to local shops. Open by 10:00 A.M., most shops close on Wednesday and Sunday.

Afterward stroll to **The Emporium at Hickory Crossing** (256–773–4972), located at 200 Railroad Street Southwest. This former freight building now houses some specialty shops, antiques, and arts.

Alabama Trivia

Alabama symbols include: the yellowhammer, the state bird; the camellia, the state flower; and the Southern pine, the state tree.

Browsing along Main Street, you'll see **Elizabeth Alexandria,** the **Zandy Zebra,** and other specialty shops, with an array of everything from bric-a-brac and potpourri to primitive antiques and quilts.

After leaving Hartselle, follow State Route 36 west, watching for the Oakville turn and signs directing you to **Jesse Owens Memorial Park** (256–974–3636) on County Route 203. The park's focal point is an 8-foot, one-ton bronze statue of Owens, who won four gold medals in the 1936 Olympics. Branko Medenica, a native of Germany who now lives in Birmingham, sculpted the piece, which depicts Owens running and incorporates the familiar Olympic rings. Mounted on a 6-foot granite base, the statue was unveiled in a 1996 ceremony attended by members of the athlete's family when the Olympic torch passed through Oakville en route to Atlanta's games.

The park also offers a visitors center, museum, Olympic-size track, softball field, basketball court, walking trail, picnic pavilions, and replicas of the 1936 Olympic torch and Owens's modest home. Owens, who was born in Oakville and spent his early life here, once said, "It behooves a man with God-given ability to stand 10 feet tall. You never know how many youngsters may be watching." The park is open during daylight hours, and admission is free. The museum is open from 11:00 A.M. to 3:00 P.M. Tuesday through Saturday and from 1:00 to 5:00 P.M. Sunday. Admission for museum.

Before leaving the vicinity, take time to visit the *Oakville Indian Mounds,* a park and museum (256–905–2494) at 1219 County Route 187. Located 8 miles southeast of Moulton just off State Route 157, the complex features a massive 2,000-year-old Woodland Indian Mound, a Copena Indian burial mound, and a museum modeled after a seven-sided Cherokee Council House. The museum contains a 12-foot wooden statue of Sequoyah plus thousands of artifacts-some dating back to 10,000 B.C. Hours are 8:00 A.M. to 4:30 P.M. Monday through Friday and 1:00 to 4:30 P.M. Saturday and Sunday. Admission is free.

Afterward, head toward Moulton, stopping by *Classical Fruits* (256–974–8813) at 8831 State Highway 157. At this combination fruit market, restaurant, gift shop, and greenhouse, Franny and Hoyt Adair offer a delightful selection of products made with their own home-grown fruits. From muscadine hull preserve and raspberry syrup to purple basil jelly and more, you'll find unique food items and gifts. Try a green apple dipped in chocolate fudge and twirled in pecans. Hoyt makes the fudge—and not just chocolate, either. The strawberry, maple nut, and peanut butter versions also prove popular. In season the Adairs offer peach and apple fudge. Franny packs the candy in beribboned boxes *almost* too pretty to open.

During their respective growing months, fresh strawberries, cherries, blueberries, blackberries, raspberries, plums, peaches, apples, pears, grapes, muscadines, and other fruits, vegetables, and herbs are available here. Hoyt's nearby 140-acre fruit-growing operation features a wide variety of fruit cultivars. He does some experimental growing for several universities and develops new fruit varieties from other countries. At the time of my visit, he was test-growing a five-acre plot with plums, apricots, cherries, peaches, and other stone fruits from Eastern Europe. "One gem," he says, "is worth ninety-nine failures."

You can opt for barbecue, which comes with a choice of three sauces, or a daily plate lunch special with fresh vegetables in season. Restaurant service starts at 11:00 A.M., but market hours are 8:00 A.M. to 8:00 P.M. except on Wednesday and Sunday, when closing time is 5:00 P.M.

Afterward, continue your journey toward Moulton. Try to hit Moulton at mealtime so you can sample the terrific lemon-pepper grilled catfish fillet at *Western Sirloin Steak House* (256–974–7191), with a huge grain-bin entrance and tin walls. Located at 11383 State Highway 157 (behind Winn Dixie), the restaurant also features charbroiled chicken breast and rib eye steak at economical to moderate rates. The restaurant, which is owned by Ann and Larry Littrell and Barbara and Ray

Chenault, is open Sunday through Thursday from 11:00 A.M. to 9:00 P.M. Friday and Saturday hours are 11:00 A.M. to 10:00 P.M.

At *Animal House Zoological Park* (256–974–8634), located about 8 miles northwest of Moulton near Hatton on Lawrence County Route 231 just off County Route 236, you'll find an unusual place where Dr. Doolittle would feel at home. The owners have been raising exotic and endangered animals for two decades and now care for some 600 pets, including Persian leopards, clouded leopards, black jaguars, African lions, Bengal and Siberian tigers, ligers, panthers, cougars, servals, bears, camels, llamas, Barbados sheep, antelope, capybaras, and a giraffe plus a varied collection of primates (who dine on fruit medleys that might rival a restaurant's salad creations).

You can visit the park between June 1 and November 15. The facility closes for repairs from November 15 to March 15 and is reserved for school tours from March through June 1. From Monday through Saturday tours start at 10:00 A.M., continuing each hour until 2:00 P.M. All tours begin on the hour. Sunday tour hours are 1:00, 2:00, and 3:00 P.M. Modest admission.

After talking to the animals, continue in the direction of Hillsboro to see "Fighting Joe" Wheeler's plantation. A Confederate cavalry commander, Wheeler later became a U.S. Army general and also served in Congress. Watch for signs directing you to the *General Joe Wheeler Plantation Home* (256–637–8513). Turning off the highway, you'll follow a secluded driveway lined with venerable oak trees. Open the wooden gate and thread your way through a maze of lovely old English boxwoods. On-site curator Melissa Beasley lives in the adjacent residence. On a tour of the two-and-a-half-story Wheeler home, run by the Alabama Historical Commission, you'll see original furniture, china, uniforms, military medals, portraits, Civil War memorabilia, books, and other family items. Wheeler's daughter, Miss Annie, who served as a nurse in Cuba and later in France during World War I, lived here until her death in 1955. Be sure not to miss the old log house and family cemetery on the grounds. The old kitchen now houses a gift shop. Currently under restoration, the Wheeler home remains open for tours from 9:00 A.M. to 4:00 P.M. Thursday through Saturday and from 1:00 to 5:00 P.M. Sunday, except for major holidays. Modest admission. For more information e-mail Wheeler@ala-net.com.

Afterward continue west on State Route 20 about 3 miles to *Courtland,* named to the National Register of Historic Places for its 1818 development of the early town plan. Local architectural styles span almost two centuries. For a brochure on Courtland, which details a driving tour of the historical district, stop by Town Hall, or call (800) 648–5381.

After exploring Courtland, continue to **Doublehead Resort & Lodge** (800–685–9267) for some relaxation and outdoor recreation. Located at 145 County Road 314 near Town Creek, the complex underscores a Native American theme from its name to its design and furnishings. A split-rail fence defines pastures, and wooden poles frame the metal entrance gate with its "Welcome Friends" greeting in Cherokee characters.

The property takes its name from Doublehead, a Cherokee chief who once lived on this land. The management wants to sustain a Native American awareness as it continues to develop this distinctive resort. The main lodge features a 5,000-square-foot deck overlooking Wilson Lake. Hammered metal designs of free-floating feathers and an upward-pointing arrowhead frame the double hand-carved front doors. A locally found Cherokee medallion inspired the lodge's unique chandelier.

Guests occupy cedar log cabins, each with three bedrooms, two baths, and a completely equipped kitchen. (After all, Doublehead's appreciation for creature comforts is well documented.) Beds are constructed from rustic cedar posts, and Indian wall hangings echo the motif. Each cabin comes with a beckoning hammock, grill, picnic table, and private pier. Recreational activities range from fishing, boating, waterskiing, and hunting to horseback riding through grazing herds of Texas longhorns. Other amenities include two tennis courts, a basketball court, and a 2½-mile walking/nature trail. The facility offers rentals for jet-skis, pontoons, canoes, and other watercraft, a sporting clays course, and a private 1,100-acre hunting preserve. Rates range from moderate to deluxe.

Afterward, head west toward Tuscumbia.

The Shoals

You will be transported back in time when you arrive in Tuscumbia. At 300 South Dickson Street stands **The Log Cabin Stagecoach Stop at Cold Water,** an authentic structure from the pioneer period. Continue to Commercial Row, located on the north side of West Fifth Street between Water and Main Streets. This block of seven bordering brick buildings, dating to the 1830s, represents local antebellum commercial architecture. During the 1880s, Capt. Arthur Keller (Helen Keller's father) published his newspaper, *The North Alabamian,* here in the corner building.

Water pump at Ivy Green

Nearby at 300 West North Commons stands *Ivy Green,* the birthplace of Helen Keller. After her graduation from Radcliffe College, Miss Keller worked tirelessly on behalf of the handicapped by lecturing, writing articles and books (some of which have been translated into more than fifty languages), and appealing to legislative bodies to improve conditions for those with impaired sight and hearing. Because she conquered her own handicaps and gained an international reputation for inspiring other handicapped persons to live richer lives, she became known as America's "First Lady of Courage."

Of Ivy Green Miss Keller wrote, "The Keller homestead . . . was called 'Ivy Green' because the house and surrounding trees and fences were covered with beautiful English Ivy." On the grounds you'll also see English boxwood, magnolia, mimosa, roses, and honeysuckle. The family home contains many original furnishings, photographs, letters, awards, books, and Miss Keller's braille typewriter.

Summer visitors can watch a miracle reenacted at a performance of

William Gibson's drama *The Miracle Worker* staged on Ivy Green's grounds and directed by Darren Butler. The play culminates with a vivid portrayal of the poignant incident at the water pump when teacher Anne Sullivan helped the blind and deaf child break through her black void into "a wonderful world with all its sunlight and beauty."

Except for major holidays, Ivy Green is open year-round. The home can be toured Monday through Saturday from 8:30 A.M. to 4:00 P.M. and on Sunday from 1:00 to 4:00 P.M. Modest admission. For more information on Ivy Green, the play, or the annual Helen Keller Festival (scheduled the last weekend of June each year), call (256) 383–4066.

At some point during your visit, you may want to learn more about this area, called *the Shoals.* Looping through north Alabama, the Tennessee River comes into its own here in the state's northwest corner. At one time navigators found the Muscle Shoals rapids too formidable to negotiate, but the Tennessee Valley Authority (TVA) solved this problem with a series of strategically placed dams. The jagged rocks that created perilous swirling currents and wrecked boats now lie "buried" far below the water's surface.

To get a good idea of the river's impact on the region, you can visit the TVA Reservation at Muscle Shoals to see *Wilson Dam.* With its north end in Lauderdale County and its south end in Lawrence County, the dam stretches almost a mile and serves as a bridge for State Highway 101. Named for President Woodrow Wilson, the dam was initiated during World War I to supply power for making munitions.

To see the dam from another perspective, head to nearby *Renaissance Tower* (256–764–5900), located at One Hightower Place in Florence on the Tennessee River's north bank. Housing an aquarium and The Renaissance Grill, the 300-foot structure overlooks Wilson Dam and offers an on-a-clear-day-you-can-see-forever kind of view for some 40 miles. For restaurant hours call (256) 718–0092. The tower is open Monday through Saturday from 10:00 A.M. to 5:00 P.M. and from 11:00 A.M. to 5:00 P.M. on Sunday. Modest admission.

Afterward follow Veteran's Drive to downtown Florence, which features a number of interesting attractions such as the *Indian Mound and Museum* on South Court Street near the river. The ancient mound looms to a height of 42 feet, the largest of several in the Tennessee Valley. Near the mound, called *Wawmanona* by Native Americans, stands a museum containing displays of tools, ornaments, pottery, fluted points, and other artifacts along with exhibits on the Mississippian culture's mysterious mound builders. Modest admission. Except for major holidays, the site is open Tuesday through Saturday from 10:00 A.M. to 4:00 P.M. For further information call (256) 760–6427.

Nearby, at 601 Riverview Drive, you'll find the only structure in the state designed by Frank Lloyd Wright. The **Stanley and Mildred Rosenbaum House,** conceived in 1939 and completed in 1940, so reflected Wright's iconoclastic approach to organic domestic architecture that the young couple could not find a local contractor to take on this project. Along with his final plans, Wright sent an apprentice to supervise the construction of this Usonian house, now on the National Register of Historic Places.

Designed for a two-acre site overlooking the Tennessee River, the architect utilized large areas of glass to take advantage of the view and innovative radiant heating because of the proximity of the Tennessee Valley

On the Coon Dog Trail

*O*ne sunny morning in August, my mother and I set out to find the Coon Dog Memorial Graveyard. Our approach led up a hill, and before reaching the top, my car developed resistance symptoms. Smoke came pouring out from some private place, and the car whimpered and gave a last gasp.

Being an auto illiterate, I knew not what to do. "You don't have AAA?!" my mother said in a slightly accusatory tone. (Mothers are born saying things like "I told you so," and yes, I now have AAA and a car phone.)

We were in a wooded area, seemingly isolated, but I saw a house in the distance. A woman answered my knock and let me use her phone. As we waited on the porch for a tow truck, she told us much about the surrounding area and its abundant wildlife, even showing us several sizable snake skins. After the arrival of the tow truck, driven by a history buff, I heard even more anecdotes and collected tips

on local sites to check out—thanks to a disaster in disguise and two good samaritans.

Anyway, back to Key Underwood's Coon Dog Memorial Graveyard, which is located south of Cherokee, via Colbert County Route 21. Now a park, the site contains markers and tombstones (some with epitaphs) for more than one hundred coon dogs.

The graveyard's origin dates to the death of Troop, a coonhound owned by Key Underwood. Here on September 4, 1937, Underwood and some friends buried the dog at a favorite hunting spot. An annual Labor Day celebration commemorating the anniversary of the graveyard's founding takes place in the park and features bluegrass music, buck dancing, barbecue, and even a liars' contest. Political hopefuls often show up for the festivities. Otherwise, the site projects a sense of serenity, and the surroundings look much as they did during the days when Troop picked up the scent of a coon here.

Authority and therefore low-cost electricity. "Mr. Wright wanted to use all natural materials," Mrs. Rosenbaum says, "no paint or plaster-only cypress wood, brick, glass, and concrete." After the couple's four sons arrived, Wright designed an addition—its clean lines flow naturally (and imperceptibly) from the original structure.

A gifted weaver, Mrs. Rosenbaum also does needlepoint and has adapted a selection of Frank Lloyd Wright designs to this stitchery medium. You'll see her weaving room, its yarn skeins making splashes of color against the wood's tawny tones, on the house tour. The house museum may be seen by reservation only. Call (256) 740–4141 for tour information. Admission is charged.

To see the birthplace of the "Father of the Blues," head for 620 West College Street, where you'll find the *W. C. Handy Home and Museum* (256–760–6434), fronted by a fence of split rails. The hand-hewn log cabin, birthplace of William Christopher Handy, contains furnishings representative of the period around 1873. The adjoining museum features Handy's legendary trumpet and the piano on which he composed "St. Louis Blues." Handy also wrote more than 150 other musical compositions, including such standards as "Memphis Blues" and "Beale Street Blues." You'll see handwritten sheet music, photographs, correspondence, awards, and other items pertaining to Handy's life and legacy. The adjacent library houses Handy's extensive book collection and serves as a resource center for Black history and culture. The museum is open Tuesday through Saturday from 10:00 A.M. to 4:00 P.M. Modest admission.

For a week of swinging jazz, plan to visit Florence during August to take in the *W. C. Handy Music Festival.* Special events include parades, jam sessions, the "DaDooRunRun" for joggers, a picnic-jazz evening on the Tennessee River's banks, the colorful "Street Strut" led by the Grand Oobeedoo, and a concert with celebrated jazz musicians.

The Handy Festival evolved from a chance meeting in the Muscle Shoals Airport when two men struck up what turned out to be more than a casual conversation. Local veterinarian David Mussleman happened to ask Willie Ruff, a Yale music professor, about the horn he carried. This led to a discussion about native son W. C. Handy and his tremendous musical contribution-and subsequently to the annual festival held in Handy's honor. For more information call the festival office at (256) 766–7642.

By now you're probably ready for a meal. If so, head to *Court Street Cafe* (256–767–4300) at 201 North Seminary Street, where owner Jake Jacobs and staff, operating on the premise that "it's the little things that count," grind their own coffee beans, squeeze fresh oranges, and give each visiting child a treat such as a balloon, coloring book, crayons, or animal crackers.

Noted for its salads, the restaurant features a grilled chicken version with almonds and fresh fruit. You might also try the chicken tenders platter, and top off your meal with one of the cafe's specialty desserts. Sunday through Thursday, the restaurant is open from 11:00 A.M. to 10:00 P.M. Friday and Saturday hours run from 11:00 A.M. to 11:00 P.M. By the way, the restaurant is *not* on Court Street.

While exploring Florence, you'll pass Wilson Park on the corner of Tuscaloosa Street and Wood Avenue. This setting serves as a backdrop for a number of local festivities, such as the ***Alabama Renaissance Faire.*** In fact, if you visit the park during this October gala, you can enjoy diversions ranging from derring-do with sword and shield to music, dance, and drama as residents bring to life some of the color, action, and excitement of the Renaissance period.

Beside the park you'll see the ***Kennedy-Douglass Center for the Arts*** at 217 East Tuscaloosa Street. This 1918 Georgian-style mansion and adjacent structures serve as a performing arts center. Stop by to view the current art exhibit and visit the gift shop.

At 316 North Court Street, you'll find ***Trowbridge's*** (256–764–1503), which offers sandwiches, salads, soups, chili, ice cream, and Oh My Gosh—a brownie piled high with vanilla ice cream and topped with hot caramel, whipped cream, and a cherry. The dessert gets its name from what most people say when they see it.

A mirrored soda fountain lists ice cream flavors and drink choices. Third-generation owner Don Trowbridge credits the eatery's longevity to keeping the menu simple. Don's grandfather built Trowbridge's Creamery in 1918, and local farmers brought their milk and cream in to be processed. The family occupied the second floor over the ice cream shop, and the dairy stood behind. The founder's original recipe for Orange-Pineapple Ice Cream, now shipped from New Orleans, remains a favorite with today's patrons.

A large painting on the rear wall depicts Trowbridge's interior from previous years—with almost no changes. Posters publicizing past local festivals pay tribute to Helen Keller and W. C. Handy, "Father of the Blues." Framed photos depict early Florence scenes and the construction of Wilson Dam, which originated as a World War I project to supply power for making munitions. Hours run from 9:00 A.M. to 5:30 P.M. Monday through Saturday.

A short distance away at 203 Hermitage Drive stands **Pope's Tavern** (256–760–6439), now a history-filled museum. Originally built as a stagecoach stopover and tavern, the attractive structure of white-painted bricks dates to 1811. Travelers on the Natchez Trace stopped here, and so did Andrew Jackson when he passed through in 1814 on his way to fight the British at the Battle of New Orleans. During the Civil War the inn served as a hospital where wounded Confederate and Union soldiers lay side by side to receive medical treatment from local doctors and the town's women.

Inside the tavern you'll see period furnishings, kitchen utensils, tools, firearms, Civil War uniforms, photos, letters, and pioneer artifacts. Be sure to notice the worn silk Stars and Bars. This flag, hand-stitched by local ladies, traveled to Virginia with the Lauderdale Volunteers (one of northwestern Alabama's first Confederate military units) when they left to fight in the first Battle of Manassas. Before you leave, notice the Florence Light Running Wagon, made in a local factory that at one time was the world's second-largest wagon-building operation. Modest admission. Except for major holidays, hours are 10:00 A.M. to 4:00 P.M. Tuesday through Saturday.

Nearby, at 658 North Wood Avenue in Florence's historic district, stands the **Wood Avenue Inn** (256–766–8441), a turreted, towered Victorian structure with a wraparound porch. Built in 1889, this Queen Anne-style home offers bed-and-breakfast accommodations

Strange As It Sounds

South of Russellville and west of Phil Campbell (that's the town's name) lies a unique attraction known locally as the Dismals. Located at 901 County Road 8, **Dismals Canyon** once served as a ceremonial ground for Native Americans and a hiding place for outlaws. In addition to caves, waterfalls, craggy rock formations, rainbows, and unusual vegetation, the canyon contains phosphorescent creatures called "dismalites" that glow in the dark.

Geologists speculate that a prehistoric earthquake produced the place's chaotic geography with its many natural grottoes and bridges. This eerie but intriguing site also features both a natural arboretum and winding staircase.

After hiking through this place primeval, you may decide to take advantage of other activities—canoeing down Bear Creek, biking a 4-mile mountain trail, or swimming in Dismals Creek. For overnight visitors the site offers lodges (with fireplaces), a country store, RV hookups, and camping facilities. Admission. For more information call (205) 993–4559.

with private bath and breakfast served in your room or suite. Standard to moderate rates.

Don't leave The Shoals without dining at *LOUISIANA The Restaurant* (256–386–0801), in spacious quarters at 1311 East Sixth Street in Muscle Shoals. Owner/chef Matthew Wood (who hails from New Orleans with impressive cooking credentials from Antoine's, Upperline, and other fine restaurants) and his wife, Pat, will make you glad you stopped. Start with Matthew's special Creole-style gumbo or crab-stuffed mushrooms. Menus change weekly, but imaginative interpretations and scrumptious selections remain constant. House specialties run the gamut from a classic fish conti, a seafood-pasta dish called shrimp and crawfish Virginia, beef medallions with chef's sauce, and spicy shrimp Louisiana. Here desserts fall in the inspired category, so plan accordingly. Louisiana is open Tuesday through Sunday from

Good Food— LOUISIANA-Style

M atthew Wood, LOUISIANA The Restaurant's award-winning chef and owner, provided the following delicious recipe for readers:

Shrimp and Corn Chowder

1 cup yellow onion, finely diced

1/2 cup celery, finely diced

1/2 cup carrots, finely diced

1 cup bell pepper, finely diced

2 ounces butter

2 bay leaves

1/8 cup garlic, chopped

1/3 cup all-purpose flour

1/4 cup white wine

2/3 cup shrimp stock (may substitute water)

2 cups milk

2 cups heavy cream (Half & Half)

1/4 teaspoon basil leaves

1/2 teaspoon salt

1/2 teaspoon ground white pepper

1/8 teaspoon Cayenne pepper

1 1/2 teaspoons parsley flakes

1/2 teaspoon dillweed

1/8 teaspoon thyme leaves

1 cup raw shrimp, peeled and deveined

2/3 pound whole kernel corn (fresh or frozen)

green onion

Sauté onion, celery, carrots, and green pepper in butter with bay leaves and garlic on a low fire. Cook until translucent. Add flour and cook for 3 minutes. Add wine and shrimp stock and simmer for 5 minutes. Add all remaining ingredients except shrimp and corn. Simmer 30 minutes on a low fire. Add shrimp and corn and simmer until shrimp are pink. Serve with finely sliced green onion. Makes about 10 servings.

11:00 A.M. to 2:00 P.M. Dinner hours run from 5:00 to 9:00 P.M. Tuesday through Thursday and till 10:00 P.M. on Friday and Saturday, with reservations recommended. Moderate prices.

Scenic Wilderness

eaving The Shoals, you might enjoy taking the **Natchez Trace Parkway.** A portion of the historic Trace cuts across this corner of Alabama through Lauderdale and Colbert Counties. Once a pioneer footpath, this route took travelers from Natchez, Mississippi, to Nashville, Tennessee. To intercept the Trace, which offers plenty of scenic stops, picnic spots, and nature trails, head northwest on State Route 20.

Exit at U.S. Highway 72 near the tiny town of **Cherokee.** At the **Wooden Nickel Restaurant** (256–359–4225), near the railroad tracks, owner Cathy Jones offers good vegetable lunches and a variety of dinner platters. Economical prices. The restaurant's hours are 7:00 A.M. to 9:00 P.M. Sunday through Thursday and until 10:00 P.M. Friday and Saturday.

Heading south to Winfield (at the juncture of U.S. Highway 78 and State Route 253) takes you to **White Oaks Inn** (205–487–4115 or 800–482– 4115). At the end of a driveway flanked by stone lions, this lovely bed-and-breakfast stands on a knoll in a parklike setting at 300 Regal Street. Owners Linda and Roger Sanders have achieved an open, airy look in their renovation of this 1918 home with a welcoming front porch (plus a bit of whimsy with the English telephone booth just inside the entrance). Accommodations include five rooms, each with private bath, in the main house and five cabins on the grounds. Guests can enjoy such amenities as a hot tub and pool (with robes and shower shoes provided). Standard rates. Call for reservations and specific directions.

In this area you'll find yet another fascinating attraction, **Natural Bridge** (205–486–5330). Located on U.S. Highway 278 about a mile west of the intersection of State Routes 5 and 13, this double-span, 60-foot-high sandstone bridge, thousands of years in the making, looms majestically in its pristine setting. Surrounding this impressive formation, presumably the longest natural bridge east of the Rockies, you'll see massive moss-covered boulders and lush vegetation. Local flora includes ferns, bigleaf magnolias, mountain laurel, and oakleaf hydrangeas. Inviting nature paths and picnic areas make this a pleasant place for an outing. Moulton photographer Charles Jordan's postcards, available in the gift

Meet Jerry Brown, Ninth-Generation Potter

*W*hile exploring this region of scenic wilderness, consider a visit to **Brown's Pottery** *(205–921–9483 or 800–341–4919), located at 1414 County Road 81, 3 miles south of Hamilton. Here, Jerry Brown carries on a family tradition of pottery making that spans nine generations. In 1992 Jerry and his wife Sandra made a trip to Washington, D.C., where he received a National Heritage Fellowship Award, presented by President and Mrs. Bush. Jerry's work is exhibited in galleries across the country as well the Smithsonian, where he has been invited several times to demonstrate pottery-making.*

The traditional Southern folk potter has captured numerous awards at shows and festivals, and his work is sought by collectors. "Folk pottery increases in value," said Jerry, who signs and dates his pieces. In a "Quest for America's Best," QVC shopping network featured his work on national television. For this show Jerry filled an order for 1,500 pitchers, which sold out in two minutes.

One of the nation's few practicing traditional potters, Jerry remembers "playing around on the potter's wheel before I was old enough to start to school." He performs his magic by combining water with local clay, which "looks almost blue. The South is known for its good clay," he added. Using a backhoe to dig the clay from a 150-year old pit, Jerry then turns the

process over to his four-legged assistant, Blue, who does the mixing by walking circles around a mule-powered clay grinder. Jerry designed and built the brick oval kiln, in which he fires his work at temperatures that exceed 3,000 degrees Fahrenheit.

The pottery's showroom features blue-speckled pitchers, bowls, churns, candle holders, crocks, mugs, pie plates, bluebird houses, and more. Face jugs, Jerry's specialty, were historically used to hold harmful substances. Sometimes called ugly jugs, the vessels feature faces that don't win beauty contests but do earn awards and are coveted by collectors. The jugs sell for prices ranging from $30 to $200 and vary in size up to the largest, a five-gallon container.

Before leaving the pottery, I purchased several gifts. The crocks do double duty, Jerry pointed out, demonstrating how to use the container's lip to sharpen a knife. Even now as I write, I am drinking coffee from a thick mug with a blue, feathered design. (Ask Jerry to tell you the story of how a mishap with flying chicken feathers inspired one of his popular patterns.)

To view the pottery-making process as it was done in the olden days or to buy unique gifts (for yourself and others), head to Hamilton, near the Mississippi border. The pottery's hours run from 8:30 A.M. till 5:00 P.M. Monday through Saturday.

shop, capture some of the site's ambience. Modest admission. The facility is open daily year-round from 8:00 A.M. till sunset.

To topple back in time a bit, drop by *Dixie Den* (205–486–8577) in nearby Haleyville for an authentic chocolate (or your own preference) mixed-in-a-metal-container milk shake. While slurping or sharing it, you can catch a glimpse of the town's past because black-and-white photos of the old Dixie Hotel and other bygone buildings line the walls; and you may also recognize hometown personality Pat Buttram's photo. Owners Judy and Toby Sherrill offer homemade chicken and tuna salads, soups and sandwiches, including the Dixie Dog for big appetites (two hot dogs on a bun plus chili, kraut, and trimmings). Hours run from 10:30 A.M. to 4:00 P.M. Monday through Wednesday and till 8:00 P.M. on Thursday and Friday. On Saturday the cafe closes at 3:00 P.M. Next door in the same 1948 complex, the Dixie Theater's nostalgic lobby beckons. If the theater is closed, you might prevail upon the Sherrills to let you have a peek.

Continuing east through Winston County, you'll find the town of Double Springs, located in the **William B. Bankhead National Forest.** This huge forest (named for the distinguished political family of actress Tallulah Bankhead) spreads over most of Winston County and north into Lawrence County.

In front of the Winston County Courthouse at **Double Springs** stands **Dual Destiny,** the statue of a Civil War soldier flanked by billowing Confederate and Union flags. Contrary to common assumption, many Alabamians remained staunch Unionists during the Civil War, and "the Free State of Winston" represented such a contingent. At **Looney's Amphitheater and Park** (205–489–5000), 7 miles east of Double Springs on U.S. Highway 278, summer visitors can watch an outdoor musical drama depicting Winston County's struggle to remain independent during the Civil War. After Alabama's secession (which passed by a narrow vote), these hill-country people, led by local teacher Christopher Sheats, took the position that if a state could secede from the Union, then a county could secede from a state.

The Incident at Looney's Tavern, based on local history, unfolds under a starry sky with a cricket chorus in the background. Researched, written, and directed by Lanny McAlister, the colorful production features a cast and crew composed of drama and music majors from colleges across the state, plus plenty of local talent. Highlights of the mountainside amphitheater production include an elaborate ballroom scene and a fireworks show. Staged from mid-June through mid-August, the action-packed performance with dancing, singing, and humor makes a delightful evening's entertainment.

The park opens at 1:00 P.M., and the play begins at 8:00 P.M. Call for information on admission rates and the monthly dinner theater productions.

Early arrivals can visit *Caroline's Gifts,* a specialty shop featuring handmade mountain crafts. To sample some tasty hill-country cookin', stop by *Sister Sarah's Kitchen,* which offers a wide selection of salads, vegetables, and meats, served buffet fashion. Moderate prices.

As a prelude to the play, you can take a sightseeing excursion aboard *The Free State Lady,* a reproduction riverboat that docks about a mile from the theater. While cruising Smith Lake, your captain will share some interesting stories about the "wild and scenic Sipsey" Wilderness Area and local history.

While visiting the Free State of Winston, take time to explore some of the surrounding *Sipsey Wilderness.* With 25,988 acres, Sipsey provides plenty of off-the-beaten-path territory, including 20 miles of hiking trails.

Afterward take U.S. Highway 278 east and head toward Cullman.

Covered Bridge Country

To see Alabama's largest covered truss bridge, continue east from Winston County on U.S. Highway 278. Watch for the left turn to *Clarkson Covered Bridge* (sometimes called the Legg Bridge), located a short distance north of the highway on Cullman County Road 11. The bridge, situated in a picturesque park setting, stretches 270 feet across Crooked Creek. Supported by four large stone piers, this "town-truss" structure features latticed timbers, clapboard siding, and a roof of cedar shingles. The bridge, restored in 1975, dates to 1904.

Once the site of a Civil War battle, the surrounding area offers picnic grounds and woodland hiking trails. During our visit my husband and I met a man who showed us a gum tree with a carving—a message left for him by a fellow Cherokee some thirty-five years earlier. The park is open year-round, and there's no admission charge.

Continuing east on U.S. Highway 278 takes you to Cullman, a city that dates to 1873 when Col. John G. Cullmann bought a large tract of land and established a colony for German immigrants here. A reproduction of the founder's Bavarian-style home (which burned in 1912) now serves as the *Cullman County Museum* (256–739–1258), located at 211 Second Avenue Northeast. The museum's eight rooms, each with a theme, preserve some of the city's German heritage and the area's history. You'll see a 7-foot wooden sculpture of a Native American warrior, china, jewelry, vintage clothing, fainting couches, early tools, a beer

Clarkson Covered Bridge

wagon, and other local items. Modest admission. Except for Thursday's schedule, which runs from 9:00 A.M. to noon, the museum is open Monday through Friday from 9:00 A.M. to noon and from 1:00 to 4:00 P.M. Sunday hours are 1:30 to 4:30 P.M.

For a good meal, stop by *The All Steak* (256–734–4322), located just a few blocks away on 314 Second Avenue Southwest on the fourth floor of the Cullman Savings Bank. (If it's raining, stop at the third level on the parking deck to stay under cover and take the elevator up one floor.) Contrary to its name, the restaurant serves a wide variety of entrees that also include seafood and poultry. In addition to its beef specialties, the eatery is famous for homemade breads and desserts, especially the orange rolls, as well as its vegetable lunches. Prices are economical to moderate. Hours are 6:00 A.M. to 9:00 P.M. Monday through Wednesday and 6:00 A.M. till 10:00 P.M. Thursday through Saturday. Sunday's schedule is 6:00 A.M. to 3:00 P.M.

For more fine fare, stop by *Provence Market* (256–734–8002) at 105 First Avenue Northeast in downtown Cullman. The cafe occupies a corner section of a warehouse that dates to around 1900. Yesteryear's touches include original windows, a high pressed-tin ceiling, and an antique oak double desk once used for warehouse transactions. Herb-filled window boxes and fanciful paintings inspired by Provence add to the ambience.

Partners Kim Calvert and Kerry Quinn, who operate Provence Market, recently started another eatery, the nearby *Deli Warehouse Cafe,* also in Cullman's historic warehouse district.

"We want people to stop by for lunch and pick up items to take home for dinner," said Kim. From their special three-salad entree to pasta selections, the lunch menu offers a variety of homemade soups, fresh bread, and home-baked desserts.

The cafe serves lunch, seating customers from 11:00 A.M. until 2:00 P.M. Monday through Friday. On Friday evening the owners offer dinner with seating from 5:00 until 7:00 P.M.

Afterward, continue to 1600 Saint Bernard Drive Southeast, off U.S. Highway 278, on the town's east side. At *Ave Maria Grotto* (205–734–4110), on the grounds of a Benedictine monastery, visitors can take a Lilliputian world tour in a unique garden filled with more than 150 miniature reproductions of famous landmarks. Brother Joseph Zoettl, a Bavarian, who arrived at St. Bernard Abbey in 1892, constructed these reduced versions of various buildings. At age eighty the gifted monk completed his final work, the Lourdes Basilica. His architectural miniatures also include the Hanging Gardens of Babylon, ancient Jerusalem, Rome's Pantheon, and St. Peter's Basilica.

Using ingenuity and an unlikely assortment of materials, from playing marbles and fishing floats to cold cream jars and even a discarded bird cage (for the dome of St. Peter's), along with the more standard cement, limestone, and marble, Brother Joe fashioned a small world that continues to delight travelers. Except for Christmas Day, the grotto can be visited daily from 7:00 A.M. until 5:00 P.M., with extended summer hours. Modest admission.

Continue east on U.S. Highway 278 until it intersects U.S. Highway 231, then turn south to see the *Blount County Covered Bridges.* Known as the Covered Bridge Capital of Alabama, this area features three covered bridges, all still in daily use and marked by road signs on nearby highways. If you're on a tight schedule, choose the Horton Mill Covered Bridge, probably the most picturesque of the bunch. Located about 5 miles north of Oneonta on State Route 75, the latticed structure looms some 70 feet above the Warrior River's Calvert Prong—higher above water than any other covered bridge in the United States. Adjacent to the highway there's a parking area with nearby picnic facilities and nature trails, making this a relaxing place to take a driving break.

Continuing your exploration, you'll find the county's shortest covered bridge southeast of Rosa. The 95-foot-long, tin-topped Easley Covered Bridge stands about a $1/2$ mile off Blount County Route 33 and spans Dub Branch.

Northwest of Cleveland, 1 mile off State Route 79, Swann Bridge appears

Alabama Trivia

Cullman acquired the title "Die Deutsche Kolonie von Nord Alabama" because the town's founder, Col. John G. Cullmann, who came from Frankweiler, Germany, attracted approximately 10,000 German settlers to north Alabama.

rather suddenly as you're rounding a curve. The three-span bridge extends 324 feet over the Locust Fork of the Black Warrior River. You can park in a turn-off lane on the bridge's opposite side to explore the nearby terrain, where Queen Anne's lace, ferns, mountain laurel, wild hydrangeas, and muscadine vines grow. You might hear a mockingbird's serenade in the background.

Each October the Oneonta area stages an annual *Covered Bridge Festival* featuring bridge tours, arts and crafts exhibits, and other festivities. For additional information on the festival, award-winning Palisades Park, or other area attractions, call the Blount County/Oneonta Chamber of Commerce at (205) 274–2153.

After seeing the bridges of Blount County, you'll probably be ready for a wonderful meal, and Charlie Bottcher promises you one at *The Landmark* (205–274–2821) in Oneonta. Described by one Birmingham visitor as "a little bit of France in the middle of nowhere," the restaurant is at 601 Second Avenue East. Charlie, who's the owner/chef, creates consistently delicious combinations and demonstrates a winning way with vegetables. Be sure to note the board specials, as these change weekly.

Depending on what's fresh, good, and available, dinner selections might mean spicy Greek snapper, filet mignon in puff pastry, or blackened amberjack. Chicken Landmark, a signature dish, features a charbroiled, marinated chicken breast topped with crabmeat, charbroiled shrimp, and clam sauce. Charlie's clientele comes from a 75-mile radius. Moderate prices. Dinner is served from 4:30 to 9:00 P.M. Thursday through Saturday.

Before leaving Blount County, head to *Benedikt's Restaurant* (205–274–0230), located on Blount County Route 27, about 8 miles southeast of Oneonta on Straight Mountain. Some folks just stumble on the restaurant by accident while taking a scenic drive; others make a deliberate effort, traveling regularly from Birmingham and surrounding areas to eat here. The restaurant's Sunday meal is served "buffeteria" style.

On her menu, Ruth Benedikt writes, "Ladies and Gentlemen, we are 12th generation Charlestonians: Scotch, Irish and German. Our recipes belong to our mother, aunts, grandmother and all who came before them." Ruth and her sister Joice have prepared their recipes for the public for three decades and consider themselves "among the last of the scratch cooks in the restaurant business."

Choices might include German pot roast, golden fried chicken, or ham steak along with side dishes of real mashed potatoes, mixed broccoli-cauliflower with cheese sauce, sweet tomato relish, fresh creamed corn, purple hull peas, and fried green tomatoes.

Closed Monday, the eatery is open 9:00 A.M. to 9:00 P.M. Call the Benedickts for Sunday reservations; serving hours are 9:00 A.M. to 5:00 P.M.

Across the road at *Capps Cove* (205-625-3039 or 800-583-4750), you'll find a country getaway with a mountain on one side and a creek

---

Shrimp 'n Grits

The Landmark's chef/owner Charlie Bottcher sometimes teaches gourmet cooking classes, demonstrating culinary techniques and sharing his much-in-demand recipes. I signed up for two series of these popular sessions. My sister (who would rather grade a hundred biology exams and judge science fair projects all day than prepare one meal) questioned my sanity: Why would anyone pay cool cash for the privilege of working in a hot restaurant kitchen? One reason: Charlie advises his students to bring good appetites, because they're required to eat all the courses prepared. It's a tough assignment, but. . . .

Charlie created the following scrumptious dish, a favorite with his patrons, and graciously granted permission to share it with my readers:

Spicy Baked Shrimp with Garlic-Cheese Grits

36 large shrimp (31/35) with tails on, peeled and butterflied

Grits:

4 cups water

1/2 teaspoon salt

1/2 teaspoon garlic, minced

1 cup quick grits

6 ounces sharp cheddar cheese, grated

In a saucepan, bring water, salt, and garlic to a boil. Add grits and stir. Turn heat to low and simmer till grits are tender and slightly thickened. Add cheese and stir until melted. Divide grits among four ramekins or individual dishes.

Dip for Shrimp:

1 cup oil

2 1/2 tablespoons K-Paul's Redfish Seasoning

2 1/2 tablespoons Old Bay Seasoning

2 tablespoons lemon juice

2 tablespoons Kikkoman soy sauce

4 tablespoons honey

Mix well. Dip 9 shrimp at one time to bottom of dip and transfer shrimp and lots of dip to each dish of grits. Place shrimp, alternating tails, in row over grits. Finish remaining three dishes. Bake in 400-degree oven till shrimp are firm and grits are bubbly, about 15 minutes. Serves 4.

on the other. Located at 4126 Blount County Route 27, the complex offers bed and breakfast and much, much more. Owners Sybil and Cason Capps, native Alabamians who have lived in several states over the past fifteen years, moved here from St. Louis when Cason retired from a broadcasting career.

"We think we're unique," Sybil says, "a country village with an antiques store, barn, wedding chapel, and two old-style country cabins." Guests can enjoy a full country breakfast—smoked ham, bacon, pancakes, grits, potatoes, the works—in the couple's lovely two-story Colonial house. Moderate rates.

Continue to the state's central section. Nearby Ashville, easily reached by taking U.S. Highway 231 south, makes an interesting stop.

PLACES TO STAY IN NORTHWEST ALABAMA

CULLMAN
Hampton Inn
6100 Highway 157
(256) 739-4444 or
(800) 426-7866

DECATUR
Country Inn & Suites (formerly Amberly Suite Hotel)
807 Bank Street Northeast
(256) 355-6800 or
(800) 288-7332

Comfort Suites Hotel
918 Beltline Road
(256) 355-9977 or
(800) 228-5150

Dancy-Polk House
901 Railroad Street
Northwest
(256) 353-3579

Hampton Inn
2041 Beltline Road
(256) 355-5888 or
(800) 426-7866

Holiday Inn Hotel & Suites
1101 Sixth Avenue
Northeast
(256) 355-3150 or
(800) 553-3150

Key West Inn
2212 Danville Road
(256) 355-1999 or
(800) 833-0555

FLORENCE
Limestone Manor
601 North Wood Avenue
(256) 765-0314

Wood Avenue Inn
658 North Wood Avenue
(256) 706-8411

KILLEN
Laurel Cottage
761 County Road 414
(256) 757-1635

ONEONTA
Capps Cove
4126 Blount County
Route 27
(205) 739-4444 or
(800) 583-4750

ROGERSVILLE
Joe Wheeler State Park
Lodge
(256) 247-5461 or
(800) 544-5639

TOWN CREEK
Doublehead Resort
& Lodge
145 County Road 314
Town Creek
(800) 685-9267

TUSCUMBIA
Key West Inn
1800 Highway 72 West
(256) 383-0700

Sharlotte House
105 East North Commons
(256) 386-7269

WINFIELD
White Oaks Inn
300 Regal Street
(205) 487-4115 or
(800) 482-4115

**PLACES TO EAT IN
NORTHWEST ALABAMA**

CHEROKEE
Wooden Nickel Restaurant
195 Main Street
Near railroad tracks
(256) 359–4225

CULLMAN
The All Steak
314 Second Avenue
Southwest
(256) 734–4322

Provence Market
105 First Avenue Northeast
(256) 734–8002

DECATUR
Big Bob Gibson's
1715 Sixth Avenue
Southeast
(256) 350–6969

Curry's on Johnston Street
115 Johnston Street
Southeast
(256) 350–6795

Shelley's Iron Gate
402 Johnston Street
Southeast
(256) 350–6795

Simp McGhee's
725 Bank Street Northeast
(256) 353–6284

FLORENCE
Court Street Cafe
201 North Seminary Street
(256) 767–4300

Eva Marie's
106 North Court Street
(256) 760–0004

Renaissance Grill
Atop Renaissance Tower
One Hightower Place
(256) 718–0092

Trowbridge's
316 North Colony Street
(256) 764–1503

HALEYVILLE
Dixie Den
907 Twentieth Street
(205) 486–8577

For More Information about Northwest Alabama

Alabama Mountain Lakes Association
25062 North Street P.O. Box 1075
Mooresville 35649
(256) 350–3500 or (800) 648–5381
Web site: www.almlakes.org
e-mail: info@almtlakes.org

*This organization covers sixteen north Alabama counties
that are home to some one hundred attractions
in a 100–mile radius.*

Colbert County Tourism & Convention Bureau
719 Highway 72 West P.O. Box 440
Tuscumbia 35674
(256) 383–0783 or (800) 344–0783
Web site: www.shoals-tourism.org
e-mail: shoalstouriism@worldnet.att.net

Cullman County Area Chamber of Commerce
211 Second Avenue Northeast (35055)
P.O. Box 1104 Cullman 35056
(256) 734–0454
Web site: www.cullmanchamber.org
e-mail: cullman@nacell.net

Decatur Convention & Visitors Bureau
719 Sixth Avenue Southeast (35601)
P.O. Box 2349 Decatur 35602
(256) 350–2028 or (800) 524–6181
Web site: www.decaturcvb.org
e-mail: info@decaturcvb.org

Florence/Lauderdale Tourism
One Hightower Place Florence 35630
(256) 740–4141 or (888) 356–8687
Web site: www.flo-tour.org
e-mail: dwilson@floweb.com

MOULTON
Classical Fruits
8831 State Highway 157
(256) 974–8813

Western Sirloin
Steak House
11383 State Highway 157
(256) 974–7191

MUSCLE SHOALS
LOUISIANA The Restaurant
1311 East Sixth Street
(256) 767–4300

ONEONTA
Benedikt's Restaurant
Blount County Route 27
(205) 274–0230

The Landmark
601 Second Avenue East
(205) 274–2821

SHEFFIELD
George's Steak Pit
1206 Jackson Highway
(256) 381–1531

New Orleans Transfer
213 North Montgomery
Avenue
(256) 386–0656

TUSCUMBIA
Claunch Cafe
400 South Main Street (in
Spring Park)
(256) 386–0222

**MAINSTREAM ATTRACTIONS
WORTH SEEING IN
NORTHWEST ALABAMA**

**Alabama Music Hall
of Fame,** *U.S. Highway
72 West, Tuscumbia;
(256) 381–4417 or
(800) 239–2643. You
can immerse yourself in
the state's musical her-
itage at this facility,
which features exhibits,
audiovisual galleries,
and memorabilia related
to musicians either from
Alabama or associated
with the state. Artists
represented include
Hank Williams, Elvis
Presley, Emmylou Har-
ris, the Temptations, and
many others. For a little
music and a Web tour of
the museum, click on
www.alamhof.org.*

Point Mallard Park,
*1800 Point Mallard
Drive Southeast,
Decatur; (256)
350–3000 or (800)
669–WAVE. Named for
nearby Wheeler National
Wildlife Refuge's winter-
ing ducks, this park for
all seasons offers aquatic
fun in the summer and
year-round golfing on a
championship course.
You may even see Capt.
Mike Mallard, a human-
size mascot in nautical
attire, wandering about.
Not only does the 750-
acre complex contain a
wave pool, an Olympic-
size diving pool, water
slides, sand beach, and
"Squirt Factory," but
you'll also find a 173-
acre campground, hiking
and biking trails, and
picnicking facilities here.*

Central Alabama

Ridges, Springs, and Valleys

Alabama's midsection presents a pleasing pastoral landscape, a panorama of ridges, springs, and valleys. Heading south, the Birmingham area serves as a convenient base from which to branch out into the state's central region. From here, too, you can easily sweep down into Alabama's southeastern section to explore the historic Chattahoochee Trace as well as the state capital area.

Start your area exploration with a trip to downtown Ashville, home of one of St. Clair County's two courthouses (the other is in Pell City). This Neoclassical Revival structure, an enlargement of an earlier courthouse, dates from the early 1840s. Two blocks from the courthouse square, on Highway 231 at 20 Rose Lane, stands a lovely bed-and-breakfast, *Roses and Lace Country Inn* (205–594–4366). Look for a Queen Anne–style home painted a muted mauve with grape and vanilla accents. Visualize a veranda with hanging Boston ferns, swings, and wicker rocking chairs, and you'll have a good idea what to expect at this Victorian home. The roses-and-lace motif echoes from the rose garden on the side lawn to the interior's floral wallpapers, lace curtains, and selected accents.

Innkeepers Wayne and Faye Payne will welcome you to this charming home. For breakfast, Faye serves homemade biscuits and jellies, bacon, sausage, country ham, and scrambled eggs. The home offers a honeymoon suite and five bedrooms with four and a half baths. Standard to moderate rates.

Ask Faye to make an appointment for you to see the circa 1852 *Inzer House* next door, a striking, white brick structure now reincarnated as a Civil War museum. A number of black cast-iron Confederate crosses dot the grounds of nearby *Ashville Cemetery.*

To learn more about local history, drive out to see the *John Looney House,* one of Alabama's oldest two-story log dogtrot structures. (The term *dogtrot* refers to a central hallway connecting two rooms also

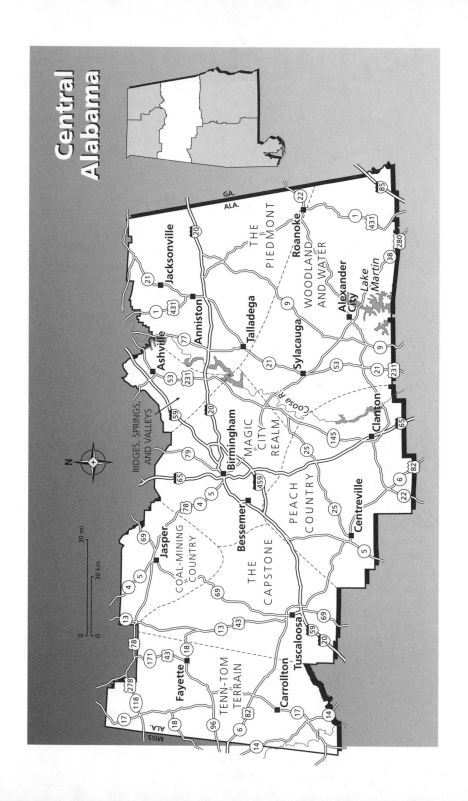

GAY'S TOP PICKS IN CENTRAL ALABAMA

Aliceville Museum and Cultural Arts Center, Aliceville

Anniston Museum of Natural History, Anniston

Birmingham Civil Rights Institute, Birmingham

DeSoto Caverns Park, Childersburg

International Motorsports Hall of Fame, Talladega

McWane Center, Birmingham

Moundville Archaeological Park, Moundville

Paul W. Bryant Museum, Tuscaloosa

Tannehill Historical State Park, McCalla

VisionLand, Bessemer

known as "pens." Although covered, this passage was left open and often proved a popular napping place for the family canines, hence its name.) Located a little over 4 miles southeast of Ashville on St. Clair County Route 24, this rare example of pioneer architecture dating to about 1820 may be visited on weekends. The Paynes at Roses and Lace Country Inn will give you a current status report on this historical site. Modest admission.

From Ashville take State Route 23 south until you reach U.S. Highway 11 leading to *Springville,* a town that takes its name from several area springs. First called Big Springs and settled about 1817, the town became Springville with the post office's establishment in 1834. On Main Street beside the 1892 *House of Quilts & Antiques* (205–467–6072), a natural spring flows; sometimes people stop to fill jugs with water or to pick the watercress growing here. Be sure to browse through the shop, owned by Beverly and Jack Crumpton, which contains several rooms of collectibles and unusual gifts. In addition to a large assortment of colorful handmade quilts and antique furniture, the Crumptons sell home accessories—everything from plant and magazine stands to wall hangings, letter openers, and hand-crafted wooden furniture. Hours are 10:00 A.M. to 5:00 P.M. Tuesday through Saturday and 12:30 to 5:00 P.M. Sunday.

Take time to explore some of this state historic district's other nostalgic shops, such as Charlotte's Web and Blackwood Gallery. Nearby Homestead Hollow, a fifty-five-acre pioneer homestead with a blacksmith shop, log cabin, barn, and gristmill, serves as a quaint backdrop for art and craft festivals throughout the year. During such events, visitors may sample sorghum and apple cider made on the premises.

The Piedmont

ocated in the Appalachian foothills, Calhoun County occupies a portion of the state's Piedmont region. Start your tour in Anniston, an attractive, arts-oriented city that named William Shakespeare its citizen of the year in 1984—before the Alabama Shakespeare Festival left its birthplace here and moved to Montgomery.

You can "expect the unexpected" at the **Anniston Museum of Natural History** (256–237–6766), located a couple of miles from downtown. Some surprises promised by the museum's slogan include a trek through jungles, deserts, and savannahs at this handsome facility surrounded by 187 acres on Anniston's northern outskirts. Entering the museum's Lagarde African Hall, you'll see a rogue elephant keeping vigil beside a towering baobab tree (the world's largest replica of an "upside-down" tree). Preserved specimens of more than a hundred creatures inhabit this African complex, most collected by Annistonian John B. Lagarde, a big-game hunter who donated his award-winning assemblage to the museum.

From antelope to zebras, all animals appear in the most realistic habitats possible. And through it all visitors see the versatility with which nature's

Strange As It Sounds

*D*eadly beauty and intrigue await at the **Berman Museum** (256–237–6261) in Anniston's LaGarde Park. Here you'll find an arsenal of rare weapons collected from all over the world by a former secret agent. Suits of armor that now stand still once clanked as knights did battle. Beheading axes and swords from ancient China and Japan hang in silence—not divulging their roles in past dastardly deeds.

A stunning royal Persian scimitar set with 1,295 rose-cut diamonds, sixty carats of rubies, and an exquisite forty-carat emerald in a three-pound gold handle mesmerizes sightseers here just as it once did Russian audiences during the reign of Catherine the Great. Other rare items include a Greek helmet dating to 300 B.C., Jefferson Davis's traveling pistols, Adolf Hitler's silver tea service, and Napoleon Bonaparte's ivory comb and brush set. Also displayed are a Korean crown and a saber used in the dramatic "Charge of the Light Brigade." The collection contains eighty-eight guns from the American West, Fraser's famous End of the Trail sculpture, and bronzes by Frederic Remington, Charles Russell, and Karl Kauba.

The man behind the arms, retired Army colonel Farley Lee Berman, worked in counterintelligence, and he and his wife, Germaine (a Parisian with a comparable position in French Intelligence), met during World War II. Afterward they traveled the world on a decades-long quest for historical weapons and art.

Personnel from several metropolitan museums approached Berman about acquiring his collection, but he chose to donate it to the city of Anniston, saying he knew "the people of Alabama would enjoy it." Located at 840 Museum Drive next to the Museum of Natural History, the Berman Museum's hours run from 10:00 A.M. to 5:00 P.M. Monday through Saturday and 1:00 to 5:00 P.M. on Sunday. The museum closes on Monday from September through May. Modest admission.

creatures adapt to their world. Every effort has been made to achieve the effect of authenticity; for example, light in the bamboo forest filters through a type of Venetian blind to create a network of slanted rays.

Spacious corridors wind from African depths to the Ornithology Hall with its impressive array of more than 600 specimens of North American birds, many now either extinct or on the endangered species list. Naturalist William Werner assembled this priceless bird collection more than a century ago, and several diorama groupings include nests (some with eggs) built by the birds themselves. The museum boasts one of the world's finest models of a pteranadon, a prehistoric flying reptile with a 30-foot wingspan. In Dynamic Earth Hall, which features a life-size model of an albertosaurus, you can explore an Alabama cave complete with waterfall, stalactites, and stalagmites. The museum's newest addition, NatureSpace, encourages children to explore beyond backyard boundaries with a unique exhibit of natural resources.

Accredited by the American Association of Museums, the Anniston facility has received national recognition for its innovative participatory exhibits. The museum also offers rotating art exhibits, a fine gift shop, picnicking facilities, and a nature trail. Modest admission. The museum is open Tuesday through Saturday from 10:00 A.M. to 5:00 P.M. and Sunday from 1:00 to 5:00 P.M. Modest admission.

Don't miss the historic Episcopal *Church of St. Michael and All Angels* (256–237–4011) on West Eighteenth Street at Cobb Avenue. With an exterior of Alabama stone, this 1888 Norman-Gothic structure features a magnificent marble altar backed by an alabaster reredos (ornamental screen). Bavarian woodworkers carved the church's entire ceiling by hand, and angels on corbels all face the altar at slightly different angles. Admission is free, and you can visit year-round between 9:00 A.M. and 4:00 P.M.

Take time to drive through the Tyler Hill Historic District and along tree-lined Quintard Avenue, where you'll see grand Victorian homes. At one such mansion, *The Victoria* (256–236–0503), you can drop in for a fine meal or an overnight stay. Look for a turreted, three-story structure, painted taupe and trimmed in white with a burgundy awning covering a walkway in front, on a hill at 1604 Quintard. This 1888 home, owned by Betty and Earlon McWhorter, now serves as a country inn. Accommodations include three lovely suites—decorated in period antiques—in the main house, a guest house, and a tasteful addition containing fifty-six rooms (all with private baths) connected to the inn by covered walkways.

The menu changes seasonally but always includes steak and fresh seafood—and by popular demand, the jumbo lump crab cakes. Appetizers might range from the chef's daily soup creation to fried green tomatoes with lime crème fraîche and tasso ham. The Victoria also offers a wide selection of wines including its own private label. Prices are moderate to expensive.

The Victoria is open to the public for dinner from 6:00 to 9:00 P.M. Monday through Thursday and till 10:00 P.M. on Friday and Saturday. Guests can enjoy a complimentary continental breakfast in the main house. Standard to moderate rates.

Much Ado in Anniston

For our first anniversary friends invited my husband and me to visit them in Anniston and take in some plays. At that time summer visitors to Anniston—the birthplace of the Alabama Shakespeare Festival (ASF)—could watch actors "strut and fret their hour upon the stage" in five rotating weekend productions.

Martin L. Platt came from Carnegie-Mellon University to direct the community theater and soon started the festival, which attracted throngs each summer. He personally picked the performers, auditioning many of them in New York.

I remember the gorgeous costumes, noted for their quality of workmanship. In a production of Romeo and Juliet, for instance, the Capulets were clothed in various shades of bronze and the Montagues in lavender and rose tones, enabling the audience to easily identify members of the feuding families. Gifted ASF Guild members spent countless volunteer hours hand-sewing seed pearls on dress hems or crocheting an army's "chain" mail headgear. Other Guild members found or provided lodging for actors, stuffed envelopes, ushered playgoers, or baked cookies for "meet the cast" parties.

We enjoyed immersing ourselves in the Elizabethan era by attending "Shakespeare Sundays" at the historic Church of St. Michael and All Angels. Filled with pomp and splendor, these services featured the use of a 1559 prayer book and the talents of the festival's company.

We continued to spend each anniversary in Anniston seeing ASF productions until the festival moved to its magnificent home in Montgomery and became a year-round theater. Although we still see occasional plays (Montgomery is much farther from our home), we miss those special summers. And on each wedding anniversary, we propose a toast to Shakespeare and all the wonderful times the curtain went up in Anniston.

Gay's Favorite Annual Events in Central Alabama

Birmingham Festival of Arts,
Birmingham, April; (205) 252–7652
or (800) 962–6453

Birmingham Heritage Festival,
Civil Rights District, Birmingham,
August; (205) 252–7652 or
(800) 962–6453

Bluegrass at Horsepens 40,
Horsepens 40, May; (800) 421–8564

Bruno's Memorial Classic, Greystone
Golf Course, Birmingham, April;
(205) 967–4745 or (800) 962–6453

**Christmas Village Arts
and Crafts Show,**
Birmingham-Jefferson Convention
Complex Exhibition Hall,
Birmingham, November;
(205) 458–8400 or (800) 962–6453

City Stages, Linn Park, Birmingham,
June; (205) 251–1272 or
(800) 962–6453

Heritage Week, Tuscaloosa, April;
(800) 538–8696

International Cityfest & Weindorf,
Downtown Tuscaloosa, August;
(800) 538–8696

Kentuck Festival of the Arts,
Kentuck Park, Northport, October;
(205) 758–1257 or (800) 538–8696

Moundville Native American Festival,
Moundville Archaeological Park,
October; (205) 371–2572,
(205) 371–2234, or (800) 538–8696

NASCAR Talledega Sears DieHard 500,
Talladega Superspeedway, Talladega,
April; (256) 362–9064 or
(800) 962–6453

NASCAR Talladega Winston 500,
Talladega Superspeedway, Talladega,
October; (256) 362–9064 or
(800) 962–6453

Sakura Festival, Tuscaloosa, March;
(800) 538–8696

Sometime during your stay stroll down to the old carriage house on the grounds, now home of an art gallery called **Wren's Nest,** which has original works and limited prints by noted wildlife artist Larry K. Martin.

While in Anniston, stop by **Cafe LeMamas** (256–237–5550) for lunch. Housed in an 1885 railroad freight station at 1208 Walnut Avenue, the eatery offers home-cooked fare with daily plate and chef specials, hickory-smoked barbecue, deli sandwiches, soups, salads, and desserts. Notice the building's attractive restoration and interior features. The entrance hall tree supposedly came from former Supreme Court Justice Hugo Black's home. The cafe's hours are 11:00 A.M. till 2:00 P.M. Monday through Friday, and prices are economical.

While in the area, head to Munford via State Route 21 for a visit at **The Cedars Plantation** (256–761–9090), located at 590 Cheaha Road. Owners Ann and Rick Price traveled widely and called many places home, including South America, before settling on this captivating country estate. "We want to share the house and its history with others," says Ann, whose research has yielded a wealth of information about the home's builder, Joseph Camp. Purchasing the property in 1833 from area Natchez/Creek chieftains, Reverend Camp completed the main house two years later.

Sometimes called the "Steamboat House," the raised cottage split-level design features long side porches and double front doors. Period antiques (and perhaps Reverend Camp's spirit) fill the high-ceilinged rooms. Guests can browse through the Price's extensive library, which includes Reverend Camp's interesting 1882 first-person account of history in the making. A post-Civil War skirmish took place at nearby Munford, and the home's east chimney still bears scars from the fire of marching Union soldiers.

Set on a sweeping lawn with stately oak and cedar trees, the home offers a tennis court, large swimming pool, and walking trails. Pleasant pastures surround The Cedars, and Tater Creek runs through the property. Ann plans to add llamas to the landscape. She recommends outings to Talladega National Forest, Cheaha State Park, and other nearby spots for nature lovers. Guests can enjoy a home-cooked breakfast in the dining room. Rates range from standard to moderate.

After basking in the country's serenity, head to nearby Talladega and immerse yourself in history. If you take the Jackson Trace Road, you'll follow a wagon route cut by Gen. Andrew Jackson and his Tennessee Volunteers as they marched southward through the Creek Indian nation. For a self-guided driving map of the town's historical sites, head to the chamber of commerce office just off the courthouse square in the old L&N Depot at 210 East Street. Start with the Silk Stocking District (outlined on your map), a sizable concentration of homes listed on the National Register of Historic Places. Stop by *Heritage Hall,* a restored 1908 Carnegie Library at 200 South Street East, for a look at its current exhibits. Afterward drive by *Talladega College,* established in 1867, to see Hale Woodruff's striking Amistad murals at Savery Library. Other points of interest include the campus chapel and Swayne Hall, the college's first building.

To explore more of Talladega's surroundings, take State Route 21 South and make *Orangevale Plantation* (256–362–3052) your base. From its grand Greek Revival-style home, built during the early 1850s, to its collection of historical outbuildings, this country estate at 1400 Whiting Road offers unique bed-and-breakfast accommodations. Dr. and Mrs.

Guests' log cabin at Orangevale Plantation

Richard Bliss and family invite guests to sample some serenity while dipping into history. If you've never slept in a dogtrot cabin, here's your chance. Authentic touches include adze marks on the log walls and free-standing fireplaces (with a supply of wood for chilly evenings). Other dependencies consist of another cozy log cabin, detached kitchen, smokehouse, and well house.

A gracious hostess, Billy Bliss invites guests to gather 'round her kitchen's big lazy Susan table or, weather permitting, on the patio or back porch for a hearty breakfast. Other enticements include a nature trail and marked walking paths, fish pond, and a house/farm tour on request. Moderate rates.

For a delightful history lesson in living color and a fun-filled family adventure, don't miss nearby *DeSoto Caverns Park* (256–378–7252 or 800–933–CAVE), 5 miles east of Childersburg at 5181 DeSoto Caverns Parkway. A one-hour tour presents highlights of the cave's role in history and features a spellbinding laser light and sound show in the magnificent onyx chamber, taller than a twelve-story building and bigger than a football field.

After the tour children can climb DeSoto's cave wall, wander through a lost trail maze, pan for gemstones, do battle with water balloons, and enjoy a picnic on the grounds. The park's hours run from 9:00 A.M. to 4:30 P.M. Monday through Saturday and 12:30 to 4:30 P.M. on Sunday (or till 5:30 P.M. from April through October). Admission.

Magic City Realm

Before exploring busy, bustling Birmingham, you can enjoy another back-to-nature experience at *Twin Pines Resort* (205–672–7575) near Sterrett. Although designed as a corporate retreat, travelers on holiday or opting to locate a serene weekend getaway will find a haven at 1200 Twin Pines Road, about 30 miles southeast of Birmingham.

Today's fast-paced world becomes a blur when you turn onto a road lined with nature's greenery and perhaps find yourself announced by a duck named Rosie. Large log lodges feature porches overlooking a forty-six-acre private lake, and you can opt for a room or a suite with fireplace and kitchen.

Outdoor recreation opportunities might focus on fishing (no license required on private property) paddleboating, canoeing, swimming, and playing volleyball, tennis, or horseshoes. While exploring the jogging/walking trails, you'll discover a covered bridge and a moonshine still and, in the process, work up a good appetite for the resort's bounteous country-cooked meals. When departure time comes, you may find it hard to tear yourself away.

Another good getaway, *Oak Mountain State Park* (205–620–2524), 15 miles south of Birmingham off I-65, offers canoeing, fishing, swimming, golfing, picnicking, horseback riding, and a demonstration farm. Children especially enjoy seeing the geese, peacocks, rabbits, pigs, calves, donkeys, horses, and other animals. The park, most of it in a natural state, occupies almost 10,000 acres. A drive to the top of Double Oak Mountain affords some sweeping views of the park's steep slopes and rugged terrain.

Other features include some 40 miles of hiking trails and four lakes. Don't miss the Treetop Nature Trail, where the Alabama Wildlife Rescue Service houses injured birds of prey. Climbing a boardwalk through woodsy surroundings takes you past large enclosures containing hawks, great horned owls, and other raptors. Call for park information or reservations at Oak Mountain's lakeside cabins or campground. Modest admission.

After basking in serenity you can pick up the pace with a jaunt to Birmingham. Named for the British industrial city, Birmingham acquired its nickname, Magic City, when soon after its 1871 incorporation it burgeoned into Alabama's major metropolis. No longer a fire-breathing, smoke-spewing dragon, the city projects a much-changed image—from gray smog to crisp skyline and green-bordered boulevards. As a leading medical and technological center, the city boasts an economic base broadened far beyond its mineral resources. The financial impact of the University of Alabama at Birmingham (UAB) Medical Center beefs up the local economy enormously.

Start your Birmingham tour at historic *Five Points South,* a charming area brimming with eateries, shops, galleries, and nightspots. Wending your way to *Cobb Lane Restaurant* (205–933–0462), you'll find Southern hospitality with a French accent. Look for an inviting courtyard with umbrella-shaded tables at 1 Cobb Lane, just off Twentieth Street between Thirteenth and Fourteenth Avenues south. You can opt for an alfresco meal here or eat in one of the restaurant's cozy rooms with murals featuring vignettes of the French countryside.

Dip into Cobb Lane's famous she-crab soup—rich and creamy with a splash of sherry. Owner Tim Kreider serves great crab cakes, too. If you can't resist dessert (and here most people can't), try the chocolate roulage, a light and delicate chocolate cake swirled jellyroll fashion with whipped cream. Those who are smitten can purchase half a roulage to carry out. Cobb Lane opens for lunch Monday through Saturday from 11:00 A.M. to 2:30 P.M. and for dinner Tuesday through Saturday from 5:30 to 10:00 P.M.

As the state's biggest city, Birmingham boasts many choice restaurants. For another memorable dinner, add *Highlands Bar & Grill* (205–939–1400) at 2011 Eleventh Avenue South to your itinerary. Classically trained chef Frank Stitt's regional Southern creations have been dubbed "New American" cuisine, and his accolades fill walls and books. Start with an appetizer of baked grits, and select an entree ranging from beef, venison, duck, and seafood to rabbit and veal. Renowned for its crab cakes, the restaurant also serves such specialties as pan roast quail with corn pudding and grilled leg of lamb with basil aioli and ratatouille. Moderate to expensive. Dinner hours are 6:00 to 10:00 P.M. Tuesday through Saturday.

While sightseeing in the Magic City, be sure to visit towering *Vulcan,* the world's largest cast-iron statue. To reach *Vulcan* park atop Red Mountain, take Twentieth Street South and watch for the sign. Just below the statue an observation deck affords a panoramic view of Birmingham and surrounding Jones Valley. Cast from Birmingham iron, *Vulcan* represents the mythological god of metalworking, fire, and forge. Designed for the 1904 St. Louis Exposition by Italian sculptor Giuseppe Moretti, *Vulcan* lifts his torch in tribute to the city's iron industry. The "Iron Man" also reminds motorists to drive safely because his torch, which normally burns green, turns red after an auto fatality.

At the base of the 55-foot statue, a museum presents *Vulcan*'s history along with an overview of steel production.

Consider stopping by **Birmingham Botanical Gardens,** at 2612 Lane Park Road, on the lower southern slope of Red Mountain. Stroll through the Japanese garden complete with a fourteenth-century teahouse reproduction. Also on the grounds, *Southern Living* magazine maintains demonstration gardens with plantings that might be duplicated at home. The museum's gift shop offers a fine selection of items from note cards and prints to unusual plants and garden statuary— great for giving or keeping.

The Tutwiler (205–322–2100 or 800–996–2426), at 2021 Park Place North, makes a comfortable and convenient base for seeing Birmingham's attractions. The staff at this charming historic hotel will make you glad you came to the Magic City. With its rose-marble foyer, original coffered ceilings, moldings, plasterwork, and brass hardware, the hotel recaptures the elegance of another era. Your room or suite, which might come with a balcony or a marble fireplace, features high ceilings, restored woodwork, marble bathrooms, and custom-designed antique reproductions. You'll also see fresh flowers but few TVs—most are tucked away in armoires.

Built in 1913 as a prestigious apartment-hotel, the redbrick, Italianate Tutwiler reopened in 1986 after a $15 million renovation. The Tutwiler's meticulous restoration resulted in charter membership in Historic Hotels of America, a select group recognized for preserving historic architectural quality and ambience. The original Tutwiler, the hotel's namesake, made news in 1974 when it became one of the country's first structures to be leveled by "implosion" (also the inspiration for the hotel's specialty drink by the same name).

The first Tutwiler hosted such dignitaries and celebrities as Eleanor Roosevelt, President Warren G. Harding, Charles Lindbergh, Will Rogers, Nelson Eddy, Tallulah Bankhead, Rocky Marciano, and Marilyn Monroe. Carrying on tradition, the current Tutwiler counts former President George Bush, Dan Quayle, Henry Kissinger, Colin Powell, Casper Weinberger, Mick Jagger, Billy Joel, and Henry Mancini among its honored guests. As another honored guest of the Tutwiler you can enjoy such amenities as complimentary shoe shines and newspapers, airport transportation, and valet parking.

For a glimpse of the city's Iron Age, take First Avenue North over the viaduct to Thirty-second Street toward the towering smokestacks of **Sloss Furnaces.** Designated a National Historic Landmark, the ironworks that served Birmingham from 1881 to 1971 now serve as a massive walk-through museum portraying the city's industrial past. Near the park gate, a visitors center features exhibits on the various aspects of combining coal, limestone, and ore at high temperatures to produce iron. In its prime, Sloss turned out 400 tons of finished pig iron a day.

For some down-home country cooking, head for *The Irondale Cafe* (205–956–5258)-the inspiration for the Whistle Stop Cafe in the movie *Fried Green Tomatoes*. Located at 1906 First Avenue North in the historic area of Irondale, the cafeteria offers a variety of meats and fresh vegetables including that Southern favorite, fried green tomatoes, that actress/writer Fannie Flagg put in the spotlight. Lunch hours run from 10:45 A.M. to 2:30 P.M. Sunday through Friday.

Heading toward the Birmingham International Airport, you'll find the *Southern Museum of Flight* (205–833–8226). Look for the big McDonnell-Douglas F–4N phantom II on the front lawn of the museum at 4343 Seventy-third Street North, 2 blocks east of the airport. Aviation buffs can spend hours here delving into the mystery and history of flying. This outstanding facility features a reproduction of a 1910 Curtis "Pusher," the second powered plane to follow on the heels of the Wright brothers' success; a 1925 Delta crop duster; a World War II Link trainer for "blind" flying; and hundreds of models that trace aviation's history. You'll see decades of military uniforms and memorabilia relating to Amelia Earhart, Gen. Claire Chennault's Flying Tigers, and the infamous Red Baron.

Visitors can view short movies, shown continuously, on such subjects as the Blue Angels, Thunderbirds, and Flying Tigers. Take time to look through the Alabama Aviation Hall of Fame on the second floor. The museum, which also offers an aviation reference library, is open from 9:30 A.M. to 4:30 P.M. Tuesday through Saturday and from 1:00 to 4:30 P.M. on Sunday. Modest admission.

Afterward return downtown to the Birmingham-Jefferson Civic Center for a spectator outing at the *Alabama Sports Hall of Fame* (205–323–6665). Located at the corner of Civic Center Boulevard and Twenty-second Street, this unique facility focuses on some of the state's greatest sports figures. Walls of bronze plaques pay tribute to athletes from Olympic diving champion Jenni Chandler to Joe Louis, who boxed his way to the World Heavyweight title. You'll also see displays on such sports luminaries as John Hannah, Joe Namath, Bo Jackson, Pat Sullivan, Bart Starr, Ozzie Newsome, Hank Aaron, Willie Mays, Jesse Owens, Hubert Green, Bobby Allison, Pat Dye, and Bear Bryant. Wall cases and displays feature trophies, uniforms, photographs, and other memorabilia from the sports world.

Even though exhibits cover Hall of Fame inductees who made names for themselves in archery, auto and harness racing, golf, baseball, boxing, track, and waterskiing, the name of the game in Alabama is Football (and yes, with a capital F). A black-and-white photo exhibit, depicting unhelmeted players in skimpy uniforms, captures some historic moments during the first Alabama-Auburn clash on February 22, 1893, in Birmingham. Football fever rages in many other parts of the country, but the intensity seems several degrees higher in the South and reaches a boiling point in Alabama during the annual collegiate battle between the Crimson Tide and the War Eagles. You can visit the hall of fame Monday through Saturday from 9:00 A.M. to 5:00 P.M. and Sunday from 1:00 to 5:00 P.M. Check out www.tech-comm.com/ashof/ for more information. Admission.

Nearby at 2000 Eighth Avenue North stands the *Birmingham Museum of Art* (205–254–2565), noted for its excellent Wedgwood collection, the finest outside England. In 1991 the museum received a $50 million collection of eighteenth-century French decorative art and furniture bequeathed by Birmingham native Eugenia Woodward Hitt, who spent most of her life in Europe and New York. This magnificent assemblage of some 500 items features paintings by Fragonard, perfume fountains, silver, textiles, ceramics, signed furnishings, and porcelain from the years 1720 to 1770. Other museum treasures include the Kress collection of Renaissance paintings and the largest collection of Asian art in the South. Check with the staff regarding current offerings. Don't miss the multilevel Charles W. Ireland Sculpture Garden, which provides a splendid backdrop for outdoor exhibits. Kathy G's Terrace Cafe serves lunch from 11:00 A.M. to 2:00 P.M. Tuesday through Saturday and features a jazz brunch the first Sunday of each month. Stop by the Museum Store for an extensive selection of books, posters, jewelry, crafts, and unique gift items. Except for major holidays, the museum is open from 10:00 A.M. to 5:00 P.M. Tuesday through Saturday and noon to 5:00 P.M. Sunday. Also, on the first Thursday of each month, the museum is open until 9:00 P.M., serves dinner, and shows a film. Check on current exhibits and other happenings at www.artsBMA.org; free admission.

Continue south on Twenty-first Street to University Boulevard and take a right to reach the University of Alabama at Birmingham campus. One of the nation's top-ranked medical centers, UAB practices a triple-thrust program of education, research, and service. Tucked in the heart of this much-trodden complex on the third floor of the Lister Hill

Library Building is a gem of a museum, the *Reynolds Historical Library* (205–934–4475). (But you probably won't find a nearby parking place, so wear your walking shoes.) With a rare and valuable collection of medical books and manuscripts (some predate the printing press), the library houses one of the country's foremost collections of its type—on par with similar collections at Harvard, Yale, Johns Hopkins, and other prestigious institutions. Incredible as it sounds, you can read actual letters (pertaining to dental matters) handwritten by George and Martha Washington. The library also owns original correspondence of Louis Pasteur, Sir William Osler, Pierre Curie, and Florence Nightingale. These letters, of course, are safely locked up, but you can ask the curator to don white gloves and show them to you.

The library owes its existence to radiologist Lawrence Reynolds, an Alabamian who grew up in a family of physicians and devoted much of his lifetime to acquiring rare medical books and manuscripts (once spending a month's salary of $600 on a single volume). In 1958 Dr. Reynolds donated his impressive collection of some 5,000 items (now doubled in size) to his alma mater. The library's collection features richly illustrated vellum manuscripts, rare first editions such as Vesalius's 1543 textbook on human anatomy, the earliest known treatise on wine, and a 1517 handbook of surgery (written in German instead of Latin) with extraordinary hand-executed illustrations. Another work, William Harvey's 1628 *De motu cordis,* accurately describes the body's blood circulation for the first time. Other interesting items include antique maps, a sizable collection of Nobel Prize Papers, and a set of four Chinese anatomical charts that date to 1668 and delineate the body's acupuncture points. Don't miss the display of exquisite ivory miniature mannequins (physicians' dolls used for medical instruction) dating from the seventeenth and eighteenth centuries. Another room contains displays of various medical instruments and equipment along with changing exhibits. The library and museum are open from 8:30 A.M. to 5:00 P.M. Monday through Friday, and admission is free. You can find more information at www.uab.edu/historical with links to the Reynolds Historical Library, the Alabama Museum of Health Sciences, and the UAB Archives.

Don't miss the *Birmingham Civil Rights Institute* (205–328–9696), located at 520 Sixteenth Street North. The focal point of the Civil Rights District, which also embraces historic Sixteenth Street Baptist Church and Kelly Ingram Park, the facility features innovative exhibits, which re-create in graphic fashion a sad chronology of segregation's inequities. Visitors start their journey through darkness with a film, followed by a startling entrance to the "Barriers" Gallery, where exhibits trace the struggle that led to the passage of civil rights laws. The new Richard Arrington Jr. Resource Gallery offers an interactive multimedia experience and creates a "living library" honoring persons who participated in the civil rights struggle. Video segments from the Institute's Oral History Project interviews are available for learning and research. Admission. Hours are 10:00 A.M. to 5:00 P.M. Tuesday through Saturday and 1:00 to 5:00 P.M. Sunday.

Nearby, on Fourth Avenue North at Seventeenth Street, stands the *Alabama Jazz Hall of Fame* (205–254–2731). Housed in the Art Deco Carver Theatre, the museum features exhibits ranging from boogie-woogie's beginnings to the current jazz scene. Displays pay tribute to native Erskine Hawkins of "Tuxedo Junction" fame, Nat King Cole, Duke Ellington, Lionel Hampton, and other musicians with Alabama connections.

While exploring the Magic City, take in nearby Homewood, where you'll find a delightful neighborhood market and cafe specializing in Mediterranean fare. *Nabeel's Cafe* (205–879–9292) at 1706 Oxmoor Road offers a menu with a global theme and a market filled with imported herbs, coffees, teas, olive oil, beans, nuts, and more. Vats of olives, bins of spices, and wedges of Greek, Italian, Bulgarian, Russian, and Lebanese cheeses tempt the shopper here.

The Krontiras family, John and Ottavia with their son Anthony, own and operate this establishment, housed in the white-painted brick building with an exterior wall mural and green canopies. The cafe evokes the intimacy of a European dining experience with a leisurely sharing of food and drink. Wine barrels and a wooden rack for wine storage along the dining room wall suggest the old country. Anthony, Nabeel's chef, focuses on family recipes and prepares food with home-cooked flavor. Nabeel's numerous awards include "Birmingham's Favorite Restaurant" in a recent readers poll conducted by *Birmingham Magazine*. "We try to treat customers as if they were guests at our home," said John.

Sip some of the cafe's celebrated and refreshing mint tea and scoop up some taramasalata dip, made of red caviar and salted carp roe, with a pita wedge while you decide what to order. From homemade soups and piquant Greek salads to sandwich specialties like fior di latte (made with fresh mozzarella cheese, roasted peppers, and fresh basil), Nabeel's crew prepares everything fresh daily. Favorites include eggplant parmesan and a spinach pie (spanakopita). Made of fresh spinach and layered with phyllo, Greek feta cheese, and herbs, spanakopita is served with a salad and pita bread. End your meal on a sweet note with baklava, cannoli, butter cookies, or honey crescents. Hours run from 9:30 A.M. until 9:30 P.M. Monday through Saturday.

Before leaving the Birmingham area, stop by *The Bright Star* (205–424–9444) in nearby Bessemer. Housed in a tall brick building at 304 North Nineteenth Street, this restaurant beckons diners with an extensive menu prepared with Greek flair. Brothers Jimmy and Nicky Koikos continue a family culinary tradition that started in 1907.

The attractive interior features roomy brass and glass-topped booths and murals dating from 1915, painted by a European artist traveling through the area. The Bright Star offers daily luncheon specials, such as fresh trout almondine or Greek-style beef tenderloin tips with such side dish choices as fresh fried eggplant, corn on the cob, and candied yams.

Moussaka on the Menu?

*T*rue, fried chicken and barbecue star on many Alabama menus. Still, you'll find ethnic variety, too. Nabeel Cafe's owner John Krontiras provided the following recipe, his family's version of moussaka enhanced by bechamel sauce—a favorite with his patrons.

Moussaka

2 pounds ground beef

3 pounds eggplants, unpeeled and sliced 1/2-inch thick

3 eggs

3 cups milk

1/2 pound kasseri cheese, grated

1 onion, sliced

1 stick cinnamon

1/2 cup extra virgin olive oil

2 pounds tomatoes, peeled and seeded

1/2 cup butter

4 tablespoons semolina (pasta flour)

salt and pepper to taste

Fry eggplants lightly and set aside. Brown onion in a saucepan with oil, then add tomatoes and cinnamon. Season with salt and pepper. Stir well and turn heat off.

Heat butter in different saucepan, then add semolina and make a roux. Beat eggs with milk and pour in saucepan, stirring constantly. (Do not let boil.) When set, turn heat off and add half of cheese.

Arrange two eggplant layers in oiled 9-by 13-inch baking pan. Sprinkle with cheese and add tomatoes, removing cinnamon stick. Add all ground beef, sprinkle with more cheese, and add remaining eggplant and tomato layers. Pour sauce over mixture. Bake in 350-degree oven for about 45 minutes or until done. Serves 10.

Christmas in Nauvoo

When Gene McDaniel planned a Christmas celebration in Nauvoo, population 249, he expected maybe 250 to 500 people. Between 2,000 to 3,000 people showed up for that first holiday festival in 1989, and that's how it's been ever since. Christmas in Nauvoo takes place the first weekend in December with an open house at the **Old Harbin Hotel** (205–697–5652), myriad lights, and attendant festivities including a fly-over, antique car show, fox hunt, and parade led by Miss Alabama, who makes the hotel her overnight base.

Once a booming coal mining town, Nauvoo takes its name from a Hebrew word meaning "pleasant." A railroad worker, who said the place reminded him of his hometown in Illinois, christened it Nauvoo. After two mines and a lumber mill closed in the 1950s, Nauvoo started to shrivel and dry up. The town's largest structure, the two-story brick Old Harbin Hotel, stands on the corner of McDaniel Avenue and Third Street. Built in 1923 at a cost of $24,574, the hotel boasted sixteen furnished rooms and seventy-six electric lights. The structure, which retains its original pine walls, downstairs pressed-tin ceilings, and four center rooms with skylights, was added to the Alabama Landmark Register in 1990.

Owners Gene and Earlene McDaniel, who live on the premises, have collected a variety of furnishings, antiques, and memorabilia to decorate each of the nine guest rooms individually.

"We don't advertise for customers," said Gene, a retired union coal miner and hardware store owner. "Don't expect a person on duty at the desk. Most weekends in summer, we're booked with family reunions because the whole clan can gather here." Gene, who owns several other buildings in Nauvoo, said he's had from 15,000 to 20,000 visitors at the hotel since 1989. Breakfast is included, and rates are standard.

About a mile from the hotel on the Carbon Hill and Nauvoo Road, you'll find some of the best barbecue in these parts at the **Slick Lizard Smokehouse** (205–697–5789). Named for a local mine, the eatery's walls are made of rough lumber edged with bark. Iced tea arrives in quart-size fruit jars with handles, and the decor features light fixtures made of wagon wheels. Farm implements, a wash pot, rub board, Buffalo Rock Cola signs, Alabama football memorabilia, old photos, and newspaper clippings add to the atmosphere.

The menu explains what's behind the name: "You're as slick as a lizard!" one miner said to another as they crawled out of the mine. That's how mining was done—on your belly through slick clay portals that were only about 25 inches high. This mine was located behind the present cafe in the mid-1920s.

"As the story continues, the name 'Slick Lizard' stuck with us. We were a coal-mining town, and we are very proud of our heritage and community. Welcome to Slick Lizard Smokehouse!" Owners Diane and James McDaniel invite you to "fill your gizzard at the Slick Lizard" on Thursday and Sunday from 10:00 A.M. to 9:00 P.M. and on Friday and Saturday till 10:00 P.M. Economical prices.

For dinner start with a cup of the restaurant's scrumptious gumbo. (All fish dishes here feature fresh seafood straight from the coast.) For the main course, you might choose broiled snapper (Greek style) or the beef tenderloin. Other enticing entrees include lobster and crabmeat au gratin, a broiled seafood platter, and a tasty blackened snapper, prepared New Orleans style, with a creamy wine sauce. Top off your meal with a slice of fresh homemade pineapple cheese or lemon icebox pie. Economical to moderate prices. Weekday hours are 10:45 A.M. to 10:00 P.M.; the restaurant serves from 10:45 A.M. to 9:00 P.M. on Sunday.

The Capstone

Traveling southwest about 50 miles takes you to Tuscaloosa. On your way to The Capstone, as the University of Alabama is often called, make a stop at the **Mercedes-Benz Visitors Center** (205–507–2266 or 888–2–TOUR–MB) in Vance, about halfway between Birmingham and Tuscaloosa. Traveling on I–59, you'll see the plant on the left. Take exit 89 onto Mercedes Drive for an up-close look at the M-class all-activity vehicle plus multimedia exhibits that span the past, present, and future of automobile technology. The company's first American manufacturing plant outside its German motherland, the operation opened in 1997. There's a modest admission for the center, but no extra charge for a factory tour. However, to take the factory tour, you must call ahead for reservations. Hours are 9:00 A.M. to 5:00 P.M. Monday through Friday and 10:00 A.M. to 5:00 P.M. on Saturday. The center closes on Sunday and holidays. Check out its Web site at www.bamabenz.com.

After dipping into the Daimler-Benz auto history, continue your trek to Tuscaloosa. This college town, rich in tradition, served as Alabama's capital from 1826 to 1846.

Before exploring the area's many attractions, you might like to fortify yourself with a slab of ribs at **Dreamland** (205–758–8135), 2 miles from the intersection of U.S. Highway 82 and I–59, off Jug Factory Road in Jerusalem Heights. Here you don't have to agonize over what to order—the choice is ribs along with slices of white bread to sop up the sauce. You'll also get a bib that says AIN'T NOTHIN' LIKE 'EM—NOWHERE, a stack of napkins, and a wet paper towel to assist you in this gustatory project that must be performed with no inhibitions. If you want more variety in your meal, get a bag of potato chips. Beer or soft drinks, followed by toothpicks, complete the feast.

True, Dreamland stays crowded and the noise level runs high, but regulars say these things add to the place's appeal. Dreamland's hours are 10:00 A.M. to 9:00 P.M. Monday through Thursday. On Friday and Saturday the restaurant is open from 10:00 A.M. to 10:00 P.M. and from 11:00 A.M. to 5:00 P.M. Sunday.

At 1400 River Road Northeast, you'll find another feast—this one for the eyes and the spirit—when you view the Warner Collection at *Gulf States Paper Corporation Headquarters* (205–562–5000). Set in the serene timelessness of Japanese gardens populated by peacocks and ducks, these corporate quarters (not your average frenetic workplace) house an excellent art collection displayed in boardrooms, corridors, and individual offices. Jack W. Warner, chairman of Gulf States's board, chose the items in this remarkable assemblage of bronze and porcelain sculpture, primitive artifacts, Oriental pieces, and paintings. Among the artists represented in the collection are Andrew Wyeth, Frederic Remington, George Catlin, Mary Cassatt, and Georgia O'Keeffe. You can also admire the talent and technique of British artist Basil Ede, world-famous for his portraits of wild birds. Warner, on behalf of Gulf States, commissioned Ede's magnificent Wild Birds of America series, the subject of two books complete with color plates.

From Monday through Friday you can visit Gulf States's headquarters for tours starting at 5:30 and 6:30 P.M. Saturday's schedule, with tours starting each hour, runs from 10:00 A.M. to 4:00 P.M., and Sunday hours are 1:00 to 4:00 P.M. Admission is free.

Continue to nearby *Cypress Inn* (205–345–6963), at 501 Rice Mine Road North. Located on the Black Warrior's banks, this restaurant offers fresh seafood, prime steaks, and traditional Southern fare as well as a relaxing river view. House specialties include Hoppin' John (a combination of black-eyed peas, rice, scallions, and bacon), smoked chicken with white barbecue sauce, crispy fried catfish, and fresh broiled red snapper. Also popular are the homemade yeast rolls, fresh raisin-bran muffins, and peanut butter pie. The Cypress Inn serves lunch from 11:00 A.M. to 2:00 P.M. Sunday through Friday; dinner hours run from 5:30 to 9:30 P.M. Monday through Thursday and from 5:00 to 10:00 P.M. on Friday and Saturday. Sunday dinner hours are 5:30 to 9:00 P.M. Economical to moderate prices.

Afterward head for the University of Alabama campus, the site of a beautiful historic district as well as the home of the Crimson Tide. Since student William Gray Little organized the college's first football club in 1892, Alabama has celebrated "A Century of Champions." A good place to learn about the school's more than one-hundred-year football history is the **Paul W. Bryant Museum** (205–348–4668). To reach the museum from U.S. Highway 82, take the University Boulevard exit and follow the signs. If you arrive via I–59, exit onto I–359, take the Thirty-fifth Street exit to Tenth Avenue, go north to Bryant Drive, and then turn east. You'll find the museum on campus at 300 Paul W. Bryant Drive next to the Four Points Hotel Tuscaloosa-Capstone by Sheraton.

For some background on the legendary figure called "The Bear," the man who became college football's most acclaimed coach, start your museum visit by viewing *The Bryant Legacy,* a film narrated by sports commentator Keith Jackson. While browsing among the displays, you'll see a replicated setting of Bear Bryant's office and a dazzling version of his famous hat. Sculptor Miraslav Havel translated the familiar crimson-and-white houndstooth pattern into a multifaceted Waterford crystal showpiece. A courier transported the real hat from Tuscaloosa to Ireland for its magic rendering-and back again.

Although dedicated to the memory of Bryant, who headed Alabama's football teams from 1958 to 1982, the museum also pays tribute to other coaches and players prominent in the school's history. You'll see photos, memorabilia, and audiovisual displays pertaining to such superstars as Joe Namath, Kenny Stabler, Cornelius Bennett, and Bart Starr. To supplement vintage film clips, montages, and recordings, the museum offers taped highlights of recent games.

In addition to the large exhibit hall, the museum houses a comprehensive library of media guides, game programs, photographs, books, films, scrapbooks, and other materials covering Southeastern Conference and college sports. Modest admission. Except for major holidays, hours run from 9:00 A.M. to 4:00 P.M. daily.

Strange As It Sounds

*C*arrollton offers a unique site-a face imprinted on a windowpane at the **Pickens County Courthouse.** To learn the strange story behind the image of a prisoner's face preserved here since 1878 (the visage remains despite repeated scrubbings and harsher attempts at removal), step inside the courthouse and pick up a leaflet that provides some background information. You can also read an intriguing account of the mysterious face in Kathryn Tucker Windham's book 13 Alabama Ghosts and Jeffrey (published by The University of Alabama press in Tuscaloosa).

While exploring campus, stop by the **Gorgas House** (205–348–5906) on Capstone Drive. One of four university buildings to survive the Civil War, this 1829 two-story brick Federal-style cottage with a curving cast-iron staircase originally served as a college dining hall. Inside you'll see period furnishings, an outstanding collection of Spanish Colonial silver, and memorabilia of William Crawford Gorgas, who was noted for his work in the prevention and cure of yellow fever. Modest admission. The Gorgas House is open Tuesday through Saturday from 10:00 A.M. to 4:00 P.M.

Housed at nearby Smith Hall, the **Alabama Museum of Natural History** (205–348–7550) features extensive fossil and mineral collections. Entering this 1909 Classical Revival building, you'll see a spacious hall and a sweeping marble staircase with iron railings. Exhibits include pottery, tools, weapons, and various artifacts from South Pacific and Central and South American cultures.

On display in the gallery upstairs, you'll find the Hodges meteorite—an outer-space missile weighing eight and a half pounds that struck a Sylacauga woman in 1954. Featured fossils include mammoth, mastodon, mosasaur, and marine turtle, to name a few. You'll also see a Studebaker buggy from the 1880s and a free-standing exhibit illustrating the research methods used by Professor Eugene Allen Smith, for whom the building is named, in gathering his geological and biological collections. Except for major holidays, you can visit the museum Monday through Friday from 8:00 A.M. to 4:30 P.M. Saturday and Sunday hours run from 1:00 to 4:30 P.M. Modest admission.

Conveniently located near the campus at 1509 University Boulevard, the **Crimson Inn** (205–758–3483) makes a handy base for travelers. Innkeeper owners Pat and Rodney LaGrone offer Southern hospitality with a crimson glow at their Dutch Colonial home, built in 1924 by Dr. Alston Maxwell, a former physician for the college football team. In fact, you can see Bryant-Denny Stadium from the window of an upstairs guest room, named for Pat's mentor and former employer, Dr. Jewitt. A floor-to-ceiling mural in the guest parlor features the University of Alabama President's Mansion, painted by local artist Lisa Godwin.

Here, all breakfasts start with dessert—Crimson soup, made with chilled strawberries. Stuffed French toast with hot orange sauce or a hearty casserole of ham, eggs, and cheese might follow. Dessert is served each evening and might be homemade cheesecake, apple dumplings, or freshly baked cookies. Moderate rates. E-mail the bed-and-breakfast at crimsoninn@aol.com. To preview the property, log onto www.bbonline.com/al/crimsoninn/.

Nearby, at *Holiday Dreams* (205–752–4528), housed in a three-story Victorian home at 1409 University Boulevard, Debbie West offers collectibles galore and Christmas cheer year-round.

Across the street at 1410 University Boulevard stands *Cocopelli Gourmet Cafe* (205–349–4033), where chef/owner James Ray serves gourmet sandwiches and such delectable creations as rosemary shrimp penne or giant seared scallops with a saffron corn sauce. Don't miss the French onion soup. Lunch hours are 11:00 A.M. till 3:00 P.M. Monday through Friday with dinner from 6:00 until 10:00 P.M. Wednesday through Saturday. Also, brunch is served from 11:00 A.M. until 3:00 P.M. on Saturday.

Downtown at 2300 University Boulevard in a building that dates to the 1890s, you'll find *DePalma's* (205–759–1879). This Italian cafe is noted for its pizzas, calzones, and dishes such as pine nut–crusted salmon, veal Marsala, or pasta DePalma—angel hair pasta baked in a cream sauce with garlic, cheeses, and Italian herbs and topped with mushrooms, mozzarella, and a choice of ham, Italian sausage, artichokes, and more. Tiramisu ranks at the top of the dessert list, and the crew offers a great wine selection, too. In fact, the owners make regular scouting trips to Italy for their selections. Here, messages don't come *in* a bottle—but *on* a bottle—because the staff invites you to sign and date your wine label and pen an appropriate message. Then your special bottle joins a long line of others on the booth-level shelf. DePalma's is open from 11:00 A.M. till 11:00 P.M. daily. Prices are economical to moderate.

After your campus tour take time to explore Tuscaloosa (a Choctaw name that means "black warrior"). While downtown, stop by the *Battle-Friedman House* (205–758–6138), a handsome Greek Revival mansion located at 1010 Greensboro Avenue. Built in 1835, this structure now serves as a house museum and city cultural center. The home may be visited Tuesday through Saturday between 10:00 A.M. and noon and 1:00 to 4:00 P.M. and from 1:00 to 4:00 P.M. on Sunday. Modest admission.

Continue to 1512 Greensboro Avenue, where you'll find *The Waysider Restaurant* (205–345–8239) in a small early-twentieth-century house. Because this is *the* place for breakfast in Tuscaloosa, you may have to stand in line, so bring along a newspaper to read while you wait for a table. No wimpy affair, breakfast at The Waysider means homemade biscuits (with a deserved reputation), eggs, grits (get the cheese version), and a meat of your choice: from sugar-cured ham to grilled pork chops or steak. An order of real country-cured ham with two eggs and red-eye gravy runs in the economical range. You can also opt for pancakes.

The Waysider opens at 5:30 A.M. Tuesday through Saturday. Sunday breakfast hours run from 6:30 A.M. to 1:00 P.M. Lunch hours are 11:00 A.M. to 1:30 P.M. Tuesday through Friday.

Next, head to nearby Northport, just a short drive across the Black Warrior River. Once called Kentuck, Northport has developed into an important craft center with a complex of studios and galleries. Each fall the **Kentuck Festival of the Arts** features more than 200 selected artists and craftspeople from all over the country. Celia O'Kelley, Steve Davis, Anden Houben, and a number of other artists maintain individual studios at **Kentuck Art Center** (205–758–1257), located at 503 Main Avenue. The gift shop, which offers photography, pottery, glass, jewelry, musical instruments, textiles, baskets, and other items, is open Monday through Friday from 9:00 A.M. to 5:00 P.M. and Saturday from 10:00 A.M. to 4:30 P.M. Call for information on the center's artists, exhibits, or Kentuck Museum's gallery.

While exploring Northport, stop by **The Globe** (205–391–0949) at 430 Main Avenue, where you'll find a menu with an international focus. As for the restaurant's name, the founding partners Jeff Wilson or Gary Wise, who met during a university production of *Richard II,* chose The Globe because Shakespeare used it for his theater, and back in the 1820s and '30s, Northport was home to a hotel called The Globe, located nearby. Spotlighting the Bard, the decor features framed page reproductions of woodcuts from the *First Folio.* Drawings of Shakespearean characters share billing with photos of downtown Northport in earlier years.

A brisk business made it necessary to enlarge the restaurant, accomplished by knocking a hole through the wall to the adjoining structure, a former dry-goods store. Both buildings date to 1909, and an archway permits easy access between them. (Some people claim a ghost roams The Globe's premises during the wee hours.)

Jeff and his wife, Kathy, later bought Gary's interest in the business, and describe the cuisine as ranging from "traditional French to fusion." The ever-popular Athenian pasta salad consists of orzo and vegetables in a balsamic vinaigrette, topped with feta cheese, Kalamata olives, and grilled shrimp. Another favorite lunch item, The Globe's special quesadillas come in a vegetarian version or with grilled chicken, shrimp, Creole crawfish, or jumbo lump crabmeat. The menu's global influence manifests itself in such items as Caribbean island stew, scallops Madrid, and Jamaican jerk chicken served over a mango rum compote and topped with red onions and fresh basil mustard. Lunch hours run from 11:00 A.M. until 3:00 P.M. Tuesday through Saturday, and dinner is served from 5:00 until 10:00 P.M. Tuesday through Thursday and until 11:00 P.M. Friday and Saturday. If you have a green thumb, be sure to stop by *the Potager* (205–752–4761), next door at 428 Main Avenue. The shop offers everything from books and tools to gardening accessories. Zebra finches provide the chirping background music.

After your Northport excursion, head for Moundville, called by *National Geographic* "the Big Apple of the 14th century." To reach *Moundville Archaeological Park* (205–371–2572 or 205–371–2234), located about 15 miles south of Tuscaloosa, take State Route 69 South. Said by archaeologists to be the best-preserved prehistoric settlement east of the pueblos, Moundville is an internationally known archaeological site with more than twenty flat-topped earthen mounds, plus other less prominent ones, spread over a 317-acre setting on the Black Warrior River. For a sweeping overview of the grounds as well as a look at a re-created temple (peopled with life-size figures performing religious rites), you can climb to the top of a 60-foot ceremonial mound. At the *Jones Archaeological Museum* you'll see hundreds of Mississippian artifacts, ceremonial vessels, and tools made by the advanced group of prehistoric people who occupied this area between A.D. 800 and 1500. One wing contains a prehistoric canoe exhibit. Don't miss the Rattlesnake disc, the most famous artifact ever found at Moundville. Although scholars disagree on the meaning of the entwined rattlesnakes on the disc, the hand with the eyelike motif in the palm is common in Mississippian art.

The park, open daily, may be visited from 8:00 A.M. to 8:00 P.M. Except for major holidays, the museum is open 9:00 A.M. to 5:00 P.M. Camping, hiking, and picnicking facilities are available. Modest admission. The annual six-day *Moundville Native American Festival,* featuring southeastern Native American crafts and cultural activities, takes place during the first week in October.

Afterward return north to U.S. Highway 82, and travel west toward Pickensville and the Tennessee-Tombigbee (Tenn-Tom) Waterway, which offers exceptional fishing, hunting, and recreational facilities.

Tenn-Tom Terrain

Don't miss the *Tom Bevill Visitor Center* (205–373–8705) at *Pickensville,* ¹/₂ mile south of the junctions of State Routes 14 and 86. The white-columned Greek Revival-style mansion you see here looks as if it dates from the mid-1800s but actually was completed in 1986. Definitely not your average rest stop, this facility primarily represents a composite of three historical homes in the vicinity, and you'll see portraits of these grand mansions in the central hall. Ascend the sweeping stairway to the second floor, where various exhibits interpret the Tennessee-Tombigbee Waterway's history. A 22-foot relief map illustrates the waterway's course through several locks and dams, and a model display demonstrates the lockage process. Even better, you can climb to the roof level and perhaps watch a vessel pass through the Tom Bevill Lock and Dam. Whether or not said event happens during your visit, the splendid view from the cupola justifies the climb.

After your house tour, put on your sea legs for another climb-one aboard the U.S. Snagboat *Montgomery,* permanently docked beside the visitors center. Recently declared a National Historic Landmark, this steam-powered sternwheeler once kept Southern rivers navigable by removing tons of debris, such as fallen trees and sunken logs, that impeded river traffic. While exploring the vessel, from pilothouse and crew quarters to engine room, you'll see displays on the Tombigbee River Valley's development.

During the third weekend in September, the Southern Heritage Festival, which depicts life in the South between 1800 and 1865, takes place at the Tom Bevill Visitor Center. Civil War reenactors stage the skirmish at Pickensville Landing, and exhibitors offer handcrafted items ranging from baskets of pine needles and white oak to dough bowls, slingshots, and wooden toys. Festival fare features Southern foods from barbecue to funnel cakes, along with storytelling and fiddle playing. Except for some federal holidays, the center is open daily year-round.

Next, head south to *Aliceville,* home of a unique museum, two lovely bed-and-breakfasts, and fine Southern fare at *Plantation House Restaurant* (205–373–8121). The eatery, located at the Highway 17 bypass across from the Piggly Wiggly supermarket, features chicken or tuna salad, vegetables, catfish, country ham, steak, and more. Owners Polly and Bill Goodwin also offer a variety of homemade desserts at their restaurant, which dates to 1905 and is listed on the Alabama Register of Historic Landmarks and Heritage. The restaurant closes on Monday.

Don't miss the *Aliceville Museum and Cultural Arts Center* (205–373–2363), downtown at 104 Broad Street Plaza. During World War II some 6,000 German prisoners—most from Field Marshall Erwin Rommel's Afrika Korps—were interned at Camp Aliceville, site of the present-day *Sue Stabler Park* about 2 miles due west of town on State Route 17. In 1993 the city hosted its fifty-year Prisoner of War Reunion.

During this three-day event, officials, residents, and visitors—including fifteen German ex-POWs and their families—gathered to dedicate the only World War II German POW museum in the United States. Exhibits include drawings, paintings, sculpture, musical instruments, furniture, newspapers, photos, and other artifacts from Camp Aliceville. Museum hours are 10:00 A.M. to 4:00 P.M. Monday through Friday, 10:00 A.M. to 2:00 P.M. Saturday, or by appointment on weekends. Modest admission. For more information check out the museum's Web site at www.pickens.net~museum; the e-mail address is museum@pickens.net.

At 501 Broad Street, Melanie and Charles Dean offer overnight accommodations at *WillowBrooke* (205–373–6133), a 1911 home they spent a year restoring. Special features of the Edwardian-style home include wraparound porches, seven fireplaces with original signature mantels, and period antiques. Breakfast can be enjoyed in the dining room or on one of the home's porches. Standard rates.

You can also enjoy some warm hospitality at *Myrtlewood* (205–373–8153 or 800–367–7891), another bed-and-breakfast at 602 Broad Street. Owned by Johnie and Billy McKinzey, this 1909 home features a minimuseum, sun porches, stained glass, and Victorian furnishings. Be sure to notice the coffee table's display of memorabilia in a front parlor. Guests can opt for an early Continental breakfast or a full plantation breakfast in the dining room. Standard rates. Johnie arranges gourmet dinners, luncheons, and area tours by request.

From Aliceville you can either dip southeast via State Route 14 to Eutaw (a charming town covered in the Southwest section of this book) or return east to tour Tannehill, about midway between Birmingham and Tuscaloosa.

Peach Country

To reach *Tannehill Historical State Park* (205–477–5711) near McCalla, take exit 100 off I-59 and follow the signs. Situated near the Cahaba River, this 1,500-acre wooded park spills into Tuscaloosa, Jefferson, and Bibb Counties. On the grounds you'll see the remains of the Tannehill Iron Furnaces and more than forty pioneer homes and farm outbuildings. A sorghum mill, cotton gin, blacksmith shop, and gristmill (that grinds cornmeal every weekend) add to the authenticity of this mid-1800s re-creation. Exhibits at the Iron and Steel Museum of Alabama spotlight the history of technology prior to 1850.

Afterward you might like to shift south to *Montevallo,* located in the middle of Alabama. Here the University of Montevallo, situated on a beautiful campus complete with brick streets, tree-lined drives, and historical buildings such as the 1823 King House and Reynolds Hall, makes a pleasant stopover. An arbor walk features thirty trees labeled by their common and scientific names. Pick up a booklet called *Guide to Campus Trees,* available on campus and at the local chamber of commerce office. The public can also attend campus concerts, plays, films, lectures, art exhibits, and sporting events; most activities are free. Call the university's information office at (205) 665–6230 to check on current happenings during the time of your visit, or stop by the Will Lyman Welcome Center (205–665–1519), located in a lovely Victorian house at 720 Oak Street.

For overnighters, **Ramsay Conference Center** (205–665–6280) offers single rooms (without TV or phones) on a space-available basis, seven days a week during the school term, at bargain rates. A short stroll away you'll find the college dining hall with cafeteria-style meals. Pay-at-the-door prices for breakfast, lunch, and dinner are economical.

While in Montevallo spend some time browsing among the treasures at **The House of Serendipity.** Housed in a downtown vintage building with a pressed-tin ceiling and wraparound balcony, this unique establishment is located at 645 Main Street. Owned by Jane and Bruce McClanahan, this shop, where "the unexpected is found," features everything from antiques, greeting cards, and art supplies to Basket Case creations by basketry instructors Faye Roberts and Mimi Lawley. Jane also offers a matching service for discontinued patterns in American crystal and dinnerware. Store hours are 9:00 A.M. to 5:00 P.M. Monday through Saturday.

Close by, you can get a great meal at the **Montevallo Grille.** Afterward, continue around the corner on Middle Street to **Willow Bend,** where Wes Cunningham creates "rustic, organic" furniture from willow and other native woods. He also displays the work of local artists.

Before leaving town, visit **Orr Park,** where you can stroll along Shoal Creek, a natural habitat for Tim Tingle's life-size carvings of birds, animals, and wizard faces.

From Montevallo head southeast on State Route 155 to the heart of Jemison for some Southern hospitality. Entering **The Jemison Inn Bed and Breakfast** (205–688–2055), located at 212 Highway 191, "is like stepping into grandmother's parlor," says hostess Nancy Ruzicka. A former librarian/business executive who gave up tailored suits for jeans, Nancy now concentrates her considerable skills on making guests glad they came. During an eighteen-month "mud, sweat, and tears" metamorphosis,

Reynolds Hall at the University of Montevallo

Nancy and husband Joe, a bookbinder by profession, transformed this house into the charming bed-and-breakfast inn they visualized.

Nancy and Joe find antiques-collecting fascinating and have furnished their home with interesting pieces. Be sure to notice the parlor's Ediphone and collection of music cylinders. Pre-breakfast coffee and juice can be enjoyed in the parlor or on the front porch, a peaceful place to sit and rock or swing while savoring the sights and sounds of a small town. Depending on "the mood of the cook at the moment," Nancy serves fresh fruit followed by pecan pancakes (the house specialty) or perhaps a sausage casserole with homemade coffee cake, biscuits, and jellies. She sets an elegant table using sterling silver, antique china, cut glass, and fine linens. Dinner packages are available, also. Adjacent to the backyard pool (also available for guests), the formal English garden can be admired, which Nancy designed. Nancy shares some of her secrets in her new book, *Embarrassingly Simple: Recipes from The Jemison Inn Bed and Breakfast,* available for purchase. For more information e-mail theinn@scott.net or set your browser to www.bbonline. com/al/jemison/. Moderate rates.

While in town, be sure to visit **Petals from the Past,** which offers antique roses and other vintage plants, and the **Jemison Trade Center,** where you can eat and shop seven days a week. The Ruzickas will direct you to these and other nearby attractions.

Continuing south to Clanton in the heart of peach country, you'll find several places to purchase this locally grown fruit. *Peach Park,* for instance, features fresh peaches (in season) along with homemade peach ice cream, milk shakes, yogurt, and other delicious desserts as well as pecans and boiled peanuts.

While in the area, plan a visit to *Confederate Memorial Park* (205–755–1990), just off U.S. Highway 31 near I–65. The site of a former home for Confederate veterans and their widows, the park features a museum with historical displays, Civil War relics, flags, Confederate uniforms, and weaponry. On the grounds you'll also find two cemeteries, a chapel, the old Mountain Creek Post Office, picnic pavilions, and hiking trails. Except for Thanksgiving, Christmas, and New Year's Day, the museum is open from 9:00 A.M. to 5:00 P.M. daily. The park may be visited year-round from dawn to dusk.

Head back north to Calera to see several antiques shops and the *Heart of Dixie Railroad Museum* (205–668–3435). From I–65 take exit 228 and travel 1 mile west on State Route 25, following signs to the museum. Exhibits include World War II photos, framed timetables, waiting room benches, old railroad lanterns, signal equipment, special tools used to repair steam locomotives, a caboose stove, and an arrival/departure board from the demolished Birmingham Terminal. A glass case contains dishes made by Marshall Field and Company in 1925 for the Rock Island Lines. You'll see a centralized train control board (CTC) with which one person, a railroad counterpart of the airline's air traffic controller, managed a large section of tracks and the trains that traveled it. Locomotives, guard cars (the museum owns four of only six in existence), passenger and freight cars, and the state's largest railroad crane stand outside the green depot museum. Hours are 10:00 A.M. to 4:00 P.M. Saturday year-round and 1:00 to 4:00 P.M. Sunday from late April through autumn. The museum sponsors train rides and special events. Call for more information on the museum and a train ride schedule. Admission is free, but donations are accepted.

Continue a few miles northeast via State Route 25 to Columbiana, where you'll find many choice items that once belonged to George and Martha Washington—the largest collection of Washington family artifacts outside Mount Vernon, in fact. The *Smith-Harrison Museum* (205–669–4545) is located behind the Shelby County Courthouse in the Mildred B. Harrison Library Building. Upon entering, you'll see beautiful table settings featuring an English punch bowl, soup tureen, and other exquisite porcelain pieces and silverware used by the *first* first lady and her family. Other treasures include family portraits, the first lady's prayer book, various personal items, an original 1787 Samuel Vaughn sketch of Mount Vernon's grounds, and some seventy letters and documents dating to the Revolutionary War period. You can read correspondence from James Madison, Lord Cornwallis, John Adams, Aaron Burr, and other historic figures. The collection's oldest item is the 1710 handwritten will of Col. Daniel Parke, the grandfather of Martha Washington's first husband. You'll also see an original tintype made by Civil War photographer Mathew B. Brady that depicts Robert E. Lee in uniform for the last time.

Vulcan, the mythical god of the forge and Birmingham's unofficial city symbol, now holds a torch indicating area traffic fatalities. In the past the iron man has promoted various products by holding up a jar of pickles, a soft drink bottle, an ice-cream cone, and other commercial items.

Amassed by Eliza Parke Custis Law, Martha Washington's granddaughter, the collection passed through six generations of Washington heirs down to Shelby County's Charlotte Smith Weaver. After giving her grandchildren selected items, Mrs. Weaver offered the remainder of her family collection for public preservation. Columbiana banker Karl Harrison acquired two-thirds of it for this museum, and the rest went to Mount Vernon, says curator Nancy Gray. The Columbiana museum has since procured additional Washington family pieces. Except for major holidays, the museum is open 10:00 A.M. to 3:00 P.M. Monday through Friday. Admission is free.

Woodland and Water

Continue to Sylacauga, sometimes called Marble City. While many cities contain marble monuments and buildings, here the entire town rests on a marble bed about 32 miles long and more than a mile wide. Sylacauga marble was used in the U.S. Supreme Court Building in Washington, D.C., Detroit's General Motors Building, and in many other distinctive edifices. "The Sylacauga area has some of the whitest marble in the world," says a local quarrying company official.

Stop by the *Isabel Anderson Comer Museum and Arts Center* (256–245–4016) at 711 Broadway Avenue North. At the museum, housed in a former library building dating from the 1930s, you'll see a big chunk of calcite quartz, unusual because it came from the middle of a local marble quarry. The museum owns several pieces by Giuseppe Moretti, the Italian sculptor who designed Birmingham's statue of Vulcan. Moretti came to Sylacauga in the early 1900s to open a marble quarry.

The museum's displays cover everything from beaded evening bags and Victorian hat pins to a reproduction of the Hodges meteorite that hurtled down on Sylacauga from outer space and struck a local woman in 1954. Here, you'll find a gallery of Native American artifacts, antique toys, handmade fabrics from the 1830s, and an extensive collection of photos and scrapbooks on local history. Pioneer exhibits are housed in the basement. One section features albums, awards, photos, costumes, and other memorabilia of native son Jim Nabors, who starred as TV's Gomer Pyle on *The Andy Griffith Show.*

The museum is open 10:00 A.M. to 5:00 P.M. Tuesday through Friday or by appointment. Although there's no admission charge, donations are accepted.

After leaving Sylacauga, follow U.S. Highway 280 southeast to **Alexander City,** home of the Russell Corporation. Employing about four-fifths of the local workforce, Russell outfits the sports world all the way from Little League through hundreds of college teams to most of the National Football League. This company handles every step of the process from cotton production to finished product. The sweat suit you don for your jog around the block may well have come from Alex City, as the locals call it.

The **Russell Retail Store** (256–500–4464), a big cheese-wedge of a building on U.S. Highway 280, sells sweatpants and tops, T-shirts, cardigans, and other leisure wear—maybe even your favorite team's togs. In addition to a university section (that carries mostly Atlantic Coast Conference and Southeastern Conference athletic apparel), the outlet offers casual clothing for ladies and children. Cross-Creek and HIGH Cotton lines feature an array of items in both heavyweight and lightweight knits. You may want to personalize your purchases with selected transfers—from SAVE THE EARTH to holiday and hunting themes—that can be applied by heat press in fifteen seconds.

Clothing sells here for one-third off the retail value. Also, a back room contains imperfect or discontinued items marked from one-half to two-thirds off the "designed to sell for" price. The store's hours are 9:00 A.M. to 6:00 P.M. Monday through Saturday and 1:00 to 6:00 P.M. Sunday.

While in Alex City, consider headquartering at **Mistletoe Bough** (877–330–3707 or 256–329– 3717), a grand Queen Anne Victorian home at 497 Hillabee Street. Built and named by Reuben Herzfeld, a leading citizen and local bank founder, the house dates to 1895. After Birmingham resident Jean Payne discovered this wonderful house "by divine appointment," she and husband Carlice bought it and embarked on a ten-and-a-half-month restoration to showcase the home's beauty and character.

Mistletoe Bough boasts its original light fixtures, parquet floors, beaded paneling, and etched glass. A stately staircase leads to five guest rooms on the second floor, and a front balcony overlooks downtown Alex City. Magnolia, pecan, and other trees dot the lovely shaded lawn with its reflection pond and masses of azaleas, camellias, gardenias, and wisteria. Jean serves guests welcoming refreshments and a full breakfast, featuring homemade biscuits with jellies and preserves made from the property's own apple, fig, and pear trees. Rates are moderate.

While in the Alex City area, you might like to explore nearby **Horseshoe Bend National Military Park,** the site of the final battle of the Creek War. Located about 12 miles north of Dadeville on State Route 49, the 2,040-acre park features a visitors center with exhibits on the battle, Creek Indian culture, and frontier life.

Other local options include boating, swimming, and fishing at **Lake Martin,** which offers a 750-mile shoreline against a backdrop of wooded hills. This body of water spills over the southern half of Tallapoosa County and even splashes into neighboring Elmore and Coosa Counties. Depending on the season and local weather conditions, fishermen haul in largemouth and striped bass, bream, bluegill, crappie, and catfish from this lake. For more outdoor recreation continue south to Elmore County.

PLACES TO STAY IN CENTRAL ALABAMA

ALEXANDER CITY
Holiday Inn Express
2945 Highway 280
(256) 234–5900 or
(800) HOLIDAY

Jameson Inn
4335 Highway 280
(256) 234–7099 or
(800) 541–3268

Mistletoe Bough
497 Hillabee Street
(256) 329–3717

ALICEVILLE
Myrtlewood
602 Broad Street
(256) 373–8153 or
(800) 367–7891

WillowBrooke
501 Broad Street
(256) 373–6133

ANNISTON
The Victoria
1604 Quintard Avenue
(256) 236–0503

ASHVILLE
Roses and Lace Country Inn
20 Rose Lane
(205) 594–4366

BIRMINGHAM
Birmingham Marriott
One Perimeter Park South
(205) 986–3775

Holiday Inn Redmont
2101 Fifth Avenue North
(205) 324–2101 or
(800) HOLIDAY

The Mountain Brook Inn
2800 U.S. Highway 280
(205) 870–3100 or
(800) 523–7771

Pickwick Hotel
1023 Twentieth Street
(205) 933–9555 or
(800) 255–7304

Sheraton Birmingham Hotel
2101 Civic Center Drive
(205) 307–3000 or
(800) 325–3535

The Tutwiler
2021 Park Place North
(205) 322–2100 or
(800) 996–2426

The Wynfrey Hotel
1000 Riverchase Galleria
(205) 987–1600 or
(800) WYNFREY

DELTA
Cheaha State Park
2141 Bunker Loop
(256) 488–5885 or
(800) 846–2654

JEMISON
The Jemison Inn
Bed and Breakfast
212 Highway 191
(205) 688–2055

MONTEVALLO
Ramsay Conference Center
University of Montevallo
(205) 665–6280

MUNFORD
The Cedars Plantation
590 Cheaha Road
(256) 761–9090

NAUVOO
Old Harbin Hotel
131 Third Street
(205) 697–5652

OXFORD
Holiday Inn
Anniston/Oxford
I–20 at intersection of U.S.
Highway 78 and
Alabama 21 South
(256) 831–3410

PELHAM
Oak Mountain State Park
200 Terrace Drive
(205) 620–2524 or
(800) ALA–PARK

STERRETT
Twin Pines Resort
1200 Twin Pines Road
(205) 672–7575

SYLACAUGA
Jameson Inn
89 Gene Stewart Boulevard
(256) 245–4141 or
(800) 541–3268

TALLADEGA
Orangevale Plantation
1400 Whiting Road
(256) 362–3052

TUSCALOOSA
Courtyard by Marriott
4115 Courtney Drive
(205) 750–8384 or
(800) 321–2211

Crimson Inn
1509 University Boulevard
(205) 758–3483

Four Points Hotel
Tuscaloosa–Capstone by
Sheraton
320 Paul Bryant Drive
(205) 752–3200

Hampton Inn
600 Harper Lee Drive
(205) 553–9800 or
(800) HAMPTON

Key West Inn
4700 Doris Pate Drive
(205) 556–3232 or
(800) 311–3811

**PLACES TO EAT IN
CENTRAL ALABAMA**

ALICEVILLE
Plantation House Restaurant
Highway 17 Bypass
(256) 373–8121

ANNISTON
Betty's Bar-B-Q, Inc.
401 South Quintard Avenue
(256) 237–1411

Cafe LeMamas
1208 Walnut Avenue
(256) 237–5550

Los Mexicanos
1101 South Quintard Avenue
(256) 238–0250

The Original Old
Smokehouse Bar-B-Q
631 Quintard Avenue
(256) 237–5200

Top O' The River
3220 McClellan Boulevard
(256) 238–0097

BIRMINGHAM
Bombay Cafe
2839 Seventh Avenue South
(205) 322–1930

Cobb Lane Restaurant
1 Cobb Lane (just off
Twentieth Street)
(205) 933–0462

Grammas'
2030 Little Valley Road
(205) 823–5825

Highlands Bar & Grill
2011 Eleventh Avenue South
(205) 939–1400

Hot and Hot Fish Club
2180 Eleventh Court South
(205) 933-5474

Jimmy's at Brookwood
509 Brookwood Boulevard
(205) 868-9180

Rossi's
2737 Highway 280 East
(205) 879-2111

The Silvertron Cafe
3813 Clairmont Avenue
(205) 591-3707

HELENA
Fox Valley
Highway 17
(205) 664-8341

HOMEWOOD
Nabeel's Cafe
1706 Oxmoor Road
(205) 879-9292

IRONDALE
The Irondale Cafe
1906 First Avenue North
(205) 956-5258

MOUNTAIN BROOK
Arman's at Park Lane
2117 Cahaba Road
(205) 939-1400

NAUVOO
Slick Lizard Smokehouse
Carbon Hill and
Nauvoo Road
(205) 697-5789

NORTHPORT
The Globe
430 Main Avenue
(205) 391-0949

Hummer's on Main
433 Main Avenue
(205) 345-2119

OXFORD
China Luck
503 Quintard Drive
(256) 831-5221

SPRINGVILLE
Cafe Dupont
619 Main Street
(205) 467-3339

TUSCALOOSA
Cocopelli Gourmet Cafe
1410 University Boulevard
(205) 349-4033

Cypress Inn
501 Rice Mine Road North
(205) 345-6963

DePalma's
2300 University Boulevard
(205) 759-1879

Dreamland
off Jug Factory Road in
Jerusalem Heights
(205) 758-8135

Kozy's
3510 Loop Road
(205) 556-0655

For More Information about Central Alabama

Alexander City Area Chamber of Commerce
120 Tallapoosa Street (35010)
P.O. Box 926 Alexander City 35011-0926
(256) 234-3461
e-mail: coc@lakemartin.net

Anniston/Calhoun County Chamber of Commerce
1330 Quintard Avenue (36201)
P.O. Box 1087 Anniston 36202
(256) 237-3536 or (800) 489-1087
Web site: www.calhounchamber.org
e-mail: carolm@calhounchamber.org

Greater Birmingham Convention and Visitors Bureau
220 Ninth Avenue North
Birmingham 35203-1100
(205) 458-8000 or (800) 458-8085
Web site: www.birmingham.org
e-mail: info@birmingham.org

Montevallo Chamber of Commerce
720 Oak Street Montevallo 35115
(205) 665-1519

Tuscaloosa Convention and Visitors Bureau
1305 Greensboro Avenue (35401)
P.O. Box 3167 Tuscaloosa 35403
(205) 391-9200 or (800) 538-8696
Web site: www.tcvb.org
e-mail tuscacvb@dbtech.net

Mezzanine
508 Greensboro Avenue
(205) 752–0020

The Waysider Restaurant
1512 Greensboro Avenue
(205) 345–8239

Wings Sports Grille
500 Harper Lee Drive
(205) 556–5658

MAINSTREAM ATTRACTIONS
WORTH SEEING IN
CENTRAL ALABAMA

Arlington Antebellum Home and Gardens, *331 Cotton Avenue, Birmingham; (205) 780–5656. This circa 1850 Greek Revival mansion contains a fine collection of period antiques.*

Birmingham Zoo, *2530 Cahaba Road; (205) 879–0408. Both big and little kids enjoy outings to this facility, the home of some 900 animals from all over the globe.*

International Motorsports Hall of Fame and Talladega Superspeedway, *Off I–20, Talladega; (256) 362–5002.*

This unique facility, which occupies a complex of circular-shaped buildings, captures the speed of movement and thrill of competitive racing. You'll see the Budweiser Rocket Car, a missile on wheels that broke the sound barrier, and record-breaking vehicles once propelled by Richard Petty, Bill Elliott, Bobby Allison, and other racing greats. Additional exhibits include vintage autos, drag racers, motorcycles, trophies, photos, and a simulator that puts you in the driver's seat. You can also tour the adjacent Talladega Superspeedway, the world's fastest speedway, which hosts the annual DieHard 500 in April and Winston 500 in October. For more information check out www.daytonausa.com.

McWane Center, *200 Nineteenth Street North, Birmingham; (205) 714–8300. Definitely not off the beaten path, this science-adventure museum occupies the historic Loveman's department store*

building in the heart of downtown. Youngsters will especially enjoy the IMAX theater's presentations and simulated space-flight experiences offered by the Challenger Center for Space Science Education, a nonprofit organization founded by the families of the seven Challenger crew members who died in the tragic 1986 space shuttle explosion. The Ocean Pool, World of Water, and various interactive science exhibits all add to the excitement. Visit the museum's Web site at www.mcwane.com.

Visionland, *Interstate 20/59 near I–459, Bessemer; (205) 481–4750. This fun-filled family park spreads across seventy-five rolling acres in Bessemer, just southwest of Birmingham. With a theme dedicated to Birmingham's early iron and steel industry, the amusement park features multiple thrills aboard a $4.5 million wooden roller coaster, The Rampage, plus rides galore. Visit the park's Web site at www. visionlandpark.com.*

Southeast Alabama

The Plains

On your way to "The Plains" (home of Auburn University) in the historic Chattahoochee Trace's upper section, you may want to follow State Route 63 south from Alex City to see *Children's Harbor* and enjoy another taste of woodland and water. Near the Kowaliga Bridge (13.8 miles from the U.S. 280 turnoff) on Lake Martin's shoreline you'll notice a reproduction of a New England lighthouse and a white-steepled church called Children's Chapel.

Across the road from Children's Harbor, just off State Route 63 at Kowaliga Marina, you'll find *Cecil's on the Lake* (334–857–2161). Beside the door stands a wooden Indian, a replacement for the one that inspired Hank Williams's song "Kowliga." (The original Indian gradually disappeared as country music fans took away small pieces for souvenirs.) Known locally as Kowaliga's, this restaurant features great steaks and seafood and attracts many boaters enjoying Lake Martin's pleasures. You might also like to sample a local catfish specialty called "the Squealer." Moderate prices.

Owned by Greg Cecil (who also runs two other area restaurants), the lakeside eatery is open for dinner year-round from 5:00 to 9:00 P.M. Wednesday through Sunday.

Afterward head south to Tallassee, just north of I-85 at State Routes 14 and 229, for some home-style mouth-watering food and a yesteryear experience at *Hotel Talisi* (334–283–2769). Located at 14 Sistrunk Avenue, this 1920s hotel brims with antiques and nostalgia-from its red-carpeted lobby with ceiling fans and crystal chandeliers to the second-floor hallway's wooden "Superman" phone booth. Three baby grand pianos (including a 1924 version), three uprights, and a player spinet add to the ambience.

In the spacious upstairs hall, you'll see Western Union writing desks,

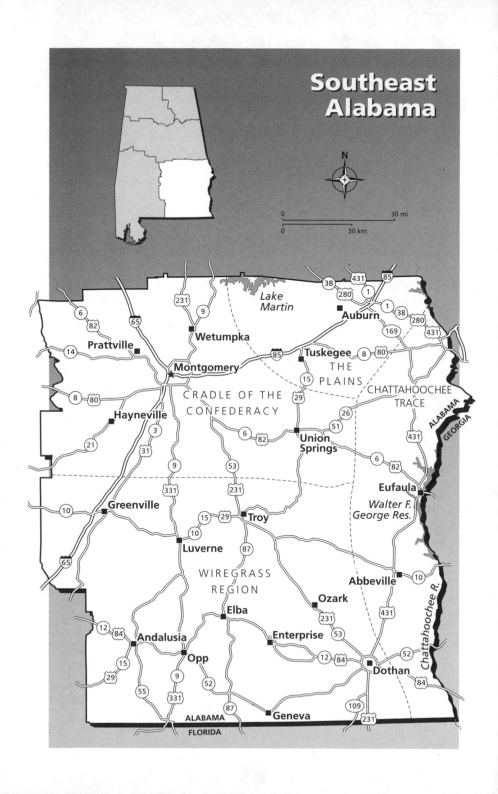

SOUTHEAST ALABAMA

interesting reading material, and an array of seating areas—great for conversation or for curling up with a mystery. Furnished in eclectic fashion with finger vases, parlor lamps, and antiques from the early 1900s, the rooms possess a uniqueness noticeably absent in today's standardized world.

Continuing the hotel's famous family-style buffet tradition, Bob Brown, Roger Gaither, and crew offer a daily feast featuring fried chicken, baked chicken with dressing, sweet potato soufflé, a medley of fresh vegetables, corn bread, hush puppies, and homemade pies accompanied by piano/organ dinner music. Except for Sunday, when the feast ends at 2:50 P.M., hours are 11:00 A.M. to 7:50 P.M. daily. Stroll across the street to the hotel's under-the-stars dining oasis, a garden setting with white lights, statuary, and olive trees. Standard to moderate rates.

GAY'S TOP PICKS IN SOUTHEAST ALABAMA

Alabama Shakespeare Festival, Montgomery

First White House of the Confederacy, Montgomery

Landmark Park, Dothan

Lovelace Museum and Hall of Honor, Auburn

Old Alabama Town, Montgomery

Pike Pioneer Museum, Troy

State Capitol, Montgomery

Town of Eufaula

Tuskegee Institute National Historic Site, Tuskegee

U.S. Army Aviation Museum, Fort Rucker

Next strike out southeast for the historic *Tuskegee Institute* (334–727–3200), where even peanut-butter buffs will be amazed to learn about the peanut's potential. The Carver Museum at 1212 Old Montgomery Road (State Route 126) pays tribute to the creative genius of the agronomist, artist, and inventor who helped change the course of Southern agriculture. George Washington Carver's agricultural experiments with peanuts, pecans, sweet potatoes, and cotton resulted in a more educated approach to farming-not to mention hundreds of new products, many featured among the museum's exhibits. You'll also see some of Carver's artwork and a model of the first lab he used to launch research that resulted in the transformation of sweet potatoes into after-dinner mints, a coffee substitute, lemon drops, starch, synthetic ginger, tapioca, library paste, medicine, writing ink, and a multitude of other items. As for the multipurpose peanut, the legendary scientist's list of possible uses ranges from beverages, foods, cosmetics, dyes, and medicines to diesel fuel, laundry soap, and insecticide. Before you leave the museum, be sure to visit the gift section. I bought a copy of a booklet (first published in June 1925) entitled *How to Grow the Peanut and 105 Ways of Preparing it for Human Consumption,* containing recipes from peanut bisque to peanut pudding. Museum admission is free. Except for Thanksgiving, Christmas, and New Year's Day, the museum is open daily from 9:00 A.M. to 5:00 P.M.

Later take a campus stroll to see some of the handmade brick buildings, which students constructed during the institute's early years. You'll also want to tour **The Oaks,** home of Booker T. Washington, who founded Tuskegee Institute in 1881. Tours start on the hour from 9:00 A.M. to 4:00 P.M. The home is furnished as it was during the time the Washington family lived there. Be sure to notice the unique hand-carved Oriental desk in Washington's upstairs den.

Head north to the "land where turtles live"—a former Creek Indian settlement called Loachapoka that once also thrived as a stagecoach junction. Seven miles west of Auburn on State Route 14, you'll find the **Loachapoka Historic District,** which features several structures dating from the decade of 1840 to 1850. **The Lee County Historical Society Museum,** housed in the old Trade Center building, contains items ranging from a unique hand-carved cedar rocking chair and an 1840s accounting desk to an oak map case, an antique medical bag, and a punch bowl and dipper made from gourds.

Way Off the Beaten Path . . . in Brazil

*T*ravel writing's overlapping projects and looming deadlines often require juggling schedules and shifting gears. Even so I found it somewhat disconcerting when a research trip to Brazil coincided with the final stages of this book's second edition. With a two-week intermission, I feared losing my focus. Instead, an odd chain of events led to the intertwining of two distinctly different destinations.

"Why don't you write about that place in Brazil where some people from Alabama settled after the Civil War?" asked a friend. "Their descendants still live there and speak Southern English—right in the middle of Portuguese country."

I found this suggestion intriguing but kept running into roadblocks—until my husband won two tickets to an Auburn football game and learned about Haley Center's Saturday Semi-

nars. Open to the public, these free pregame lectures covered topics from financial planning to gardening. On the day of our visit, the session featured Dr. Cyrus Dawsey and Dr. James Dawsey, speaking on the subject of a book they coedited: The Confederados: Old South Immigrants in Brazil (available from the University of Alabama Press).

Their comments and videotape provided background on Americana, founded and settled by Confederate refugees. Located about 80 miles from Sao Paulo, Americana remains home to a number of descendants from several southern states whose families moved there during the 1860s. Through the generations, they made valuable contributions to their adopted homeland, especially in the area of agriculture. So instead of fragmenting my focus, a trip to Brazil added another facet to my Alabama research.

Gay's Favorite Annual Events in Southeast Alabama

A-Day Football Game, Auburn, April; (334) 844–4040 or (800) AUB–1957

Alabama Highland Games, Wynton M. Blount Cultural Park at the Alabama Shakespeare Festival, Montgomery, fourth Saturday in September; (334) 361–4571

Auburn Floral Trail, Auburn, late March or early April; (334) 887–8747 or (800) 321–8880

Azalea-Dogwood Trail and Festival, Dothan, late March or early April; (334) 793–0191 or (888) 449–0212

Festival in the Park, Oak Park, Montgomery, early October; (334) 241–2300

Historical Fair and Ruritan's Syrup Sop in Loachapoka, Loachapoka, October; (334) 887–8747 or (800) 321–8880

Jubilee Cityfest, downtown Montgomery, May; (334) 834–7220

Opelika Arts Festival, Opelika, third Saturday in April; (334) 749–8105 or (800) 321–8880

National Peanut Festival, Dothan, November; (334) 794–6622 or (888) 449–0212

Rattlesnake Rodeo, Opp, first Saturday and Sunday in March; (334) 493–9559 or (800) 239–8054

Spring Pilgrimage, Eufaula, late March or early April; (888) 383–2852

Victorian Front Porch Christmas, Opelika, December; (334) 887–8747 or (800) 321–8880

Upstairs, rooms with individual themes feature vintage costumes such as an 1877 wedding dress, an exhibit on Ella Smith's Roanoke doll creations, antique quilts, and a melodeon. Other displays include military uniforms and equipment, kitchen utensils and gadgets, and an almost complete section of Auburn annuals that date to the 1890s.

On the grounds you'll see a steam-powered cotton gin, gristmill, working blacksmith shop, bandstand, doctor's buggy, and dogtrot cabin (moved here from rural Tallapoosa County and reconstructed). If you visit in October, don't miss the *Loachapoka Syrup Sop and Historical Fair.* Folks at this event, harking back to yesteryear, demonstrate the entire process of converting sugar cane into syrup— from cane crushing by mule-drawn press to syrup sampling on homemade sweet potato biscuits (sometimes called "cat head biscuits" because of their large size). For information on making an appointment to see the museum, call the Auburn-Opelika Convention and Visitors Bureau at (800) 321–8880 or (334) 887–8747.

Afterward head east to "sweet Auburn, loveliest village of the plain." This line from Oliver Goldsmith's poem "The Deserted Village" inspired the university town's name. Founded by the Alabama Methodist Conference in 1856, the school later became a land-grant institution. (Incidentally, if you enter Auburn by way of I–85, a trail of big orange tiger paws takes you all the way to the university campus.)

Start your tour of the **Auburn University Historic District** at Toomer's Corner, a busy intersection that gets layered so deeply with toilet tissue after each Tiger victory that sometimes vehicles cannot pass through for an hour or two while a celebration takes place. Before embarking on your campus trek, you might like to step into Toomer's Drugstore, a local landmark, to see the antique marble soda fountain and to order a lemonade.

Alabama Trivia
Isabella de Soto planted America's first fig trees, which came over from Spain, at Fort Morgan.

This section of campus features several buildings that date from the 1850s to the early 1900s. You'll see the Gothic Revival University Chapel, Langdon Hall, and Samford Hall. The latter, a four-story brick structure of Italianate design, dates to 1888 and stands on the site of Old Main, a building that burned the year before.

To explore a tucked-away corner on campus, search out the **Donald E. Davis Arboretum,** with pavilion, lake, and some 200 labeled botanical specimens ranging from red Japanese maples and chinquapin oaks to Southern magnolias and chinaberry trees.

Don't miss the **Lovelace Athletic Museum and Hall of Honor** (334–844–4750), located at the corner of Samford and Donahue in the Athletic Complex. Honoring Auburn's athletes, the museum recognizes their sports achievements with high-tech interactive exhibits, life-size figures in talking dioramas, and a cavalcade of fascinating displays. Trip along the Tiger Trail and experience a vicarious but thrilling football victory with the crowd's roar and take a look at a replicated Toomer's Corner, triumphantly decorated with toilet paper.

Athletes represented include Heisman Trophy winner and football/baseball hero Bo Jackson, NBA star Charles Barkley, Chicago White Sox player Frank Thomas, and Heisman Trophy winner/coach Pat Sullivan. Museum hours are 8:00 A.M. to 4:30 P.M. Monday through Friday, 9:00 A.M. to 6:00 P.M. Football Saturdays, and 9:00 A.M. to 3:00 P.M. on Football Weekend Sundays.

While in Auburn consider headquartering at **Crenshaw House Bed and Breakfast** (334–821–1131 or 800–950–1131), 2 blocks north of Toomer's Corner. Shaded by giant oak and pecan trees, this blue Victorian gingerbread-style house stands at 371 North College Street in Auburn's Old Main and Church Street Historic District. Owners Fran and Peppi Verma, who furnished their two-story 1890 home with lovely antiques, offer six units for overnight guests. The Vermas wanted to start a small family business and purchased the house "knowing it would lend itself well to a bed-and-breakfast facility," Fran says, adding that her husband had enjoyed bed-and-breakfast lodging while traveling in Europe. As for breakfast, guests receive a room-service menu and indicate their choices along with a serving time. The Web site is www.auburnalabama.com. Standard to moderate rates.

For lunch or dinner try the *Terra Cotta Cafe* (334–821–3656) at 415 East Magnolia Avenue. You'll find the entrance and parking off Ross Street. This eatery, decorated with a garden theme of clay pots and hand-painted wall designs, offers patio seating. Appetizers might range from black bean and corn salsa served with tortilla chips to fried green tomatoes drizzled with a fresh herb sauce. Chef Billy Lee's menu changes seasonally but always includes chicken pie, a pasta bowl such as red chile linguine, and nightly dinner features—perhaps shrimp cakes or a grilled meat or chicken entree. "We depend heavily on what's in season and locally grown," he says, "and make all our desserts from scratch." Prices are moderate. Lunch hours run from 11:00 A.M. to 2:30 P.M. Monday through Saturday. Dinner is served from 5:30 to 9:00 P.M. Monday through Thursday and till 10:00 P.M. on Friday and Saturday.

Also, golfers will want to check out *Auburn Links at Mill Creek* (334–887–5151), a $5 million facility that occupies 274 acres located about 3 miles south of town near the intersection of U.S. Highway 29 and I–85 at exit 51. (The eighteenth hole's sand traps form a giant tiger paw print.)

Nearby at 2780 South College Street, the kids will enjoy *Surfside Water Park* (334–821–7873) with all its splashing, swimming, and dunking possibilities. Hours are 10:00 A.M. to 7:00 P.M., and the facility opens daily from Memorial Day through Labor Day. Admission. LeisureTime Campground offers RV campsites adjacent to the park.

Auburn's sister city, *Opelika,* makes a good place to continue your area exploration. In Opelika's "olden days," passengers traveling through by train sometimes saw shootouts across the railroad tracks. Fortunately, today's visitors don't have to dodge stray bullets, so you can relax as you explore the Railroad Avenue Historic District.

As a result of Opelika's participation in Alabama's Main Street program (a project of the National Trust for Historic Preservation), many once-forgotten structures have been rescued and reincarnated as charming shops such as *Easterday Antiques.* Helen Easterday, who's been called "the quintessential town person," and her husband, Kenneth, have embraced the local downtown revitalization program to the point of converting the enormous upper level of their shop into a wonderful home. Mrs. Easterday's passion for art may be observed in the exquisite antique furnishings, paintings, and accessories displayed in her shop. For health reasons, she limits her schedule and operates by appointment only. For more information or an appointment, call (334) 749–6407.

During mid-December, the *Victorian Front Porch Christmas* features self-driving and walking tours through the streets of North Opelika Historic Neighborhood. More than thirty homes and porches serve as backdrops for unique decorations and life-size holiday figures designed by local artist Jan Jones, who maintains a studio in downtown Opelika.

After your Railroad Avenue stroll, head to *The Museum of East Alabama* (334–749–2751), located nearby at 121 South Ninth Street. Here you'll see glass milk bottles, baby bonnets, Shirley Temple and Roanoke dolls, toys, and collections of vintage typewriters, pianos, farm implements, war memorabilia, and surgical instruments. Other unusual exhibits include a foot X-ray machine (typical of those once used in shoe stores) and a bicycle-propelled ice-cream cart. The museum's collection also includes an early-twentieth-century kitchen and a full-size fire truck. Hours are 10:00 A.M. until 4:00 P.M. Tuesday through Friday and 2:00 to 4:00 P.M. on Saturday. Admission is free.

Looking to the right as you exit the museum, you'll see the lofty clock tower of the *Lee County Courthouse,* a ¹/₂ block away. Listed on the National Register of Historic Places, the handsome, white-columned, two-story brick structure dates to 1896 and features marble floors and decorative arched windows.

Take time to drive around a bit to see Opelika's lovely homes, which exemplify a wide range of architectural styles. Better yet, make reservations to stay in one of them—*The Heritage House* (334–705–0485), at 714 Second Avenue. Barbara Patton, Opelika's mayor and an advocate of historic preservation, appealed to various parties to step in and preserve this fine old 1914 neoclassical tan brick home during the years it stood vacant. Finding no volunteers, she called a family conference to discuss its purchase. With the help of her son Richard, Barbara turned the thirteen-room home into a bed-and-breakfast. Guests will enjoy Richard's Mexican baked eggs, grits casserole, orange-French toast, and other specialties. The Pattons converted the home's carriage house, located in the rear, into a gift shop with several lines of collectibles, gourmet foods and coffees, men's shirts and ties, and other items. Standard to moderate rates.

While in the area, golfers will enjoy playing the *Grand National,* one of Alabama's fine courses on the award-winning Robert Trent Jones Golf Trail. For more information on this award-winning course, built on 1,300 acres encompassing a 650-acre lake, call (334) 749–9042 or (800) 949–4444.

After your local tour consider an outing to a bona fide "kissin' bridge" (so called because of the privacy it afforded courting couples who once traveled through in horse-drawn buggies). One of only three such structures still left in the lower Chattahoochee Valley, the *Salem-Shotwell Covered Bridge* can be reached by traveling east for about 8.7 miles via U.S. 280 and turning left on Lee County Route 254 (the Wacoochee School Road). The barn-red, single-span bridge is located 1.3 miles off Lee County Road 252.

Once part of a stagecoach route, this 75-foot bridge made of heart pine features latticed trusses, a wooden shingled roof, and round wooden pegs, surprisingly still intact. A master-and-slave team, John Godwin and Horace King, introduced the "town-truss" bridge design into the Chattahoochee Valley and built many of the area's early wooden bridges. Some local sources speculate that King may have drawn the plans for the Salem-Shotwell bridge. Whether or not he did, this bridge typifies the town-truss construction for which the team gained recognition in Alabama and neighboring states. Acting on Godwin's request, the Alabama legislature granted King his freedom in 1846. The two men then became business partners, and the former slave went on to serve as a member of the Alabama House of Representatives from 1869 to 1872. After Godwin's death in 1859, King erected a marble monument that may still be seen at Godwin Cemetery in nearby Phenix City. The inscription reads IN LASTING REMEMBRANCE OF THE LOVE AND GRATITUDE HE FELT FOR HIS LOST FRIEND AND FORMER MASTER.

Chattahoochee Trace

After touring War Eagle country, head south toward Eufaula. Along the way you'll see Pittsview (if you don't blink). Stop by the *Mayor's Office* (334–855–3568) on U.S. Highway 431 for a friendly chat with Frank Turner (who's the unofficial mayor) and a look at his folk art gallery. You'll find paintings by an area folk artist, signed "Mr John Henry Toney" along with his age. Frank also features the work of Butch Anthony, James (Buddy) Snipes, and other folk artists. Hours are by chance or appointment.

Afterward, continue south toward Eufaula, sometimes called the "Natchez of Alabama." You may want to make your base at lovely **Lakepoint Resort** (800–544–LAKE), about 7 miles north of town just off U.S. Highway 431. Located on the shores of Lake Eufaula (also known as Lake George), this complex offers accommodations ranging from campsites, cabins, and cottages to resort rooms and suites along with a restaurant, coffee shop, lounge, and gift shop. Recreation options include swimming, golfing, tennis, hiking, picnicking, biking, waterskiing, and boating—not to mention fishing in a 45,200-acre lake known as the Big Bass Capital of the World.

Just south of Lakepoint you'll find **Tom Mann's Fish World** (334–687–3655), which boasts a 38,000-gallon aquarium where you can watch largemouth bass, albino catfish, turtles, spotted gar, and other native fish swimming about; the observation process gets particularly interesting at feeding time. Local fishing expert Tom Mann also runs a pro shop here and posts current lake conditions for anglers in pursuit of trophy largemouths.

You'll enjoy browsing through Fish World's museum with its enormous collection of arrowheads—most found within a 200-mile radius. Other exhibits include mounted wildlife specimens, pottery, a

Strange As It Sounds

*S*peaking of bass, don't miss Leroy Brown's marble monument—the inscription reads:

MOST BASS ARE JUST FISH, BUT LEROY BROWN WAS SOMETHING SPECIAL.

And indeed he was. From a baby bass, Leroy ate from Tom Mann's hand. (The owner of Tom Mann's Fish World, south of Lakepoint.) "He could jump through a hoop. I've never found another fish as intelligent," says Mann, adding that Leroy never struck a lure and even tried to keep other fish away from these enticing but deadly objects. Leroy also proved to be an exemplary father, guarding the nest until all babies hatched.

Perhaps the esteem in which the big bass was held could be measured in some degree by his final rites. Some 700 persons attended Leroy's funeral. Professional bass fishermen, outfitted in tie and black tails, served as pallbearers, and Leroy's large tackle-box coffin contained a red velvet lining. The choir sang about "big bad Leroy Brown, meanest bass in the whole damn town . . ." Leroy was survived by eight wives. Following the funeral, a grave snatcher made off with Leroy's remains and sent a ransom note demanding $10,000. After several days and no reward, the thief abandoned his quest (and Leroy's coffin), apparently concluding that this scheme was neither fruitful nor fragrant.

Leroy Brown

MOST BASS
ARE JUST FISH
BUT
LEROY BROWN
WAS
SOMETHING
SPECIAL

Leroy Brown Monument

totem pole, a trophy collection, and a gallery featuring art by John Andrews, noted for his watercolor portraits of Native Americans. Modest admission. Except for Christmas, the facility is open daily year-round from 8:00 A.M. to 5:00 P.M.

Continue to Eufaula, a city filled with multiple versions of the perfect Southern mansion. Located on a bluff above the Chattahoochee River, Eufaula boasts the state's second-largest historic district and offers a feast for architecture aficionados. During the *Eufaula Pilgrimage,* an annual event that takes place in early April, visitors can enjoy home tours, antiques shows, concerts, and other festivities.

Stop by the *Hart House* (334–687–9755) at 211 North Eufaula Avenue, an 1850 Greek Revival structure that serves as headquarters for the Historic Chattahoochee Commission. Here you can pick up visitors information about the Trace, a river corridor running through portions of Alabama and Georgia. Throughout this bi-state region, travelers will discover a wealth of historic sites, natural attractions, and recreation facilities. Except for holidays, the Hart House may be visited from 8:00 A.M. to 5:00 P.M. Monday through Friday.

Continue to *Shorter Mansion* (334–687–3793), at 340 North Eufaula Avenue. This elegant structure dates to 1884 and features seventeen Corinthian-capped columns and an elaborate frieze of molded acanthus leaves and scrolls beneath its lofty balustraded roof. Be sure to notice the front door's beveled leaded glass and the entrance hall's parquet floor and molded plaster cornices. This Neoclassical Revival mansion, furnished in fine Victorian period pieces, houses the Eufaula Historical Museum and serves as headquarters for the Eufaula Heritage Association.

One upstairs room contains portraits of six state governors who were either born in or later lived in Barbour County. Another upstairs room pays tribute to retired Adm. Thomas H. Moorer, a Eufaula native who served two terms as chairman of the Joint Chiefs of Staff. Displays include Admiral Moorer's portrait, uniform, awards, and a number of mementos from his naval career.

You'll also see Waterford crystal and cut-glass chandeliers, antiques, Confederate relics, period wedding dresses, Alabama memorabilia, and decorative arts. You may browse through the mansion at your leisure or take a guided tour. Modest admission. Except for major holidays, the home is open Monday through Saturday from 9:00 A.M. to 4:00 P.M. and on Sunday from 1:00 to 4:00 P.M.

To sample some classic Southern hospitality, make reservations at *Kendall Manor Inn* (334–687–8847), a grand Italianate-style house atop a hill at 534 West Broad Street. Distinctive features of this 1860s mansion include fifty-two exterior columns, sixteen-foot ceilings, original gold-leaf cornices in both front and back parlors, and a crowning belvedere. This tower, which overnight guests can tour, boasts a commanding view, and its walls still bear poems, names, dates, and ditties that go back to June 6, 1894. One inscription, written by the original owner's grandson, says: "I, Joe Kendall came up here on Sunday, January 15, 1905, to keep from going to church with my mother." Another family member, Pearl, recorded: "No one loves me. I'm going to the garden and eat worms."

Barbara and Tim Lubsen found Kendall Manor, the third historic home they've owned, by accident while on a house-sleuthing expedition to a nearby town. Tim says that when Barbara saw the FOR SALE sign, she leaped out of the car almost before it stopped. While many people might find running this grand home a daunting task, Barbara obviously enjoys the challenge. The large rooms, each with sitting area and private bath, are named for places that played roles in the Kendall family's history—Alabama, England, Georgia, North Carolina, South Carolina, and Virginia. An entry board in the hall welcomes guests and lists their room assignments. The Lubsens serve refreshments on arrival and a full breakfast.

Ask Barbara about her local tour and golf packages. Popular pastimes range from relaxing on the upstairs sitting porch to croquet and bicycling—the latter a great way to see some of Eufaula's Seth Lore and Irwinton Historic District with more than 700 buildings on the National Register of Historic Places. For a preview visit Kendall Manor Inn at www.bbonline.com/al/kendall/index.html. You can e-mail the innkeepers at kmanorinn@aol.com. Moderate rates.

Before leaving Eufaula be sure to visit *Fendall Hall* (334–687–8469), at 917 West Barbour Street. Built between 1856 and 1860, the home features stenciled walls and ceilings painted by a nineteenth-century Italian artist, and the original decor with High Victorian colors remains relatively unchanged. Also noteworthy are the entrance hall's striking black-and-white marble floor and the home's early plumbing system, supplied by attic cisterns. Rumor has it that a ghost named Sammy makes his presence known here from time to time. Currently the house is open for tours Monday through Saturday from 10:00 A.M. to 4:00 P.M. Modest admission.

At 317 South Eufaula Avenue, you'll find *Fagin's Thieves Market* (334–687–4100), with a name inspired by Dickens's *Oliver Twist*. The Beasley family operates this business and rents space to a dozen or so antiques dealers. Browsing through various rooms, you might see children's sleighs, late 1800s cross-country skis, a red wooden rocking horse, bird cages, punch bowls, Depression glassware, books, old phonograph records, lamps, tables, cast-iron stoves, kerosene lamps, and weather vanes. Hours are 9:00 A.M. to 5:00 P.M. Monday through Saturday and 1:00 to 5:00 P.M. on Sunday.

If you need a little Christmas cheer or some hand-packed pecans, a gift basket, candies, jams, and jellies, stop by **Superior Pecan Company** (334–687–2031) at 303–317 Britt Street. Surrounded by a Santa Claus collection that rivals that of any Christmas boutique for originality and sheer numbers, manager Renée Ellis celebrates the holiday season every day of the year. Business goes on as usual here—and has for more than fifty years—but not in the typical office setting. Renée's computer looks like an alien among her multiple versions of Father Christmas. Hours are 8:00 A.M. to 5:00 P.M. Monday through Friday from September through April.

After touring this town of lovely mansions, head to **Clayton,** a small town with some unique attractions, such as the **Octagon House** at 103 North Midway Street. Listed on the National Register of Historic Places, this unusual structure is the state's sole surviving antebellum octagonal house. The ground floor served as the original kitchen (and also as the setting for a mystery, *The Rusty Key,* written by one of the home's owners). Four chimneys extending above the cupola enclose the staircase of this eight-sided structure. The first floor features four main rooms, two small rooms, and two halls that open to the surrounding porch. To arrange a tour call Thelma Teal at (334) 775–3546 or Sharon Martin at (334) 775–3254. Admission.

At nearby Clayton Baptist Church Cemetery (also on North Midway Street), you'll find the **Whiskey Bottle Tombstone,** once featured on *Ripley's Believe It or Not* television show. The bottle-shaped headstone and footstone, which mark the final resting place of William T. Mullen (1834–63), still contain their original removable stone stoppers. Such a memorial obviously tells a story, and the story behind the stone goes something like this: Mr. Mullen, a local accountant, acquired a reputation as a heavy drinker. His wife, Mary, a devout teetotaler, threatened that if he drank himself to death, she would let the world know by erecting an appropriate memorial. The Whiskey Bottle Tombstone testifies that she kept her promise.

Wiregrass Region

Continuing south along the Chattahoochee Trace takes you to Dothan, in the state's southeastern corner. Here, in a region called the Wiregrass, early settlers battled the odds to cultivate this large stretch of land once completely covered by clumps of stiff, dry grass growing under longleaf pines. To learn more about the Wiregrass region's roots, stop by **Landmark Park** (334–974–3452), in Dothan on U.S. Highway 431, 3 miles north of Ross Clark Circle. At this living-history farmstead, you may be greeted by sheep, goats, pigs, chickens, cows, and a mule. You'll see a blacksmith shop, pioneer log cabin, smokehouse, cane mill syrup shed, and other authentic outbuildings of an 1890s farm.

"We want to preserve the natural and cultural heritage of the Wiregrass region," says William Holman, Landmark Park's executive director, who calls the one-hundred-acre park an outdoor classroom. The cozy clapboard farmhouse looks as if its occupants just stepped out to milk the cows and may return any minute. An apron hangs on a cupboard door, and a shaving mug and brush wait beside the wash stand. Oblivious to onlookers, a cat naps on the back porch.

> **Alabama Trivia**
>
> *George Washington Carver invented peanut butter during his experiments at Tuskegee Institute.*

The park offers a full schedule of special events with demonstrations of seasonal farming activities, pioneer skills, and various crafts. In addition to the farmstead, you'll see a country store, church, gazebo, interpretive center, planetarium, nature trails, boardwalks, beaver ponds, and picnic areas. Modest admission. Hours are 9:00 A.M. to 5:00 P.M. Monday through Saturday and noon to 6:00 P.M. Sunday.

Continue to downtown Dothan, the area's major trade center. Proclaimed Peanut Capital of the World, this region produces one-fourth of the nation's peanuts. Each fall Dothan stages the **National Peanut Festival** with a full calendar of events, from demonstrations of square dance rounds by the Goober Gamboleers to a contest for prize-winning peanut recipes.

Across the street from the Civic Center, you'll see the **Wiregrass Museum of Art** (334–794–3871) at 126 Museum Avenue. This facility features a full schedule of rotating exhibits attractively displayed in two galleries flanking the entrance atrium. The museum contains a classroom/studio and a children's hands-on gallery. Youngsters will find the activity area entertaining as well as educational. The museum's hours are 10:00 A.M. to 5:00 P.M. Tuesday through Saturday and 1:00 to 5:00 P.M. Sunday. Admission is free.

First known as Poplar Head, Dothan took its present biblical name in 1885. Around that time, concerned citizens decided to tone down the town's rowdy image and hired a marshal and deputies to enforce new laws designed to terminate the saloons' regular Saturday-night brawls.

The *Mule Marker* in Poplar Head Park pays tribute to the animal that played a major role in the Wiregrass region's early development. Nearby at North Saint Andrews Street, you'll notice the impressive *Dothan Opera House,* a Neoclassical Revival structure that dates from 1915. Although it is not open on a regular basis, you can arrange a free tour of the opera house by calling (334) 793–0126. Another downtown historic site, *Porter Hardware,* with its rolling ladders, still exudes the nostalgic flavor of its late 1800s origin.

While in Dothan be sure to stop by *Garland House* (334–793–2043), at 200 North Bell Street, for a delicious lunch. Try the chicken divan and peanut paradise pie. Serving hours are 11:00 A.M. to 2:00 P.M. Monday through Friday. Prices are moderate.

Afterward, head to nearby Ozark, home of the *Claybank Church* on East Andrews Avenue just off State Route 249. This 1852 log church with hand-split board shingles and original pews is open daily during daylight hours.

You might like to continue your exploration of the Wiregrass region with a visit to Enterprise. If so, don't miss the *Boll Weevil Monument.* Actually, you can't miss this memorial because it stands in the middle of Main Street. And if you aren't sure you'd recognize a boll weevil (a bug about a ¼-inch long with a snout half the length of its body), just watch for a statue of a woman clad in classic drapery who stands on an ornamented pedestal and holds a magnified version of the pest high above her head. A streetside plaque explains that in 1919 the citizens of Enterprise and Coffee County erected the statue IN PROFOUND APPRECIA- TION OF THE BOLL WEEVIL AND WHAT IT HAS DONE AS THE HERALD OF PROSPER- ITY. After the boll weevil demolished two-thirds of Coffee County's cotton in 1915, local farmers started to diversify, planting other crops such as sugar cane, corn, hay, potatoes, and peanuts. Particularly suited to the Wiregrass, peanuts played a primary role in saving the local economy after the boll weevil's destruction and soon became the region's principal cash crop.

Opp, in neighboring Covington County, hosts a unique annual event: the *Rattlesnake Rodeo.* This spring festival, scheduled the first full weekend in March, features the world's only rattlesnake race along with arts and crafts (including several made from rattlesnake skins), a buck dancing contest, and programs on rattlesnake education and safety. For specific information call (334) 493–9559. You can also write to the Opp

Boll Weevil Monument

Jaycees at P.O. Box 596, Opp 36467 or contact the chamber of commerce at (800) 239–8054.

To reach *Troy* follow State Route 87 north from Enterprise. On the southern outskirts of this town, the home of Troy State University, you'll find the *Mossy Grove School House Restaurant* (334–566–4921) just off U.S. Highway 231. Set among moss-draped trees, this rustic structure started out as a one-room schoolhouse in 1856. Later enlarged and renovated, the building still contains its original stage, now part of the back dining room.

Diners can order fried dill pickles to nibble on while waiting for their entrees and admire memorabilia ranging from Confederate money, swords, and a cannonball to antique tools, barrels, and even bear teeth. Also displayed here are an old-fashioned telephone, cheese cutter, barber chair, and many other items.

Popular entrees include broiled shrimp scampi, charbroiled chicken tenders, and charbroiled rib eye. All dinners include hush puppies, cole slaw or salad, wedge fries or baked potato, and white beans with a special pepper relish. Moderate prices. Hours are 5:00 to 9:00 P.M. Tuesday through Saturday.

Continuing north through Troy takes you to **Pike Pioneer Museum** (334–566–3597), located at 248 U.S. Highway 231. Situated on ten wooded acres, this fascinating folk museum contains thousands of items contributed by some 700 local residents. You'll find extensive collections, all well organized and attractively displayed. Household items range from lemon squeezers, sausage stuffers, and butter molds to cookware, fluting irons, spittoons, and an Edison phonograph with a morning glory-shaped speaker. Although the lovely period furnishings of the three Bass Rooms reflect an upper-class lifestyle, the museum's collections focus on items that played a part in the daily existence of the community's middle- and lower-class members.

Alabama Trivia
Alabama's forest acreage ranks as third largest in the nation and second largest in the South.

Other exhibits include newspaper typesetting and printing machines, an enormous collection of farm equipment, blacksmith and carpenter shop displays, and several horse-drawn vehicles, including an antique hearse. One exhibit, *When Cotton Was King*, features a mule with "a lean and hungry look." Upon seeing the sculptor's interesting armature, museum officials had the artist stop working at once to preserve the unique look of the unfinished piece. Other objects on display include a portable boll weevil catcher, a peanut sheller, and a moonshine still.

Don't miss the early-twentieth-century street setting featuring storefronts of barber and millinery shops, a bank, and offices for a dentist, doctor, and lawyer—all appropriately equipped. Save plenty of time for exploring the grounds, too. On your way to see the furnished dogtrot log cabin and nearby tenant house, you'll pass a loblolly pine known as the Moon Tree—the seed from which it grew journeyed to the moon and back with the Apollo astronauts. Before leaving the museum, stop by the country store stocked with essentials such as snuff, castor oil, patent medicines, and bone buttons. You'll also find a restored 1928 schoolhouse, a working gristmill, a corncrib made of hand-hewn logs, a covered bridge, a nature trail, and a picnic area on the grounds. Admission is modest. Hours are 9:00 A.M. to 5:00 P.M. Monday through Saturday and 1:00 to 5:00 P.M. Sunday.

Cradle of the Confederacy

For a really great meal at **Red's Little School House** (334–584–7955), located at blink-and-you've-missed-it Grady, travel north on U.S. Highway 231, then turn onto State Route 94 in the direction of

Alabama Trivia

Nat King Cole was born at the Cole-Samford House on St. John Street in Montgomery.

Dublin and Ramer. At the intersection of Route 94 and Gardner Road, look for a tall water tower, labeled Pine Level, with a small red structure beside it. At this restaurant (housed in a former school), now owned by Jeanette and Red Deese and managed by their daughter Debbie, you'll find a buffet selection of all-you-can-eat, fresh, home-cooked vegetables such as sweet potato soufflé, fried okra, and collards. (Red grows acres and acres of vegetables each season and reaps a huge harvest.) The menu also features fried corn bread, chicken and dumplings, barbecue, and fried chicken. If you manage to save room for dessert, the choices are listed on the blackboard.

Even though the nation's presidents look sternly from their frames over the chalkboard and old maps suggest geography-test anxiety, this is a place to relax. Schoolmarm Debbie banters with the customers, who obviously enjoy both the food and the friendly surroundings. Debbie, who calls herself "a half-decent guitar player," sometimes sings for the crowd. "Everyone brags on the food, and laughs at the entertainment," she writes in the preface of her cookbook.

When her daughter, Raeanne, left home for college, Debbie compiled a book of recipes as a survival manual. At the urging of her customers, she published this as *Red's Little Schoolhouse Country Cookbook,* and you can pick one up for $5.00.

Debbie converted two school buses into traveling kitchens and takes her catering show on the road for large gatherings. She has cooked for four governors and one president. "I think food is the answer to everything," she says. School starts at 11:00 A.M. and ends at 9:00 P.M. Wednesday through Saturday and closes at 3:00 P.M. on Sunday. Prices are economical.

Afterward, continue north on one of several roads that lead to Montgomery, about thirty minutes away. Montgomery offers a wealth of attractions appealing to all interests. In the past the city has been home to such luminaries as Tallulah Bankhead, Hank Williams, and Nat King Cole. Montgomery served as a launching ground for the Wright brothers, who gave early flying lessons here; a playground for Zelda and F. Scott Fitzgerald; and a battleground in the Civil Rights Movement. This city also pioneered the nation's first electric trolley system, the Lightning Route, which made its successful trial run in 1886.

While in the city stop by the ***Montgomery Visitor Information Center,*** on the corner of Madison and Hull Streets. Housed in a grand home dating from the 1850s, the center offers a short video to whet your sightseeing appetite, along with maps and brochures on local attractions.

On the city's southeast side, you'll find the *Alabama Shakespeare Festival* (334-271-5353 or 800-841-4ASF). Just off East Boulevard on Woodmere Boulevard in the Wynton M. Blount Cultural Park, ASF presents works ranging from familiar classics to world-premiere Southern Writers' Project productions. You can take in a performance of works by such writers as Sir Noel Coward, Anton Chekhov, Eugene O'Neill, George Bernard Shaw, Tennessee Williams, and, of course, the Bard. The only American theater invited to fly the same flag as that used by England's Royal Shakespeare Company, ASF attracts more than 300,000 visitors annually from all fifty states and sixty foreign countries and is the world's fifth largest Shakespeare festival.

Situated in a 250-acre, landscaped, English-style park, the $21.5 million performing-arts complex houses two stages, rehearsal halls, and a snack bar along with costume, property, and gift shops. The grounds, perfect for strolling or picnicking, feature a reflecting lake complete with gliding swans. For information, brochures, or tickets, call or write to Alabama Shakespeare Festival, One Festival Drive, Montgomery 36117-4605. You can also e-mail ASF at asfmail@mindspring.com or visit its Web site at www.asf.net to check on current productions.

Before leaving the park you may want to browse through the *Montgomery Museum of Fine Arts* (334-244-5700). Located at One Museum Drive, this facility features the fine Blount Collection with works representing more than 200 years of American art. Admission is free. Except for major holidays, the museum's hours are 10:00 A.M. to 5:00 P.M. Tuesday through Saturday. Thursday hours extend to 9:00 P.M. The Sunday schedule is noon to 5:00 P.M.

Sometime during your Montgomery visit, consider searching out an off-the-beaten-path place called *Panache at Rose Hill* (334-215-7620), in the Mt. Meigs community at 11250 Highway 80 East. A winding tree-lined driveway leads to the restaurant, which occupies a white frame Colonial-style home on the rolling grounds of an 1814 plantation northeast of Montgomery. Originally a 4,000-acre estate, Rose Hill was built by Henry Lucas, a wealthy landowner in Montgomery County. The surrounding forty acres of rose gardens gave the estate, listed on the Alabama Historical Register, its name.

Using their flourishing catering business, Panache, as a springboard to a restaurant partnership, Barbara Duke and Shirley Sandy bought Rose Hill in 1989 with the goals of preserving the home and offering fine dining. Using indigenous Southern ingredients, they create a spectrum of delectable dishes like spicy black-eyed pea soup, topped with scallions and tomatoes and served with corn-bread muffins. Typical dinner selections might include prime rib, orange roughy, beef tenderloin, or glazed Cornish hen. Although Panache opens only for private events, add-on diners are accepted once minimum lunch reservations of twenty-five or dinner reservations of fifteen are reached. The restaurant opens for Mother's Day, Easter brunch, and Valentine's Day with no minimum reservation. Moderate to expensive.

Back in downtown Montgomery, across the street from Cloverdale park, stands the former home of a famous couple who personified the Jazz Age. Housed in the lower right section (Apartment B) of a circa 1910 two-story brown structure at 919 Felder Avenue, you'll find the *Scott and Zelda Fitzgerald Museum* (334–264–4222 or 334–262–1911). Francis Scott Key Fitzgerald met Zelda Sayre, a native of Montgomery and daughter of an Alabama Supreme Court judge, at a local dance in 1918. The couple married in 1920, soon after Scott published his first novel, *This Side of Paradise.*

The Fitzgeralds and their daughter, Scottie, lived here from October 1931 to the spring of 1932. While here Scott worked on his novel *Tender Is the Night* and the screenplay for a Jean Harlow movie. At the same time Zelda, whose writings include a play as well as several short stories and articles, started her only novel, *Save Me the Waltz.* Beautiful, flamboyant,

A Sweet Ending

*P*anache *owners Barbara Duke and Shirley Sandy shared the recipe for their signature dessert, Buttermilk Pie with Blackberry Sauce.*

Panache at Rose Hill's Buttermilk Pie with Blackberry Sauce

Mix together:

3 eggs

1 cup sugar

2 tablespoons flour

Add: 1 cup buttermilk

1 stick melted butter, slightly cooled

Add: 2 teaspoons vanilla

Pour into a fluted 9-inch deep-dish pie crust. Cook at 350 degrees for 45–50 minutes. Center will still be soft but will set as it cools. Serve warm.

Sauce:

¹/₂ cup seedless blackberry preserves

2 tablespoons Chambord liqueur

Use a small whisk to mix preserves and liqueur until the mixture is smooth. Heat in microwave about 20 seconds. Spoon 2 teaspoons over each pie slice. (Note: Use the best preserves possible. In place of Chambord, you may substitute Razzamatazz, a less expensive raspberry liqueur.)

and driven, Zelda also excelled at painting and ballet. Unfortunately, her recurring mental collapses played havoc with the family's lives and prevented her from realizing more of her creative potential.

Exhibits include some of Zelda's original paintings, family photos, autographed books, letters, and other personal memorabilia. Plans were afoot to tear down this historic home until local attorney Julian McPhillips and his wife, Leslie, purchased it and set about creating this museum. In the sunroom you can watch a twenty-five-minute video that provides some glimpses into the lives of the author of *The Great Gatsby* and his talented but tormented wife. Museum director, Elena Aleinikov, shares anecdotes with visitors. No admission is charged, but contributions are accepted. Hours are 10:00 A.M. to 2:00 P.M. Wednesday through Friday and 1:00 to 5:00 P.M. Saturday and Sunday.

Afterward head downtown to Montgomery's capitol complex, where you can easily spend a full day. If you enjoy digging into the past, you'll find this area fascinating to explore. From here Jefferson Davis telegraphed his "Fire on Fort Sumter" order, beginning the Civil War. Rising impressively above its surroundings on Dexter Avenue, the 1851 capitol reflects the period's prevailing architecture—Greek Revival. In this building Jefferson Davis took his presidential oath for the Confederacy, and a six-pointed brass star now marks the spot.

At 644 Washington Avenue, just across the street from the capitol, stands the *First White House of the Confederacy* (334–242–1861). Occupied by the Jefferson Davis family during the early days of the War Between the States, this Italianate-style home built by William Sayre dates to the early 1830s. Elegant downstairs parlors and second-floor bedrooms (including a charming nursery) contain Davis family possessions and period antiques. Other displays include Civil War relics, letters, and glass-cased documents. Hours are 8:00 A.M. to 4:30 P.M. Monday through Friday.

Next door to the Davis home, you'll find a treasure-filled museum, the *Alabama Department of Archives and History.* This building houses an enormous manuscript collection and exhibits spanning the gap from the Stone Age to the Space Age.

A short jaunt takes you to the *Dexter Avenue King Memorial Baptist Church* (334–263–3970). Located at 454 Dexter Avenue, the church became a National Historical Landmark in 1974. It was at this church, pastored by Dr. Martin Luther King Jr., that the Montgomery bus boycott was organized on December 2, 1955, launching the American Civil Rights Movement.

A forty-five-minute tour covers the church's early history as well as the more recent role it played as a rallying place for civil rights activists. On the ground floor, a six-section folk mural illustrates major events from Dr. King's life. Tours start at 10:00 A.M. and 2:00 P.M. Monday through Thursday and at 10:00 A.M. only on Friday. Call for the weekend schedule. Admission is free.

Nearby, in front of the Southern Poverty Law Center at 400 Washington Avenue, stands the **Civil Rights Memorial.** Designed by Maya Lin, who also served as the architect for the Vietnam Memorial in Washington, D.C., this black granite memorial documents major events in the struggle for civil rights.

Also downtown, at 301 Columbus Street, you can step back into the nineteenth century at **Old Alabama Town** (334–240–4500 or 888–240–1850). This fascinating concentration of historical buildings provides glimpses of city and country living in the nineteenth century. Start your tour at the **Loeb Center,** where you can also visit the museum store. Continue your excursion into the past at **Lucas Tavern.** As you exit through the tavern's back door, Alabama author and storyteller Kathryn Tucker Windham takes you on a tour (via cassette) through this historical complex, starting with an orientation under the scuppernong arbor. You'll see an 1850s dogtrot house (a dogtrot is a form of Southern architecture that features an open central hall connecting two rooms, sometimes called pens). Other stops include such buildings as a grange hall, carriage house, grocery store, church, country doctor's office, and a one-room schoolhouse—complete with *McGuffey's Readers* and slates.

You'll also see the nearby **Rose-Morris House,** with craftspeople at work, and the **Ordeman-Shaw House,** a handsome townhouse with elegant furnishings and backyard dependencies. Admission. Except for major holidays, hours are 9:00 A.M. to 3:00 P.M. Monday through Saturday. A special program is offered the first Sunday of each month.

Cap off your stroll through history with a delectable repast at nearby **Amy's Young House** (334–262–0409), diagonally across the street from Lucas Tavern, at 231 North Hull Street. The restaurant features fried chicken, soups, salads, and sandwiches. For dessert order the apple dumplings or bread pudding. Economical prices. The restaurant is open for lunch from 11:00 A.M. to 2:00 P.M. Monday through Friday.

Montgomery's colorful past is only part of its appeal. The city offers contemporary attractions such as the **W. A. Gayle Planetarium** in Oak Park and the **Montgomery Zoo,** located at 329 Vandiver Boulevard,

Ordeman-Shaw House

which houses many rare and endangered species among its animal community of some 700 birds, mammals, and reptiles.

"Your Cheatin' Heart" immediately brings Hank Williams to mind for all country music lovers, and fans from throughout the world travel to Montgomery to pay tribute at his grave site. Set in *Oakwood Cemetery,* the marble memorial is sculpted in the shape of two large music notes and a cowboy hat. You can also see a life-size bronze statue of the musician in Lister Hill plaza, across from City Hall.

Stop by historic Union Station for an in-depth look at the legacy of Alabama-born Hank Williams Sr. Paying tribute to the memory of this country music legend, the *Hank Williams Museum* (334–262–3600) at 300 Water Street contains recordings, albums, musical instruments, clothing, a saddle with silver trim, family photos, and other personal items. The museum's focal point is the robin's-egg blue 1952 Cadillac convertible in which the singer/songwriter died while being driven to his scheduled performance in Canton, Ohio, on January 1, 1953. Other exhibits showcase memorabilia of family members and associates. A carved Kowliga, created by the Wood Chippers (with a time investment of 559 hours), looms 8 1/2 feet tall. Museum hours are 9:00 A.M. until 6:00 P.M. Monday through Saturday and 1:00 to 4:00 P.M. on Sunday. Admission.

Nearby, *Sassafras Tea Room* (334–265–7277), at 532 Clay Street, overlooks Union Station and the Alabama River and makes a lovely setting for lunch. This striking circa 1888 Victorian brick home, originally known as The Mills' House, is listed on the National Register of Historic Places. Built by Alfonzo Mills, a carpetbagger from Michigan, the home stands in the historic Cottage Hill district. The builder's son, John Proctor Mills, became Alabama's first poet laureate.

Jim and Mary Wallace, who purchased the home in 1990, spent more than a year restoring it. Their daughter Shannon and her husband, Russell Houlden, help run the business. A tower room, hand-painted murals, and period antiques add to the ambience. Before or after your meal, you may browse through the antiques-filled rooms. Many of the home's pieces are for sale.

The menu, which changes daily, features soup and quiche selections, specialty sandwiches, and salads such as the popular crunchy chicken salad served with seasonal fruit. Also, Sassafras offers Southern lunches, which might mean chicken supreme, beef Stroganoff, or smothered pork steak. Plates come with a choice of three home-cooked vegetables—sometimes pobagas, Mary's own tasty creation of mashed potatoes and rutabagas. Save room for dessert—chocolate chip or buttermilk pie, cheesecake, or another delectable finale. Lunch hours run from 11:00 A.M. until 2:00 P.M. Monday through Friday. The restaurant opens evenings and weekends by group reservation. Prices are economical.

Across the street at 551 Clay Street, Anne and Mark Waldo dispense warm hospitality at *Red Bluff Cottage* (334–264–0056 or 888–551–CLAY), a perfect place to headquarter in Alabama's capital city. In fact, the upstairs porch of this raised cottage offers fine views of the State Capitol and the Alabama River. Furnished with family antiques, the comfortable home was planned with guests in mind. Special spots for relaxing include the porch, gazebo, TV room, and music room. Anne might be persuaded to play the harpsichord for you and will provide information on the current offerings at the Alabama Shakespeare Festival Theatre, other local sites, and directions on getting there the easiest way. A retired Episcopal priest, Mark makes a superb host, and guests tend to linger at breakfast—savoring the delicious meal and enjoying the conversation. The couple grew accustomed to having a bunch for brunch while parenting six children, and they welcome youngsters as guests. E-mail the Waldos at RedBlufBnB@aol.com or pay a virtual visit to www.bbonline.com/al/redbluff. Standard to moderate rates.

After exploring the Capital of the Old South, head about 12 miles north to Wetumpka to visit **Jasmine Hill Gardens and Outdoor Museum** (334–567–6463). Located just off U.S. Highway 231 at 3001 Jasmine Hill Road, this magical place features twenty acres of flowers, shrubs, and trees, providing a lovely backdrop for Greek statuary and a full-size reproduction of the Temple of Hera, which stood in Olympia near the stadium home of the ancient Olympic Games. In 1996 the Olympic Flame made its way to Jasmine Hill en route to Atlanta's games. Sometimes called "Alabama's little corner of Greece," this outdoor museum contains reproductions of renowned works such as the Dying Gaul, Venus de Melos, Mourning Athena, and Nike of Samothrace. Jasmine Hill's original owners made more than twenty trips to Greece to commission and collect these reproductions of classic works of art. In the new Olympian centre, visitors can watch an audiovisual introduction for more background on the complex.

You can visit Jasmine Hill Tuesday through Sunday between 9:00 A.M. and 5:00 P.M. year-round. Admission. To see the gardens at your convenience, browse your way to www.jasminehill.org or e-mail jasmine-hill@mindspring.com.

After seeing Jasmine Hill you might enjoy exploring **Fort Toulouse-Jackson Park** (334–567–3002). To reach the park, the site of two forts from different centuries, return to U.S. Highway 231 North and watch for the turnoff sign across from the Food World supermarket. Continue 2.4 miles down this road to the main gate. After entering the park you'll see the visitors center on the left. Inside, displays of artifacts unearthed in archaeological digs, from brass uniform buttons and silver earrings to French wine bottles and cannonballs, provide background on the site's history.

The original 1717 French fortress, named for the Compte de Toulouse (son of Louis XIV), served as a trading post where Native Americans exchanged furs and deerskins for European goods. This French outpost also helped keep the British at bay. Gen. Andrew Jackson's forces later built a larger nineteenth-century counterpart while fighting the Creek Indians. From here Old Hickory plotted his campaign against the British and Spanish that ended with the Battle of New Orleans.

Fort Toulouse living-history programs, staged on the park's grounds the third weekend of each month (except in August), present aspects of the French occupation. Fort Jackson living-history programs are conducted the first weekend of each month (except January). Visitors might observe costumed volunteers engaged in making hominy, constructing dugout canoes, or firing muskets and cannons.

This 164-acre park also offers a picnic area, campground, and launching ramp. Another attraction is the thirty-acre arboretum with boardwalk, footbridges, and study decks. Nearby, the Coosa and Tallapoosa rivers—with their cache of bass, bream, catfish, and crappie—beckon anglers. (A state fishing license is required.) Modest admission. Except for major holidays, the park is open from sunup to sundown, year-round.

After your park outing follow State Route 14 west to **Prattville.** Daniel Pratt, for whom the town was named, came here from New Hampshire in the 1830s and established an industrial center—still the site for the manufacture of cotton gins. A drive through Pratt Village takes you past a section of restored nineteenth-century buildings. For a driving tour map, which highlights about forty homes in the historic district along with area churches and industrial sites, stop by the chamber of commerce at 1002 East Main Street or City Hall at 101 West Main Street.

Head to Lowndesboro, south of Prattville. This small town, founded by cotton planters in the 1830s, contains some thirty surviving antebellum structures. If you'd like to visit **Marengo** (334–278–4442 or 334–272–8508), an 1835 plantation home with an interesting history, take U.S. Highway 80 west. At the flashing caution light 13 miles past Dannelly Field Airport, turn right and travel 1.3 miles. You'll find Marengo on the left. Owned by the Lowndesboro Landmarks Foundation, this historic home serves as an intimate restaurant for dinner parties. Operated by Virginia and Art Moody along with their son Mark, who lives on the premises and performs the duties of chef, the facility opens when a minimum of thirty guests make a dinner party reservation. Once that quota is reached, individual diners are accepted.

After guests arrive around 6:30 P.M. for appetizers, drinks, and socializing, Virginia shows them through the historic home. When the dinner bell rings about an hour later, Mark serves a multicourse dinner starting with homemade soup that's followed by a seasonal salad and a palate-cleansing sorbet. The entree might be a chargrilled tenderloin filet, beef kabobs, or Cornish hen with homemade rolls, vegetables, and dessert. After dinner Art tells guests about Marengo's history and shares some intriguing ghost stories. Call for reservations and rates.

Traveling south, Greenville—also known as Camellia City—offers special treats for history lovers and golfers. Many of the town's lovely homes, churches, and public buildings are on the National Register of Historic Places and the Alabama Historic Register. Also, Cambrian Ridge, one of the award-winning courses on the Robert Trent Jones Golf Trail, beckons nearby. To collect information on what to see and do in

Butler County, make your first stop the Greenville Area Chamber of Commerce (334–382–3251 or 800–959–9717), housed in the old CSX depot on Bolling Street.

The Martin House (334–382–2011 or 877–627–8465), a bed-and-breakfast inn at 212 East Commerce Street, offers overnight visitors an opportunity to relax in charming surroundings. Owner Jo Weitman spent a year putting "her heart and soul" into restoring this striking Queen Anne–style home listed on the Alabama Historic Register and National Register of Historic Places. Also, she spent countless hours researching the ideal location and collecting antiques and art to fill the handsome inn. The original portion dates to 1853, and a Victorian-era remodeling took place in 1895. Painted shell pink, the inviting house features a wraparound porch and nine fireplaces. A side porch, tearoom, sunroom, deck, and parlors all make lovely retreats for guests. Jo named her guest rooms for the town's famous camellias: The Pink Perfection Suite, The Pride of Greenville, and The Purple Dawn Suite. A downstairs suite honors the home's builder, Porter Martin, who owned the Greenville Ice Factory and produced the town's first electricity.

Breakfast might feature homemade waffles with fruit topping and sausage on the side or other tempting combinations to start your day. E-mail Jo at martinbb@alaweb.com or log onto www.bbonline.com/al/martin/index.html to view the home and get some of Jo's favorite recipes. Standard to moderate rates.

From Greenville, a short drive south takes you to Georgiana and the *Hank Williams, Sr. Boyhood Home and Museum* (334–376–2396). Located at 127 Rose Street, the home contains six rooms filled with walls of family photos, original posters, albums, 78 RPM recordings, a church pew, piano, and 1923 Victrola. Fans from all over the world donated many of the items on display. Draperies, custom made for the musician's Nashville home, feature an overall design of lyrics and music from "Your Cheatin' Heart." Volunteers staff the museum, and hours are 10:00 A.M. until 5:00 P.M. Monday through Saturday and 1:00 until 5:00 P.M. on Sunday. Admission. During the first Friday and Saturday in June, Georgiana hosts an annual Hank Williams Day Celebration with country music concerts, food concessions, and street dances.

PLACES TO STAY IN SOUTHEAST ALABAMA

AUBURN
Auburn University Hotel and Conference Center
241 South College Street
(334) 821–8200 or
(800) 228–2876

Chewacla State Park
124 Shell Toomer Parkway
(334) 887–5621 or
(800) 252–7275

Crenshaw House
Bed and Breakfast
371 North College Street
(334) 821–1131 or
(800) 950–1131

Jameson Inn
1212 Mall Parkway
(334) 502–5020 or
(800) 526–3766

DOTHAN
Best Western Dothan Inn
& Suites
3285 Montgomery Highway
(334) 793–4376 or
(800) 528–1234

Comfort Inn
3593 Ross Clark Circle
(334) 793–9090 or
(800) 474–7298

Courtyard by Marriott
3040 Ross Clark Circle
(334) 671–3000 or
(800) 321–2211

Holiday Inn South
2195 Ross Clark Circle
(334) 794–8711 or
(800) 777–6611

EUFALA
Jameson Inn
136 Towne Center Boulevard
(334) 687–7747 or
(800) 541–3268

Kendall Manor Inn
534 West Broad Street
(334) 687–8847

Lakepoint Resort
Highway 431 North
(334) 687–8011 or
(800) 544–LAKE

GREENVILLE
Jameson Inn
105 Cahaba Road
(334) 382–6300 or
(800) 541–3268

The Martin House
212 East Commerce Street
(334) 382–2011 or
(877) 627–8465

MONTGOMERY
Comfort Inn
5175 Carmichael Road
(334) 277–1919

Embassy Suites
300 Tallapoosa Street
(334) 269–5055 or
(800) EMBASSY

Fairfield Inn
5601 Carmichael Road
(334) 270–0007 or
(800) 228–2800

Holiday Inn East
1185 Eastern Boulevard
(334) 272–0370 or
(800) 351–7742

Red Bluff Cottage
551 Clay Street
(334) 264–0056 or
(888) 551–CLAY

Studio Plus
5115 Carmichael Road
(334) 273–0075 or
(800) 646–8000

OPELIKA
The Heritage House
714 Second Avenue
(334) 705–0485

TALLASSEE
Hotel Talisi
14 Sistrunk Street
(334) 283–2769

PLACES TO EAT IN SOUTHEAST ALABAMA

ALEXANDER CITY
Cecil's on the Lake
Kowaliga Marina, just off
State Route 63
(334) 857–2161

AUBURN
Auburn Grille
104 North College Street
(334) 821–6626

Mellow Mushroom
128 North College Street
(334) 887–6356

Terra Cotta Cafe
415 East Magnolia Avenue
(334) 821–3656

DOTHAN
Garland House
200 North Bell Street
(334) 793–2043

Hunt's Steak, Seafood, and
Oyster Bar
177 Campbellton Highway
(334) 794–5193

Old Mexico
2920 Ross Clark Circle
(334) 712–1434

The Old Mill Restaurant
2557 Murphy Mill Road
(334) 794–8530

Poplar Head Mule Co.
Brewpub & Grill
155 South St. Andrews
Street
(334) 794–7991

EUFALA
Airport Restaurant
1720 North Eufaula Avenue
(334) 687–3132

Boux Rae's Four Beans Cafe
Bluff City Inn
(334) 616–0008

Chewalla
Highway 431 North
(334) 687–8858

Lakepoint Resort
Highway 431 North
(334) 687–8011

Old Mexico
114 North Eufaula Avenue
(334) 687–7770

GRADY
Red's Little School House
State Route 94 and Gardner
Road
(334) 584–7955

LOWNDESBORO
Marengo
Broad Street
(334) 278–4442 or (334)
272–8508

MONTGOMERY
Amy's Young House
231 North Hull Street
(334) 262–0409

Lek's Railroad Thai
Union Station, 300 B Water
Street
(334) 269–0708

Martha's Place
458 Sayre Street
(334) 263–9135

Panache at Rose Hill
11250 Highway 80 East
(334) 215–7620

Sahara Restaurant, Inc.
511 East Edgemont Avenue
(334) 262–1215

For More Information about Southeast Alabama

Auburn/Opelika Convention & Visitors Bureau
714 East Glenn Avenue (36830)
P.O. Box 2216; Auburn 36831–2216
(334) 887–8747 or (800) 321–8880
Web site: www.auburn-opelika.com
e-mail: maria@auburn-opelika.com

Dothan Area Convention & Visitors Bureau
3311 Ross Clark Circle Northwest (36303)
P.O. Box 8765; Dothan 36304
(334) 794–6622 or (800) 449–0212
Web site: www.dothancvb.com
e-mail: dothancvb@mail.ala.net

Eufaula/Barbour County Chamber of Commerce
102 North Orange Avenue (36027)
P.O. Box 697; Eufaula 36072
(334) 687–6664 or (800) 524–7529
e-mail: ebctour@hotmail.com

Montgomery Convention & Visitors Bureau
401 Madison Avenue (36104)
P.O. Box 79; Montgomery 36101
(334) 261–1100
Web site: www.montgomery.al.us
e-mail: tourism@montgomerychamber.org

Sassafras Tea Room
532 Clay Street
(334) 265–7277

Sinclair's
1051 East Fairview Avenue
(334) 834–7462

Vintage Year, Inc.
405 Cloverdale Road
(334) 264–8463

OPELIKA
Venable's
913 Railroad Avenue
(334) 745–0834

Warehouse Bistro
105 Rocket Avenue
(334) 745–6353

TALLASSEE
Hotel Talisi Restaurant
14 Sistrunk Street
(334) 283–2769

TROY
Mossy Grove School House
Restaurant
U.S. Highway 231
(334) 566–4921

MAINSTREAM ATTRACTIONS
WORTH SEEING IN
SOUTHEAST ALABAMA

Montgomery Zoo,
*2301 Coliseum Parkway,
Montgomery;
(334) 240–4900.
Observe more than
800 animals from five
continents in the zoo's
naturalistic settings and
take a train ride around
the park.*

**U.S. Army Aviation
Museum,** *Andrews
Avenue and Novosel
Street, Fort Rucker;
(334) 255–3036 or
(334) 598–2508. This
museum is in Fort
Rucker, a training base
for military helicopter
pilots located 5 miles
west of Ozark. Covering
the complete history of
Army Aviation, this com-
plex contains one of the
world's largest collections
of helicopters. Exhibits
include maps and photos
of Army Aviation's role
in the Louisiana Maneu-
vers through Operation
Desert Storm, a full-scale
model of the Wright B
Flyer, and unusual pieces
such as a Sopwith Camel
and a Nieuport 28.*

Black Belt

Alabama's Black Belt, so called because of a strip of dark, rich soil that stretches across part of the state's south-central section, covers 4,300 square miles. This fertile farmland became the setting for a host of plantations prior to the Civil War, and you'll see many antebellum structures throughout the area. From Selma, which retains a lingering flavor of the Old South's cotton-rich aristocratic past, you can easily make a loop of several small Black Belt towns with their treasure troves of architecture. Situated on a bluff above the Alabama River, Selma served as a major munitions depot, making battleships as well as cannonballs, rifles, and ammunition for the Confederate cause.

U.S. Highway 80 west from Montgomery to Selma leads across the *Edmund Pettus Bridge,* a landmark that figured prominently in the civil rights struggle. In 1965 marchers followed Martin Luther King Jr. across this bridge on their trek to Montgomery during voting rights demonstrations.

Located near the bridge, the *National Voting Rights Museum* (334–418 0800) at 1012 Water Avenue presents a visual history of the Selma-to-Montgomery march and related events. Upon entering, viewers see themselves reflected in a mirrored "I Was There" wall with a display of cards recording firsthand observations by individuals. A series of rooms focus on reconstruction, suffrage, and other aspects of the voting-rights struggle. A large window, etched with the names Andrew Young, Martin Luther King Jr., Thurgood Marshall, Dick Gregory, and other museum Hall of Fame inductees, provides a fitting vantage point for viewing the historic Pettus Bridge. Hours are 9:00 A.M. to 5:00 P.M. Tuesday through Friday, 10:00 A.M. to 3:00 P.M. Saturday, and Sunday by appointment. Admission.

Take time to stroll along historic Water Avenue, a restored nineteenth-century riverfront warehouse district with brick streets, arcades, and

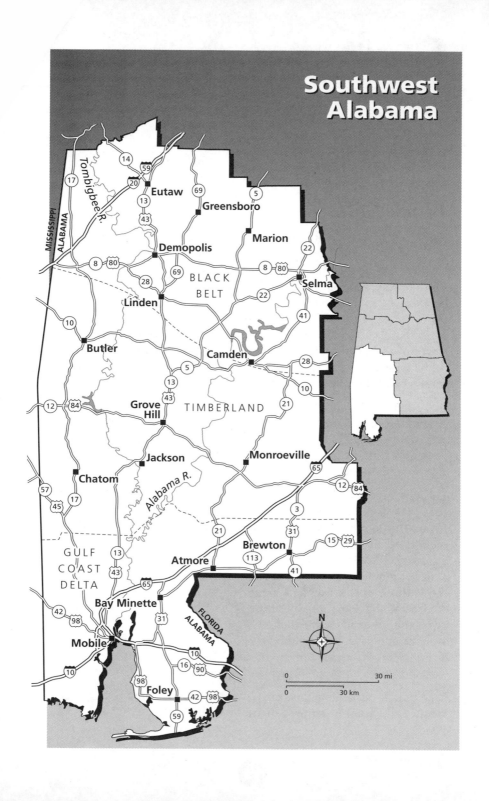

GAY'S TOP PICKS IN SOUTHWEST ALABAMA

Battleship U.S.S. Alabama, *Mobile Bay*

Bellingrath Gardens and Home, Theodore

Fort Morgan, Mobile Bay

Gulf Coast beaches

Mobile's historic districts

Old Cahawba Archaeological Park, Cahaba

Town of Demopolis

Town of Fairhope

Town of Marion

Town of Selma

parks overlooking the river. Nearby, at 1124 Water Avenue, you'll find a mini-mall with an eatery and several interesting shops.

Settle into a room at the newly restored *St. James Hotel* (334–872–3234) and map out your Selma itinerary. One of the country's few remaining antebellum riverfront hotels, the St. James occupies a corner at 1200 Water Avenue. Lacy iron grillwork traces the balconies of the camel-colored structure, which surrounds a courtyard with fountain. The original 1837 hotel served passengers from paddle wheelers and steamboats that plied the Alabama River and also those from the nearby railroad station. Jesse and Frank James (under assumed names) once stayed at the St. James.

Many of the rooms' balconies overlook the historic Edmund Pettus Bridge and nearby Bridgetender's House, where TV camera crews stationed themselves, plugging into the house's electrical outlets while reporting on the Selma-to-Montgomery march. Furnished with antebellum and Victorian pieces, the hotel boasts a ballroom; elegant guest rooms and suites; a Drinking Room with handsome, marble-topped mahogany bar; and a white-tablecloth dining room. The latter, called *Troup House Restaurant,* features regional specialties to savor against a backdrop of teal, ivory, and gold with a rose-patterned carpet. Moderate.

During your waterfront excursion, saunter into *Major Grumbles* (334–872–2006), a restaurant named for a local character in Selma's storybook of history. You'll find this eatery at 1 Grumbles Alley, a few steps from the Bridgetender's House. Be sure to notice the restaurant's two original black iron gates (believed to be slave doors) that weigh about 400 pounds each. And don't get the wrong idea from the century-old skeleton, attired in a Confederate uniform, seated on the stair landing—starving is not something you have to worry about here.

Everything served here, including the bread for sandwiches and the dressings for salads, is made from scratch. Some customers claim Major Grumbles serves the best Reuben sandwiches they ever ate. You might instead opt for the restaurant's justly famous marinated chicken breast sandwich or hearty red bean and rice soup. Dinner entrees include such items as baked shrimp stuffed with crabmeat dressing and a variety of steak cuts. Economical to moderate prices. Every day except Sunday, the restaurant is open from 11:00 A.M. to 11:00 P.M.

To dip into more of the city's interesting history, stop by the hand-some **Old Depot Museum** (334-874-2197), located on the corner of Martin Luther King Street and Water Avenue. Built in 1891 by the Louisville and Nashville Railroad, this arched and turreted two-story redbrick structure stands on the site of the Confederate Naval Foundry, which Union troops destroyed during the Battle of Selma in 1865. The museum houses everything from a 1908 portrait camera used by psychic Edgar Cayce (who once lived in Selma and operated a photography studio here) to Victorian hair combs, plantation records, quilts, Confederate bills, cannonballs, early medical equipment, and antique tools.

In the Black Heritage Wing, you'll see sculpture by Earl Hopkins, nationally recognized for his wood carvings and leather crafts. Hopkins, who uses exotic woods in his creations, worked at Colonial Williamsburg before retiring to his native Selma. A not-to-be-missed rare display of photographs, made between 1895 and 1905 by Selmian Mary Morgan Keipp, depicts daily life on a Black Belt plantation. Curator Jean Martin calls this wonderful series "one of the finest and most complete collections of photos covering that period in history."

Behind the museum you'll see a boxcar, caboose, and old farm equipment. Monday through Saturday the museum is open from 10:00 A.M. to 4:00 P.M. or by appointment. Modest admission.

Nearby at 410 Martin Luther King Street stands **Brown Chapel African Methodist Episcopal Church,** another significant structure in Selma's history. This 1908 Byzantine-style building served as headquarters for the civil rights activists who played a pivotal role in bringing about the passage of the National Voting Rights Act during the turbulent decade of the 1960s. Visitors may take a self-guided walking tour of the surrounding historic area.

Sometime during your local tour, be sure to stop at 109 Union Street to tour the white-columned, three-story, brick **Joseph T. Smitherman Historic Building** (334-874-2174), named in honor of Selma's mayor, who plays an active role in historic preservation. Crowning Alabama Avenue, this impressive building opened its doors in 1848 as the Central Masonic Institute and later served as a hospital for wounded Confederates (escaping the fate of many Selma buildings when Union general John Harrison Wilson's raiders, disobeying orders, embarked on a wholesale campaign of wanton destruction in April 1865). The building later served as a courthouse, military school, and private hospital.

Gay's Favorite Annual Events in Southwest Alabama

Alabama Deep Sea Fishing Rodeo,
Dauphin Island, July; (334) 471–0025

Alabama Tale Tellin' Festival,
Selma, October; (800) 45–SELMA

Arts & Crafts Festival, Fairhope, March;
(334) 928–6387

Azalea Trail Run and Festival,
Mobile, March; (334) 473–7223 or
(800) 5MOBILE

Bayfest Music Festival, Mobile, late
September or early October;
(334) 470–7730

Blessing of the Fleet, Bayou La Batre,
May; (334) 824–2415

Christmas on the River, Demopolis,
December; (334) 289–0270

Festival of Flowers, Mobile, March;
(334) 639–2050 or (800) 5MOBILE

Historic Selma Pilgrimage, Selma,
March; (800) 45–SELMA

Magic Christmas in Lights, Bellingrath
Gardens & Home, late November
through December; (334) 973–2217

Mardi Gras, Mobile, February;
(334) 434–1858

National Shrimp Festival, Gulf Shores,
October; (334) 968–6904 or
(800) 982–8562

Old Cahawba Festival, Cahaba, May;
(334) 872–8058 or (800) 45–SELMA

Pow Wow, Atmore, November;
(334) 368–9136

The Original German Sausage Festival,
Elberta, last Saturday in March and
October; (334) 986–5805

Inside you'll see a large collection of Civil War relics, Confederate money, medical artifacts, and period furnishings from the mid-1800s. Hours are 9:00 A.M. to 4:00 P.M. Tuesday through Saturday or by appointment. Modest admission.

To sample the city's architectural medley of historic homes and churches, you can take the hour-long taped or written "Windshield Tour" in your own vehicle. Stop by the chamber of commerce at 513 Lauderdale Street for a cassette and map. (Your $5.00 deposit will be refunded when you return the tape.) While here you can also collect brochures on local attractions.

Across the street stands *Grace Hall* (334–875–5744), a lovely antebellum mansion. Located at 506 Lauderdale Street, this historic bed-and-breakfast inn dates from about 1857. Owners Joey and Coy Dillon spent more than four years restoring the home, "twice as long as the original construction took," says Coy. During the restoration (certified by the Department of the Interior), the Dillons maintained scrapbooks that chronicle the project. Near the entrance of each room, a framed "before" photo provides a graphic illustration of the enormity of their task.

Now beautifully decorated, the home is furnished with period antiques.

A central courtyard fountain sounds like soft rain falling, especially soothing for overnight guests. Breakfast often starts with a fruit compote accompanied by a variety of homemade breads, jellies, and preserves. Afterward Joey might serve a ham and cheese croissant or a vegetable omelet with bacon. Other specialties include crepes, pancakes, and traditional Southern fare with biscuits. Guests also receive a mansion tour. Moderate rates. Call for reservations or tour information.

On a drive through the Old Town Historic District, you'll see block after block of antebellum and Victorian architecture. The **Historic Selma Pilgrimage** provides visitors with opportunities to tour many of the city's outstanding homes each spring. A reenactment of the Battle of Selma is another popular springtime event.

For a memento of your visit, consider purchasing a cookbook called *Tastes of Olde Selma,* available in several places throughout the city. Compiled by Selma's Olde Towne Association, the book contains line drawings and brief histories of many of the town's significant structures along with a selection of wonderful recipes. The front cover features a color illustration of **Sturdivant Hall** (334–872–5626), a Neoclassical mansion located at 713 Mabry Street. Designed by Thomas Helm Lee (Robert E. Lee's cousin), this magnificent home that took three years to build boasts elaborate ceilings and decorative moldings with a motif of intertwined grape leaves and vines. You'll also see a spiral staircase, marble mantels, and servant pulls—each with a different tone. Other treasures include period furnishings, portraits, silver, crystal, china, and a rare French-made George Washington commemorative clock of ormolu and gold—one of only seven in existence.

Coral vines climb the home's back walls, and mock lemons perfume the air. You may be presented with a sprig or cutting of lavender, mint, or sage from the mansion's herb garden outside the backyard kitchen. The home's formal gardens, which feature a variety of native flowers, shrubs, and trees, serve as a lovely backdrop for the pilgrimage's annual grand ball. Except for major holidays and Mondays, Sturdivant Hall is open from 9:00 A.M. to 4:00 P.M. Tuesday through Saturday. Admission.

By the way, some Selmians say the ghost of John McGee Parkman, one of Sturdivant Hall's former owners, roams the mansion. You may or may not see house ghosts here, but you can certainly find several in Sturdivant Hall's gift shop—sandwiched between the covers of some of Kathryn Tucker Windham's books, such as *13 Alabama Ghosts and Jeffrey* or *Jeffrey's Latest 13.* For a souvenir or gift, you might like to buy *Alabama—One Big Front Porch,* an engrossing collection of stories compiled by Mrs. Windham. To hear her in person-along with other famous Southern storytellers-plan your visit to coincide with the **Alabama Tale Tellin' Festival,** an annual fall event staged in Selma. (In great demand as a speaker, Alabama's famous First Lady of Folk Tales and Ghost Stories travels frequently, so if you see someone behind the wheel of a Dodge Spirit with a license plate that reads JEFFREY, be sure to wave.)

Driving along Dallas Avenue (which becomes State Route 22), you'll pass the **Old Live Oak Cemetery,** filled with ancient trees festooned by Spanish moss. During spring, dogwoods and azaleas make this site even more spectacular. A number of Confederate graves and unique monuments may be seen here, including the mausoleum of William Rufus King, who named Selma and planned its layout. King, on the Democratic ticket with Franklin Pierce, died shortly after being elected vice president of the United States.

During your Selma sightseeing tour, stop by the **Siegel Gallery** (334–875–1138) at 706 Broad Street. This 1840 Greek Revival cottage houses outstanding collections of national, regional, and local art. Originally built at Cahaba, the home was dismantled around 1850 and transported to Selma, where its numbered boards were reassembled.

You'll enjoy seeing the gallery's fine collection of paintings, prints, batik, and sculpture. "We have a little of everything," says Mr. Siegel. Gallery hours run from 10:00 A.M. to 5:00 P.M. Monday through Friday, from 10:00 A.M. to 1:00 P.M. on Saturday, and by appointment.

While sightseeing you'll probably pass **The Candy Store** (334–875–1575) at 1205 Broad Street. You may want to dash inside and buy a big bag of bargain-priced candies from Liz and Billy Bond, who carry some of American Candy Manufacturing Company's locally made varieties. You'll find old-fashioned stick candy, giant lollipops, mints, chocolate bars, and other confections here.

For dinner strike out for the **Tally-Ho Restaurant** (334–872–1390), located on Mangum Avenue, just off Summerfield Road in the northern section of town. Owner Bob Kelley's entrees run the gamut from seafood and chicken to London broil and prime rib au jus. A blackboard features daily specials, which might include grilled pork chops with rosemary sauce. (The rosemary, thyme, and other herbs used in several dishes come from the restaurant's herb garden on the grounds.) Homemade zucchini muffins accompany entrees. For dessert try the chocolate cheesecake or amaretto soufflé. The restaurant's hours are 5:00 to 10:00 P.M. Monday through Saturday.

During your Selma visit, swing southwest about 9 miles on State Route 22 toward **Cahaba** (Cahawba is the historical spelling). Watch for a sign that says to CAHABA, then turn left and travel 3¹/₂ miles. When you reach a dead end, turn left again and continue 3 miles to **Old Cahawba Archaeological Park** (334–872–8058), the site of Alabama's first permanent state capital. Here, near the place where the Cahaba and Alabama Rivers merge, once stood a thriving town. Today's visitors will have to use some imagination to visualize the remaining ruins as grand mansions that surrounded a copper-domed capitol, completed in 1820. A large stone monument and interpretive signs in conjunction with old street markers, brick columns, cemeteries, and domestic plants growing wild offer the few clues that this off-the-beaten-path spot once flourished as a political, commercial, and cultural center. You'll also see an artesian well (where watercress grows), the source of water for the elaborate gardens surrounding the Perine family mansion, which once stood nearby. "We are currently restoring a standing slave quarters, which will be opening in the year 2000," said project manager Linda Derry.

The visitors and education centers provide information on Cahaba's glory days. In 1825 legislators voted to move Alabama's capital to Tuscaloosa. While local lore holds that frequent flooding caused Cahaba to lose its position as the state's seat of government, evidence suggests that sectional politics probably played a larger role. Gradually Cahaba became a ghost town, and by 1900 most of its buildings had disappeared. Log onto www.olcg.com/selma/cahawba.html, the park's Web site.

You might like to visit the site the second Saturday in May during the **Old Cahawba Festival,** a fun-filled day of living history with storytelling, children's games from long ago, bluegrass music, craft displays, and barbecue. Except for major holidays, the park is open daily from 9:00 A.M. to 5:00 P.M. Admission is free.

Afterward, follow U.S. Highway 80 west from Selma until you reach Dallas County Route 45; then turn north to **Marion,** one of Alabama's oldest towns and a leading cultural center for planter society. The city is home to both **Judson College** and **Marion Military Institute.** The latter's chapel, Old South Hall, and Lovelace House on campus served as hospitals during the Civil War. The graves of more than a hundred Southern and Union soldiers were later relocated from campus to **Confederate Rest,** a cemetery behind St. Wilfrid's Episcopal Church. The miniature Old Marion City Hall (moved to MMI's campus from the downtown square), houses the **Alabama Military Hall of Honor.** For an appointment to see the exhibits, call (334) 683–2346.

Downtown you'll see several historical churches and the handsome Perry County Courthouse dating from the early 1850s. Be sure to drive down Green Street, the setting for a number of antebellum residences, including the *Lea-Kramer Home* (circa 1830), where Texas hero Sam Houston married Margaret Lea (their marriage license is recorded in the courthouse). With some 200 sites (in a wide variety of architectural styles) listed on the National Register of Historic Places, Marion promises plenty to see.

During your Marion excursion take a stroll across the Judson College campus and stop by the *Alabama Women's Hall of Fame,* which occupies the first floor of Bean Hall. Formerly the school's library, this Carnegie-built structure stands on the corner of Bibb and East Lafayette Streets. Bronze plaques pay tribute to Helen Keller, Julia Tutwiler, Lurleen Burns Wallace, Tallulah Bankhead, Zelda Sayre Fitzgerald, her daughter Frances Scott Fitzgerald Smith, and many other women of achievement with Alabama connections. Former first ladies Barbara Bush and Rosalynn Carter have spoken at past induction ceremonies. Except for major holidays, hours are 8:00 A.M. to 4:30 P.M. Monday through Friday. For a tour call (334) 683–5109.

At 303 and 305 West Lafayette Street, you'll find *Myrtle Hill* (334–683–9095), which consists of neighboring antebellum homes surrounded by twelve acres of Victorian gardens. Elegantly furnished with period antiques, the homes offer spacious accommodations for bed-and-breakfast guests and the option of a Continental or plantation breakfast. Owners Wanda and Gerald Lewis sometimes treat guests to ghost-story and folk-tale sessions. Moderate rates.

The Gateway Inn (334–683–2582), located at 1615 State Route 5 South, offers a hearty noon buffet or sandwiches (available for takeout) Monday through Friday from 11:45 A.M. to 1:30 P.M. The restaurant also opens for dinner from 5:00 to 10:00 P.M. Friday and Saturday. Save room for the luscious homemade lemon icebox pie. Prices are economical to moderate.

Marion's early-twentieth-century train depot serves as a visitors center complete with walking trail along the former railroad tracks. For more information on Marion, call the chamber of commerce at (334) 683–9622.

After exploring Marion follow State Route 14 west to Alabama's Catfish Capital, Greensboro. Because this Black Belt town managed to escape the Civil War's ravages, a large number of its antebellum homes and churches have been preserved. In fact the entire downtown district, featuring some

150 nineteenth-century structures, is on the National Register of Historic Places. More than sixty of the town's homes predate the Civil War. Be sure to drive along Main, Tuscaloosa, and South Streets, all of which offer interesting architecture. At Market and South Streets, you'll see the **Noel-Ramsey House.** Built between 1819 and 1821, this is the only remaining residence of French settlers from nearby Demopolis's Vine and Olive Colony (see page 148).

Don't miss **Magnolia Grove** (334–624–8618), a two-story Greek Revival house built around 1840 by a wealthy cotton planter, Col. Isaac Croom. Located at 1002 Hobson Street, the home stands among lovely magnolia trees and landscaped gardens on a twelve-acre setting. Magnolia Grove was also the home of Croom's nephew, Rear Adm. Richmond Pearson Hobson, recently inducted into the Alabama Men's Hall of Fame. A naval hero in the Spanish-American War, Hobson later served in Congress and introduced legislation (the Hobson Amendment) that became the basis for the Constitution's prohibition amendment. My guide explained that this amendment, generally understood to refer only to alcohol, was also directed at drug control because, prior to aspirin's advent, the use of potent pain relievers such as morphine and opium commonly led to addiction. The Museum Room contains memorabilia from Hobson's military and political careers.

The house also features family portraits, heirlooms, and furnishings from the 1830s to the early 1900s. You'll see an 1866 piano, a Persian rug from the late 1800s, a chaperon's bench, and antique quilts. Outbuildings include a kitchen, slave cottage, and a structure that probably served as a classroom or library and office. Modest admission. Hours are 10:00 A.M. to 4:00 P.M. Tuesday through Saturday and 1:00 to 4:00 P.M. Sunday.

From Greensboro head south on State Route 25 toward Faunsdale—population 98. Housed in an 1890s mercantile building on the town's main street, **Ca-John's Faunsdale Bar & Grill** (334–628–3240) serves great steaks and seafood, and owner John (Ca-John) Broussard, originally from Louisiana, offers a variety of crawfish specialties in season. The food speaks for itself, attracting diners from distant towns. Windows sport red-and-white checkered cafe curtains. A pot-bellied stove and fireplace add to the ambience. Saturday night patrons can enjoy live music until the wee hours. Hours are 5:00 to 10:00 P.M. Wednesday through Friday and 10:00 A.M. until the crowd thins out on Saturday evening. From Faunsdale return to U.S. Highway 80 and head west toward Demopolis.

Sometime during your visit to the area, make an outing to Prairieville, the site of **St. Andrews Episcopal Church.** Located a short distance off

U.S. Highway 80, this red Carpenter Gothic structure dates from 1853 and is a National Historic Landmark. Nearby you'll see a picturesque old cemetery, where many of this area's early settlers are buried.

Peter Lee and Joe Glasgow, master carpenters and slaves of Capt. Henry A. Tayloe, supervised a crew of slaves belonging to church members in the construction of this edifice, built to serve settlers from the Atlantic seaboard.

Craftspeople created the mellowed appearance of interior wood walls by applying a brew made from the stems of tobacco plants. Pokeberry weeds provided color for some portions of the lovely stained-glass windows. Ragweed, chewed and molded, forms the decorative relief letters of a biblical quotation near the altar. Be sure to notice the pipe organ (which still plays) and the choir gallery. Closed as a regular parish in 1927, the church hosts annual spring and fall services, followed by picnic dinners on the grounds. For more information or to schedule an appointment to see the interior, phone (334) 289–3363.

Traveling 9 miles west on U.S. Highway 80 takes you to *Gaineswood* (334–289–4846), a gorgeous cream-colored mansion with white-columned porticos. Once the centerpiece of a huge plantation, the home

St. Andrews Episcopal Church

now stands in the suburbs of the town of Demopolis at 805 South Cedar Avenue. Gen. Nathan Bryan Whitfield, a gifted inventor, musician, artist, and architect, started construction on the house in 1843. He spent almost two decades planning and building this elegant Greek Revival home and continued to refine it until the Civil War's outbreak.

Stepping into the columned ballroom, you'll see yourself reflected thirteen times in the vis-à-vis mirrors. Be sure to notice the glass ceiling domes and the elaborate friezes and medallions. The home contains its original furnishings, family portraits, and accessories. Don't miss the flutina (invented by Whitfield), a one-of-a-kind musical instrument that sounds something like a riverboat calliope.

In many ways Gaineswood reminded me of Thomas Jefferson's splendid Monticello, and my guide said visitors often make that observation. Except for state holidays, Gaineswood is open Monday through Saturday from 9:00 A.M. to 5:00 P.M. and on Sunday from 1:00 to 5:00 P.M. Admission.

Continue to downtown Demopolis, "the City of the people," a town with an interesting origin that goes back to 1817 when 400 aristocrats, fleeing France after Napoleon's exile, landed here at the white limestone bluffs overlooking the Tombigbee River. They acquired a large tract of land along the river and set about establishing the Vine and Olive Colony. The agricultural experiment, however, yielded little more than frustration for the colonists, who lacked essential farming skills and found the local climate and soil unsuitable for cultivating their imported grape vines and olive trees.

You'll see a display on this early colony in the French Room at *Bluff Hall* (334–289–9644 or 334–289–0282). Located on North Commissioners Avenue next to the Civic Center, this 1832 brick home takes its name from its position overlooking the Tombigbee River. Originally built in the Federal style, the home took on a Greek Revival appearance after later additions. Furnishings are Empire and mid-Victorian.

As you start upstairs notice the newel post's amity button, symbolizing a state of harmony between the owner and builder. In addition to documents, crystal, silver spoons, cannonballs, portraits, and other memorabilia of the Vine and Olive Colony, you'll see a room filled with period costumes, such as an 1831 wedding dress. Bluff Hall is noted for its extensive collection of vintage clothing.

The kitchen's interesting gadgets range from an egg tin, sausage stuffer, and fluting iron to the "humane" rat trap on the hearth. Adjacent to the home, a gift shop offers a choice selection of items including posters depicting a European artist's imaginative conception of the early Vine and Olive Colony, handmade split-oak baskets, and eye-catching pottery by Susan Brown Freeman. Bluff Hall is owned and operated by the Marengo County Historical Society. (The county's name was inspired by Napoleon's victory at the Battle of Marengo in northern Italy.) Except for major holidays, Bluff Hall is open Tuesday through Saturday from 10:00 A.M. to 5:00 P.M. and on Sunday from 2:00 to 5:00 P.M. During January and February, the home closes at 4:00 P.M. Admission.

While sightseeing stop by the Demopolis yacht Basin on U.S. Highway 43 for a meal at *The Jolly Roger.* If you sit near a window, you can still see a portion of the white chalk bluffs where the French Bonapartists landed. (This landmark is less prominent since the Demopolis Lock and Dam raised the river level by 40 feet in 1954.)

Here you can meet and eat with "the boat people," members of the city's maritime community, who live aboard their yachts and play active roles in the town's civic and social life. The restaurant serves a variety of sandwiches, salads, and dinner entrees. Generally open for lunch and dinner, the restaurant has seasonal hours that vary. When you leave, take along some bread to feed the fish and turtles that congregate below the boardwalk—they expect it.

Demopolis offers more than mansions and water recreation. You'll find plenty of interesting places to shop, too, such as *Landmark Gallery,* a restored 1909 building that houses several stores. Also downtown, at 109 West Washington Street, *The Mustard Seed* offers fine gifts, china, crystal, housewares, collectibles, dolls, and toys. *Maison de Briques,* a flower and gift shop at 102 Highway 80 East, offers a variety of decorative items.

Local festivals include a July the Fourth Fireworks Celebration at City Landing and Art in the park, an annual May arts and crafts show staged at Confederate Square. The grand finale, December's *Christmas on the River,* features a weeklong festival of parades, tours, and events culminating in an extravaganza of decorated, lighted boats gliding down the Tombigbee River. For more information on these or other special events, including productions by the Canebrake Players (a local theater group) or on other area attractions, call (334) 289–0270.

Traveling north from Demopolis to *Eutaw,* watch for Greene County farmer Jim Bird's hay-bale sculptures along U.S. Highway 43. His environmental art often gets double takes from passersby. After all, one does not expect to see a pasture populated by dinosaurs or a giant octopus, pig, rabbit, spider, snail, caterpillar, and dragon. Jim uses an assortment of driftwood and discarded objects to transform the large hay rolls into his whimsical creations.

Eutaw, a charming hamlet situated around a courthouse square, dates from 1838. The town boasts fifty-three antebellum structures, with many on the National Register of Historic Places. Head first to the Visitor Information Center, located in the Vaughn-Morrow House at 310 Main Street, where you'll find information on both Eutaw and Greene County. If the museum is not open, look for a telephone contact number posted on the porch.

Beside the visitors center stands the *First Presbyterian Church.* Organized in 1824 as Mesopotamia Presbyterian Church, the congregation's current home dates from 1851. This white-steepled structure looks as if it belongs on a Christmas card (without the snow, of course—a rare commodity in most of Alabama). Original whale-oil lamps, stored for a time in the slave gallery, have been wired for electricity and again grace the church's interior. For a tour, inquire at the church office in the adjacent Educational Building.

Nearby, on the corner of Main Street and Eutaw Avenue, stands *St. Stephen's Episcopal Church.* The handsome brick structure features a hand-carved lectern, an elegant white marble baptismal font, and beautiful stained-glass windows. To see the lovely interior, check with the church office.

Don't miss *Kirkwood* (205–372–9009), a restored 1860 mansion located at the intersection of State Route 14 and Kirkwood Drive. This impressive American Greek Revival home, topped with a belvedere, features eight massive Ionic columns, Carrara marble mantels, Waterford crystal chandeliers, and original furnishings. Built by Foster Mark Kirksey, the mansion was on the verge of completion when the Civil War brought construction to a halt. After a century of neglect, the house was rescued by Mary and Roy Swayze, who moved here from Virginia and set about transforming Kirkwood into the elegant home you see today. In 1982 Nancy Reagan, on behalf of the National Trust for Historic Preservation, presented the Swayzes with the National Honor Award in recognition of their outstanding restoration of Kirkwood. The mansion is open for bed-and-breakfast guests. Beautifully furnished with period pieces, the home may be toured by appointment. Current owner/innkeeper Sherry Vallides offers six guest rooms with private baths and serves afternoon refreshments plus a full plantation breakfast. She will give you some insider tips on what to see and do in this area, rich in fishing and hunting. Rates are moderate.

Kirkwood

After relaxing at Kirkwood, head west to **Gainesville,** a delightful "piece of the past" populated by 307 people. Most places like this charming town have vanished from today's landscape. Retired teacher Kathryn Harrison, better known as Miss Kitty, often volunteers to take visitors on a "loopity-joopity" tour of town, sharing anecdotes about its historic churches, cemeteries, and citizenry. (She's been known to greet visitors with her homemade tea cakes.)

Don't miss **The Presbyterian Church,** which dates from 1837. Interior features include whale-oil lamps, pews with doors, and the altar's original chairs. To give the bell its tone, a member melted 500 silver dollars, says Miss Kitty, who remembers helping extinguish flames with a hand-to-hand bucket brigade during one of three times the church caught fire. Because several denominations share this church (one per Sunday), Miss Kitty labels herself a "Metho-bap-terian."

Other sites of interest include the 1872 **Methodist Church; St. Alban's Episcopal Church,** founded in 1879; and the **Confederate Cemetery.** For more local information stop by one of the downtown stores. You can contact Miss Kitty at P.O. Box 9, Gainesville 35464; or call (205) 652–7629.

Afterward, continue south to nearby Livingston. The town was named for Edward Livingston, who served as Andrew Jackson's secretary of state.

On your way into town, stop by Sumter County's **Alamuchee Covered**

Bridge, across from the Baptist Student Union on the campus of Livingston State University. Capt. W. A. C. Jones of Livingston designed and built this 1861 structure, one of the South's oldest covered bridges. Made of hand-hewn heart pine held together by large wooden pegs, the bridge originally spanned the Sucarnochee River, south of town. In 1924 the bridge was taken down and reconstructed across a creek on the old Bellamy-Livingston Road, where it remained in use until 1958. The bridge was moved to its present location and restored in 1971. You might enjoy seeing more of the campus, which also boasts two lakes.

Downtown you'll see a lovely square surrounding the impressive domed *Sumter County Courthouse* (circa 1900). This area remained Choctaw

An Accidental Discovery

*W*ithin shouting distance of Kirkwood stands a delightful Greek Revival cottage called **Sipinn on Ashby** *(205–372–3516). Lucky is the guest who headquarters here. This "small Greek temple" contains everything one needs to be comfortable, with some elegance thrown in for good measure. Trisha and Walter Griess built the guest cottage on the grounds of Sipsey, the home they rescued and moved from its original site on Pleasant Ridge overlooking the Sipsey River. Beautifully restored and decorated, the circa 1835 Greek Revival raised one-story cottage features a four-columned portico and two formal entrances. During her two decades of research and restoration, Trish became a Greek Revival virtuoso.*

I first discovered Sipinn by mistake. Somehow, I dialed the cottage's unlisted and unadvertised number. The surprised guests, an attorney and his wife from Colorado, gave me a rave review of the property, describing its charm and the friendliness of Eutaw's residents. So captivated were they that they extended their stay.

Their glowing recommendation reminded me of my first research visit to Eutaw when former resident Deb Knowles took me under her wing, showed me around, and coordinated a potluck supper in one of the town's lovely historic homes. About six couples brought wonderful food and shared some background on this delightful town. Then, on my recent return, two golden retrievers met me in Sipinn's driveway. One started licking my hand before I got out of the car, and the other presented me a stick for a toss-and-fetch game. And they probably would have carried my bag to the cottage.

Trisha decorated the cottage with architectural antiques, a custommade bed, and wide plantation shutters. Guests get breakfast and a tour of the main house. For a glimpse of Sipsey, search out Bob Vila's American Home (March 1998), which chronicles the restoration, and Veranda (Winter 1998), featuring Sipsey along with several more of Eutaw's historic treasures. Moderate rates.

country until 1830, when the United States acquired it in the Treaty of Dancing Rabbit Creek.

Local businesswomen Mary Tartt, Molly Dorman, and Louise Boyd find *The Dancing Rabbit* (205–652–6252) is a good name for their shop near the courthouse square. Located at 307 Monroe Street, the charming store features silver, crystal, antique linens, wicker items, china, Christmas ornaments, and other collectibles along with a variety of rabbits (but not the real live kind). Hours are 10:00 A.M. to 5:30 P.M. Tuesday through Friday and 10:00 A.M. to 4:00 P.M. Saturday.

Head southwest to York, about 11 miles southwest of Livingston. In this small town near the Mississippi border, you'll find a wonderful art museum inside *The Coleman Center* (205–392–2005), at 630 Avenue A. The museum, a library, genealogical room, and a cultural center occupy an early-twentieth-century general store. On an exterior wall of the building, a repainted vintage ad shows silent film star Clara Bow promoting an early brand of gasoline. You'll enter The Coleman Center through a courtyard on the opposite side.

Director Kaye Kiker, an artist specializing in stained glass, describes the four-building complex as a community effort and the only facility of its kind in Sumter County. Local citizens contributed the land, building, services, and funds for the center. Tut Altman Riddick (who grew up in York but now lives in Mobile) and her husband Harry were early promoters of this project, and their outstanding contemporary art collection may be seen at the museum. In addition to its permanent collection, which includes an original etching by Renoir, prints, paintings, pottery, and other items, the museum features traveling exhibits. The facility closes each day from noon to 1:00 P.M. and also on Thursday and Saturday afternoons. Otherwise, hours are 9:00 A.M. to 4:30 P.M. or by appointment. The museum closes on Sunday. Admission is free.

Timberland

Timber is big business in this part of the state, and hunting and fishing are popular pastimes. If you're in the mood for a feast, head for *Ezell's Fish Camp* (205–654–2205) near Lavaca. This out-of-the-way restaurant is definitely worth adding some extra miles to your trip. In fact, some customers fly in, and an Ezell's staffer meets them at the airport. The restaurant also gets a lot of river traffic and often provides transportation into town for boating customers who need motel lodging.

To reach the restaurant from Lavaca, take State Route 10 east toward Nanafalia and turn left just before reaching the big bridge. Located on the west bank of the Tombigbee River, this family operation is the granddaddy of "catfish cabins" you might see while driving through the state. Following family precedent, each of the Ezells' three children went into the restaurant business.

As you arrive, you'll see a large rustic structure with a roof of wooden shingles. The restaurant started out as a Civil War-era dogtrot cabin, and the Ezells added more rooms for their brisk business. The rambling structure now seats 400 people. Mounted deer and moose heads line the walls. (Mr. Ezell, an avid fisherman, hunter, and trapper, used to ship his furs to New York's garment district.)

The back porch, a favorite spot for eating, overlooks the river. Start with an appetizer of onion rings, crab claws, or fried dill pickles. In addition to catfish, the restaurant serves seafood specialties such as shrimp and oysters. Entrees come with slaw, potatoes, and hush puppies. Moderate prices. Open seven days a week, Ezell's has flexible hours, but the typical schedule is 11:00 A.M. to sometime between 9:00 and 10:00 P.M., depending on the crowd.

Traveling south from Lavaca takes you through large expanses of timberland. Forestry and related industries play major roles in the area's economy. Clarke County holds the title of Forestry Capital of Alabama, and Fulton, a small town south of Thomasville, pays tribute to this important industry by hosting a *Sawmill Days* celebration each fall.

If you visit *Camden* during the Wilcox Historical Society's biennial (slated for odd-numbered years) Fall Tour of Homes, you can survey some of the area's antebellum structures. The stately *Wilcox Female Institute,* which dates from 1850, serves as tour headquarters. Located at 301 Broad Street, the former school (open by appointment) houses a small museum of local history.

For a Southern taste treat, make reservations at the *Gaines Ridge Dinner Club* (334–682–9707), located about 2 miles east of Camden on State Route 10. Housed in Betty Gaines Kennedy's two-story circa 1830 family home, the restaurant seats about one hundred guests in five dining rooms. From shrimp bisque to spinach salad and steak or seafood, everything on the menu is well prepared and tasty. (Ask Betty about the home's ghosts.) Prices fall in the economical to moderate range, and hours are 5:30 to 9:00 P.M. Wednesday through Saturday.

Wilcox County, which promises good fishing, attracts out-of-state deer and turkey hunters, and many make their headquarters at nearby **Roland Cooper State Park.** If you're in the area during harvest season, consider purchasing some fresh-shelled pecans from Joe C. Williams. To order the local product, write P.O. Box 640, Camden 36726; or call (334) 682–4559. For more information on Camden and Wilcox County, call Dick Kinne at (334) 682–4929.

Traveling south from Camden on State Route 265 takes you by **Rikard's Mill,** just north of Beatrice. Stop by to browse through the Covered Bridge Gift Shop and watch the old-fashioned water-powered gristmill in operation. You'll also find a restored blacksmith shop and hiking trails. Modest admission. For seasonal hours, April through mid-December, call (334) 789–2781 or (334) 575–7433.

Continue south to Monroeville (where Alabama authors Truman Capote and Harper Lee played as children) for a stop at the **Old Monroe County Courthouse.** This 1903 three-story brick structure served as a model for the courthouse in the film *To Kill a Mockingbird,* based on Harper Lee's Pulitzer prize-winning novel (and starring Gregory Peck in the role of Atticus Finch). During my visit, I entered the courthouse and asked to see Atticus Finch. While applauding myself on being so imaginative, I learned that "everyone wants to meet Atticus Finch."

During the first three weekends in May, visitors can watch the stage version of *To Kill a Mockingbird* in a bona fide courtroom setting. Produced by the Monroe County Heritage Museum under the direction of Kathy McCoy, who heads up the museum staff, the local stage adaptation

Monroeville—Literary Capital of Alabama

*I*n recognition of the exceptional literary heritage of Monroeville and Monroe County, the Alabama legislature designated this region the Literary Capital of Alabama in a 1997 joint resolution. Author of "A Christmas Memory," In Cold Blood, Breakfast at Tiffany's, *and other classics, Truman Capote spent idyllic hours roaming the town as a youngster along with friend Harper Lee, who penned the Pulitzer prize–winning novel,* To Kill a Mockingbird. *Other writers who have called Monroeville home include nationally syndicated columnist Cynthia Tucker and novelist Mark Childress. The small town of Monroeville, which packs a rich literary history, hosts an Alabama Writers Symposium each May. For more information on this event, contact the Alabama Southern Community College at P.O. Box 2000, Monroeville 36461; or call (334) 575–3165, extension 223.*

boasts the authenticity of the story's actual location plus cultural awareness and genuine Southern accents.

As guests of the government of Israel in 1996, the talented performers (and only amateur group ever invited to participate) presented this classic drama on stage in Jerusalem at the International Cultural Festival. In September 1998 the production traveled to England and was staged at the Hull Theater. For more information visit the Web site at www.tokillamockingbird.com, or call or visit the **Heritage Museum** (334–575–7433), which also features changing exhibits related to Monroe County's past and a gift shop with works by area artists. Hours run from 8:00 A.M. to noon and 1:00 to 4:00 P.M. Monday through Friday and from 10:00 A.M. to 2:00 P.M. Saturday.

While downtown, stop by **Finishing Touches** at 107 East Claiborne Street on the square's south side. You'll enjoy browsing through this shop with lovely handmade items, antiques, kitchen accessories, gifts, clothing for children and ladies, customized baskets, and books. While here you might like to purchase a copy of *To Kill a Mockingbird,* which author Harper Lee (who divides her time between New York and Monroeville) will sign when she's in town. The staff will then send you the autographed book. For more information call (334) 575–2066.

Before leaving the area, you might want to visit the **River Heritage Museum,** housed in the old Corps of Engineers building at the Claiborne Lock & Dam. The surrounding region is a great place for camping and fishing, too. Located about 18 miles from the square in downtown Monroeville, the museum can be reached by taking State Route 41 to County Road 17 and then following the signs to the Claiborne Lock & Dam. The museum's exhibits feature fossils, Native American artifacts, and steamboat relics. With seasonal hours, the museum is open April through October. Hours run from 9:00 A.M. to 4:00 P.M. Thursday through Saturday and 1:00 to 5:00 P.M. on Sunday. For more information call (334) 575–7433.

Gulf Coast Delta

After your timberland excursion head south to Escambia County, where traveling pilgrims can spend an authentic Thanksgiving Day with the Poarch Band of Creek Indians at their annual Pow Wow. Tribal members welcome friends, relatives, and visitors to help them celebrate the Thanksgiving holidays on the **Poarch Creek Reservation,** 8 miles northwest of Atmore at 5811 Jack Springs Road. Festivities include exhibition dancing by tribes from throughout the country, a greased pig chase, turkey shoot, and much more. You can feast on roasted corn, Indian fry bread, ham, fried chicken, or traditional turkey and dressing. Booths feature beadwork, basketry, silver work, and other Native American crafts. Take a lawn chair, camera, and your appetite. Modest admission. For more information on this two-day event, call (334) 368–9136.

Continue southwest toward the Eastern Shore and stop by Malbis, 12 miles east of Mobile on U.S. Highway 90. On Baldwin County Route 27, you'll find the **Malbis Greek Orthodox Church.** This magnificent neo-Byzantine-style structure, built at a cost of more than $1 million, was dedicated to the memory of Jason Malbis. A former monk who emigrated from Greece in 1906, Malbis traveled through thirty-six states before selecting this Baldwin County site to establish Malbis Plantation (virtually a self-supporting colony that grew to cover 2,000 acres).

The marble in this edifice came from the same Greek quarries used to build Athens's ancient Parthenon. The majestic interior features a dark blue 75-foot domed ceiling, stained-glass windows, mosaics, and murals.

Strange As It Sounds

*W*hether or not you hear the cry of "Jubilee!" during your visit to the Eastern Shore of Mobile Bay, you can see this strange spectacle depicted in a photo display at **Manci's Antique Club** in downtown Daphne. Located at the corner of Daphne and Bellrose Avenues, this combination bar-museum (originally opened as a gas station in 1924 by Frank Manci, converted to its current status in 1947 by Arthur Manci, and now operated by a third-generation family member, Alex Manci) houses a rickshaw, oxen yokes, and Victrolas. You'll also see collections of antique tools, cowbells, political campaign buttons, and Native American artifacts. The club boasts the biggest assemblage of Jim Beam decanters outside the distillery's own collection. Claiming the title Bloody Mary Capital of the Eastern Shore, the house serves its specialty garnished with a pickled string bean. A sign over the bar promises FREE BEER *tomorrow.*

Those who visit the ladies' room at Manci's will see the wooden figure of a man—dressed only in a fig leaf. The observant will notice the fig leaf is hinged, and the curious might go even further. Unrestrained curiosity can soon turn to horror, however, because a blaring alarm alerts all within hearing distance that one possesses an inquisitive nature. One then must make the uncomfortable choice of exiting—red-faced—to the merriment of Manci's patrons or occupying the ladies' room till closing time. Manci's hours are 10:00 A.M. till 11:00 P.M. Monday through Thursday, and closing time is 2:00 A.M. Friday and Saturday.

Greek artists spent eight months completing the paintings that extend from the cathedral's entrance to its altar. The church is open daily, and admission is free. Hours run from 9:00 A.M. to noon and 2:00 to 5:00 P.M. For more information call (334) 626–3050, extension 155.

Next swing westward to Daphne, perched on Mobile Bay's Eastern Shore, where you might hear someone shout "Jubilee!" When you do, people will grab buckets and rush to the water's edge for flounder, shrimp, and crabs—theirs for the scooping. This natural phenomenon might occur several times a summer, usually during the wee morning hours. Some natives claim they can predict an approaching jubilee by watching weather conditions and studying certain indicators in the moon, tide, and winds. Although not unique to the area, this "shoreward migration of bottom-living organisms"—to put it in technical terms—surprises most visitors.

After exploring Daphne continue south to Fairhope, a charming flower-filled town founded about 1894 on the "single tax" concept of economist Henry George, who considered land the source of all wealth. The Fairhope Single Tax Colony still functions today, one of the country's few model communities operating on George's taxation theories. A percentage of the town's property is held by the Fairhope Single Tax Colony office, and a resident can lease his or her land for ninety-nine years (or perpetuity). The resident pays a single annual tax on the land only—not on improvements—and this yearly payment covers school district, city, county, and state taxes as well as community services.

Save plenty of time for browsing through Fairhope's downtown area, where baskets of cascading blossoms adorn every street corner. You'll see art galleries, eateries, boutiques, and shops offering everything from antiques, toys, and clothing to crafts and nautical gear. Located at the foot of Fairhope Avenue, the attractive Fairhope Pier attracts strollers and joggers.

The *Church Street Inn* (334–928–8976) makes a lovely and convenient base for travelers. Located at 51 South Church Street, the white stucco-and-brick home contains five generations of family photos and antiques. Visitors can relax on the front porch and watch passersby (who often wave hello) or retreat to the back-garden courtyard. The living room's window seat makes a cozy spot for reading about local history. Guests may help themselves to ice cream when hunger pangs strike and enjoy an ample serve-yourself Continental breakfast when they choose. Moderate rates.

SOUTHWEST ALABAMA

Hosts Becky and Bill Jones also welcome visitors to **Bay Breeze Guest House** on historic Mobile Bay, where they can watch the glorious sunsets, go beachcombing or fishing, and feed the resident ducks. Ask Becky, a former biology teacher, about the local Jubilee phenomenon. From May through September, guests can enjoy breakfast served on Bay Breeze's pier. Moderate rates. For reservations at either property, call (334) 928–8976.

Before leaving Fairhope, stop by the **Eastern Shore Art Center**, at 401 Oak Street, to see its current exhibits. You might also enjoy visiting a unique museum on Faulkner State Community College's Fairhope campus that houses memorabilia from the early days of the **Marietta L. Johnson School of Organic Education** (334–990–8601). Counselor Clarence Darrow, who summered in Fairhope, lectured at this nontraditional school, which was noted for its progressive curriculum promoting creativity. The museum occupies the west wing of the historic Bell Building at 440 Fairhope Avenue. Hours are 1:00 to 5:00 P.M. Monday through Friday and 2:00 to 5:00 P.M. Sunday.

South of Fairhope at Point Clear (designated "Punta Clara" on sixteenth-century maps of Spanish explorers), you'll find Marriott's **Grand Hotel** (334–928–9201 or 800–544–9933) on scenic U.S. Highway 98. This legendary resort on Mobile Bay offers facilities spreading over 550 lovely acres studded with moss-festooned oaks more than 300 years old. The locale has long attracted generations of wealthy Southern families—the site's first resort dates from the mid-1800s. Today's guests continue to enjoy "the Grand's" traditions, such as afternoon tea in the wood-paneled lobby.

The hotel's three restaurants offer delightful dining options. Recreation choices range from golf, boating, tennis, swimming, and fishing to croquet. Call for a rate schedule on current package offerings or reservations.

Be sure to visit a candy shop called **Punta Clara Kitchen** (334–928–8477), located in an 1897 gingerbread house 1 mile south of the Grand Hotel. Here you can sample confections from pecan butter crunch and divinity to chocolate-covered bourbon balls and buckeyes (balls of creamy peanut butter confections hand-dipped in chocolate). The shop also sells jellies, recipe books, pickles, and preserves. Before leaving, take a few minutes to look around this historic home, furnished as it was during the late 1800s. Hours are 9:00 A.M. to 5:00 P.M. Monday through Saturday and 12:30 to 5:00 P.M. Sunday.

Behind the Victorian home stands a weathered cedar and cypress structure that originally served as a laundry and wine cellar. It now houses *The Wash House Restaurant* (334–928–1500), where you can enjoy a delicious dinner. You might start with an appetizer of crab claws, fried crawfish tails, or escargot. Entrees include chef-created specialties that Norris, a waiter there who is known for his tempting food descriptions, will describe in mouth-watering detail, as well as menu items such as sautéed shrimp on fettucini. Noted for its Continental specialties and sophisticated sauces, the restaurant also features soft-shell crabs, raised exclusively for The Wash House.

While here you might bump into a governor, an ambassador, or another visiting celebrity—Dolly Parton, Stacey Keach, Jimmy Buffett, and Steven Seagal have all dined at The Wash House, says Wanda Taylor, who along with her husband, John, owns and operates this eatery. Their daughter, Joni Baecher, serves as chef and creates delectable desserts such as Bread Pudding with Southern Comfort Nutmeg Sauce, Biscotti Pie, and Fried Apple Dumplings with Caramel Sauce and Whipped Cream. Prices are moderate to expensive. Guests are seated from 5:00 to 9:00 P.M. Sunday through Thursday and till 10:00 P.M. Friday and Saturday.

Ready for an antistress kind of place? Then head for nearby Magnolia Springs, where you can unwind in a serene setting of dappled sunlight and live oaks. The *Magnolia Springs Bed & Breakfast* (334–965–7321 or 800–965–7321), once known as the Sunnyside Hotel, exudes a friendly aura with inviting front porch and comfortable ambience. Committed to providing warm hospitality, owner David Worthington welcomes guests to his 1897 home at 14469 Oak Street and recommends local excursions. You may have seen this property before; it was featured on a past Alabama Public Television special. E-mail David at msbbdw@gulftel.com. For a virtual tour and more information, log onto www.bbonline.com/al/magnolia.

Don't miss *Foley,* situated around the intersection of U.S. Highway 98 and State Route 59. The town offers not only factory-outlet shopping but a host of attractions such as antiques malls, arts centers, and charming eateries.

Start your tour at 111 West Laurel Avenue with the *Baldwin Museum of Art* and the *Holmes Medical Museum* (334–970–1818), housed in a building that dates to the early 1900s. After viewing the current downstairs art exhibits, climb to the second floor for a close-up look at instruments and memorabilia from medicine's earlier years. Once a hospital for Baldwin County residents, the rooms contain an operating suite complete with table, bone-breaking apparatus, Kelly pad, ether container, and attendant tubes. Also on display are X-ray equipment and medical cabinets filled with delivery forceps, tonsil guillotine and snare, and other instruments. In addition to patient quarters, you can inspect a room devoted to quackery paraphernalia—a color spectrum device for treating everything from headaches to kidney infections, barber bowl for bleeding patients, and diagrammed phrenology skull. Hours are 10:00 A.M. to 4:00 P.M. Tuesday through Saturday. Admission is free.

Continue to the *Performing Arts Center* (334–943–4381) at 119 West Laurel Avenue. Step inside the lobby of the former Foley Hotel, which dates to 1928, for a look at exhibits of juried fine art and browse back through the dining room filled with more art and crafts by area artists. The facility sponsors a sales gallery (a great place to buy unique gifts) as well as cultural events and art classes. Staffed by an all-volunteer organization, the center's hours run from 10:00 A.M. to 4:00 P.M. Monday through Friday and 11:00 A.M. to 2:00 P.M. on Saturday.

Take a break next door at *Stacey Rexall Drugs* (334–943–7191), with its "Old Tyme Soda Fountain." In this delightful pharmacy at 121 West Laurel Avenue, you can savor a banana split, slurp on an ice-cream soda, cherry Coke, or chocolate milk shake and listen to old favorites from the jukebox or player piano while watching a toy train make its rounds above the soda fountain. A penny scale reveals your weight and fate. Owners Kathi (the "druggist") and John J. Henderson (the "fizzician"), with the help of Adam (the soda jerk), will treat you to an old-fashioned good time. Hours run from 8:00 A.M. to 6:00 P.M. Monday through Friday and 9:00 A.M. to 6:00 P.M. on Saturday.

Continuing to the next block, you'll find *The Gift Horse* (334–943–3663 or 800–FOLEYAL), located at 209 West Laurel Avenue. Beyond the restaurant's leaded-glass doors, you'll see a grand banquet table with a buffet of salads, vegetables, meats, breads, and desserts. House specialties include fried biscuits, spinach soufflé, mystery crab-shrimp salad, and the restaurant's famous apple cheese—all prepared from owner Jackie O. McLeod's recipes. Lunch is served from 11:00 A.M. to 4:30 P.M. Monday through Sunday. Dinner hours run from 4:30 to 9:00 P.M. Monday through Sunday. Jackie's cookbook, available in the gift shop, makes a great souvenir and divulges some of her culinary secrets. While in Foley you may want to visit The Gift Horse Antique Centre, too.

Follow U.S. Highway 98 east to Elberta. During the first half of the century, this fertile area attracted families from central, northern, and southern Europe, as well as Quebec. At Elberta's *German Sausage Festivals,* staged in March and October, descendants of early settlers dress in native attire to perform Old World dances.

To learn more about the ethnic diversity and lifestyles of the county's early settlers, stop by the *Baldwin County Heritage Museum* (334–986–8375), ¹/₂ mile east of Elberta on U.S. Highway 98. In front of the five-acre wooded setting called "Frieden Im Wald," you'll see a working windmill and several outdoor agricultural exhibits.

Displays inside the museum feature the Kee tool collection and vintage farm equipment, a printing press, and an interior section of a post office from Josephine, Alabama. Household items include an Edison phonograph, antique sewing machines, stoves, cooking utensils, and washing machines. Also on display are old-fashioned school desks, folk sculpture, and a moonshine still. The museum is staffed entirely by volunteers, many of them snowbirds from Minnesota, Wisconsin, Michigan, New York, and other northern states, who contribute their time and skills to restoring artifacts and putting old machinery in running order again. Modest admission. Hours are 10:00 A.M. to 5:00 P.M. on Friday and Saturday and 1:00 to 5:00 P.M. Sunday. Weekday tours can be arranged by appointment.

For some great food, including some of the best soups on the Gulf Coast, continue east on U.S. Highway 98 to Lillian. At Kit's Marina on Perdido Bay, you'll find *Miss Kitty's Restaurant* (334–962–2701 or 800–844–2701). Watch for signs directing you to turn right just before reaching the Lillian Bridge, then left soon after. Popular dinner choices include snapper or veal with a choice of sauces, roast duck with blackberry sauce, and barbecued baby back ribs. All soups, sauces, and desserts are prepared daily. Owner/operators Rose and Chris Russo, along with son Bob, will be on hand to make your dining experience one to remember. The restaurant is open Wednesday through Saturday for dinner. On Sunday a brunch is served from 11:00 A.M. to 2:00 P.M. and dinner until 7:00 P.M. during winter months and 7:30 P.M. in summer. Reservations are recommended.

To see some secluded portions of the area, sign up for a *Dolphin Ecology Tour* aboard the *DAEDALUS* with Captain Fred. Based at 6816 South Bayou Drive near Elberta, architect Fred Saas designed and built the 50-foot sailboat *DAEDALUS* and navigated it from California to its home in Alabama. Because the big vessel performs in shallow water, passengers can visit hidden bayous and bays and even venture onto an uninhabited beach.

Local wildlife that may be glimpsed includes osprey, blue herons, and dolphins. The crew keeps records of dolphin sightings for a dolphin scientist in Mobile and gives out information sheets on these fascinating creatures.

Such a grand scenario calls for background music—happily provided by the birds with perhaps Mozart, Linda Ronstadt, or Jimmy Buffett filling in. Captain Fred, who's made many trips to Central America, offers week-long tours to Guatemala. A licensed minister, he often performs weddings aboard the sailboat at no charge. Call (334) 987–1228 for reservations and rates or for information on either the ecology tour or another family venture, the *Biophilia Nature Center.* You can e-mail the owners at daedalus@gulftel.com or pay a Web visit to www.gulftel.net/daedalus.

At 12695 County Road 95 in Elberta, you can study carnivorous plants like Venus's-flytrap, pitcher bog plants, and other unusual botanical specimens at the Biophilia Nature Center. "We have an 11-foot alligator and turtles that can be seen year-round," said Carol Lovell-Saas, who promotes environmental education and takes you on a walk through her "open book of nature" that spreads across twenty acres. Tours offer a mini-course in butterfly gardening for the South and the Midwest and include free pamphlets on each plus literature on ecogardening.

From spring through early winter, several kinds of showy native butterflies are raised indoors and outdoors, allowing visitors to observe all stages from egg to adult. You'll see forest wildflower meadows and swamps, now being restored with 300 native species, and can stop by a plant nursery and bookstore on the premises. Contact Carol for specific directions and hours.

From Perdido Bay you're just a hop and a skip (or a short boat ride) from the glistening white sands of *Gulf Shores.* Although a Diners' Club publication once conferred highest honors on the stretch of shoreline along the Florida panhandle between Destin and Panama City, calling it "the world's most perfect beach," fewer people know about the other end of the Southern Riviera-Alabama's toehold on the Gulf of Mexico. In fact, the relatively new town of Gulf Shores did not appear on Alabama's official highway map until the sixties. But a retreat offering sugar-sand beaches and a balmy climate cannot remain a secret forever, and this 32-mile crescent known as Pleasure Island (once a peninsula) now attracts vacationers from across the country.

Some one hundred charter boats dock at nearby *Orange Beach* marinas, offering outings from sunset cruises to fishing excursions. Surrounding waters feature world-class fishing throughout the year. (For information about state fishing licenses, call 800–262–3151.)

FLORA-BAMA—Home of the Annual Mullet Toss

Jimmy Buffett used to come here and jam. John Grisham wrote about it in a novel. It's the area's hottest hangout—the FLORA-BAMA, boasting an identity all its own. Located ten minutes from Gulf Shores on the Alabama/Florida line, the place bills itself as "one of the nation's last great roadhouse watering holes."

"You never know what'll be going on here," says a local. The crowd is mixed, and so is the music—everything from country to rock and roll—and mostly original music. FLORA-BAMA offers entertainment every day of the year and attracts throngs including now-and-future-famous musicians and songwriters.

Regulars claim good music is the big draw here. You might happen on a folk singer holding court or six bands on three stages in different sections nightly (in season). They swap sets, so it's possible to hear up to twelve bands in one evening. Several Nashville regulars perform and record at FLORA-BAMA.

"There's more original music here than anyplace I've ever been," says soundman Rodeo Joe (aka the "Sound Clown"). "It's one of the things that appeals to me. We make and sell a lot of different albums here."

The party heats up after five, and the parking lot gets full fast. Though success often invites duplication, FLORA-BAMA's idiosyncratic style and haphazard floor plan make cloning a remote possibility. Beyond the storefront package shop through room after rambling room, one ultimately finds a large deck overlooking the Gulf of Mexico. Here's the best vantage point for watching the annual Interstate Mullet Toss, held the last weekend in April. (What's a mullet toss? An event on the beach where people vie for the dubious distinction of pitching a dead fish the greatest distance—from Florida to Alabama.)

If your April calendar is too full to fit in the Mullet Toss, there's always next January 1 and the Polar Bear Dip. After testing the Gulf of Mexico's cold waters, you can warm up with a serving of black-eyed peas—the traditional Southern dish declared to bring good luck throughout the year. (The luck intensifies if you consume collards or other greens, and adding hog jowl almost guarantees more luck than you can stand.)

Otherwise you can meander around, buy souvenirs, consume beverages, visit the Beach Oyster Bar, eat crab claws or Royal Reds (the very best of steamed shrimp), purchase lottery tickets, or converse with other patrons. The person standing next to you might have a total of five dollars in his jeans pocket or five million on his Personal Worth statement.

Located at 17401 Perdido Key Drive, FLORA-BAMA (334–980–5119 or 904–492–0611) opens daily 8:30 A.M. and shuts down at 2:30 A.M. Those who celebrate with too much abandon can take advantage of the Flora-Bama Taxi/Limo (904–492–7664) for a ritzy ride back to their quarters.

While exploring Orange Beach, once home to myriad orange trees, search out **Bayside Grill** (334–981–4899) at Sportsman Marina. Located at 27842 Canal Road, the eatery promises lunch, dinner, and sunsets on the deck. Owner/chef Greg Bushmohle features Creole and Caribbean cuisine in a casual setting. Ask about the fresh catch of the day with several choices, grilled to perfection, and served with Cuban yellow rice and steamed fresh vegetables. (During my visit, cobia, a migratory fish that passes through the area during certain months— April and May are the best times to catch it—was on the menu.) Moderate prices. Hours are 11:30 A.M. to 9:00 P.M. Monday through Thursday and 11:30 A.M. to 10:00 P.M. on weekends.

You might want to headquarter at **Gulf State Park Resort,** about 4 miles east of Gulf Shores. The park's facilities include a restaurant, golf course, fishing pier, tennis courts, and campsites with all the amenities plus miles of bright white beaches, sea oats, and sand dunes.

During the second weekend of October, seafood lovers flock to **Gulf Shores' National Shrimp Festival.** Speaking of shrimp, this is the place to walk into a seafood outlet, just after the fleet has docked, and buy your dinner fresh from coastal waters. Many area fish markets will ice-pack local seafood for travel. Just off Highway 59 in Gulf Shores, you'll find **South Port Seafoods** (334–968–7268) on the Intracoastal Waterway's north bank, east of W. C. Holmes Bridge. Third-generation owners Marilyn and Dale Lawrenz will help you select crabmeat or live crabs, shrimp, grouper, flounder, and oysters to go. Pick up some of Dale's Bama Boil seafood seasoning, too. Hours are 9:00 A.M. to 5:00 P.M. daily.

The tiny fishing village of **Bon Secour,** located west of State Route 59 between Foley and Gulf Shores, is home to several shrimp-packing operations. At some of these, you can crunch your way through oyster shells to watch the unloading process and buy the day's freshest catch directly off the boat. Look for signs along Baldwin County Route 10 that lead to several of these markets with their colorful shrimp boats on the Bon Secour River.

During the late 1700s French settlers staked a claim here, naming the area Bon Secour for "Safe Harbour." While driving around, notice the lovely little church, Our Lady of Bon Secour, framed with Spanish moss in its tree-shaded setting.

Several area eateries will cook your catch. Mike Spence, owner of **Fish Camp Restaurant** (334–968–CAMP) at 4297 Baldwin County Route 6, offers a "You hook 'em and we cook 'em!" option. Try the bottomless house salad, garlic bread, and corn fritters with a Caribbean-style

A Sunken Treasure—Discovered by Mistake

*O*nce upon a time, a Spanish ship named El Cazador *went sailing on the Gulf of Mexico. The ship, loaded with a fortune in minted silver coins, never reached its destination—New Orleans. Then on an ordinary fishing trip in August 1993, Jerry Murphy, captain of a fishing vessel named* Mistake, *brought up his nets to find—not butterfish—but ballast and clusters of encrusted coins. He'd discovered "the wreck that changed the world." This significant find prompted Murphy to call his uncle, Jim Reahard, who soon set wheels in motion by claiming the wreck (located outside state and federal boundaries) and forming the Grumpy Partnership.*

After hearing this engrossing story about a museum where visitors could see, touch, and purchase silver coins dating back to 1783, I set out for Grand Bay near the Mississippi border. And, sure enough—treasure! I saw the anchor, ship's bell, gold and silver coins, sword handles, jewelry, china, silverware, brass buttons, and other artifacts recovered from the Spanish brigantine of war.

Jim brought me a cup of coffee, and his wife, Myrna, showed me displays of photographs documenting the recovery. The Reahards spend much of their time these days dealing with matters from research to reclaiming the treasure. Their daughter, Debbie Hale, works as preservationist. Through a painstaking process she transforms clumps of corroded coins into shiny polished pieces of eight and reales.

Working with the Spanish archives in Seville, Jim started fitting the puzzle together. He explained that the El Cazador sailed from Veracruz, Mexico, on January 11, 1784, bound for New Orleans in Spanish-owned Louisiana with silver to bolster the sagging economy. "We don't know why the ship sank," Jim says. "We can only speculate." The silver's loss drained a declining economy even more, and Spain's North American grip gradually weakened, forcing the Spanish king to sell his holdings to Napoleon.

I found both a treasure and a fascinating history lesson at **El Cazador Museum** *(334–865–0128), housed in a former bank building at 10329 Freeland Avenue. Museum hours run from 10:00 A.M. to 4:00 P.M. Thursday through Saturday. Admission is free.*

To peep into the museum's treasure trove, visit its Web site at www.elcazador.com.

seafood and pasta dish or a house specialty like sautéed scallops or crawfish tails. Open daily at 11:00 A.M., the restaurant serves till 9:00 P.M. every night except Saturday, when closing time is 10:00 P.M. Moderate prices. Call for specific directions.

After dipping into the Gulf of Mexico's foaming waves and basking in the sunshine, you may want to sally forth to other points of interest, such as historic ***Fort Morgan*** (334–540–7125). Located at the end of a scenic drive 22 miles west of Gulf Shores on State Route 180, the fort—built to guard Mobile Bay-played a major role during the Civil War. At the Battle of Mobile Bay on August 5, 1864, "torpedoes" (underwater mines) were strung across the channel to stop the Union fleet from entering. This strategy failed when Adm. David Farragut issued his famous command, "Damn the torpedoes—full speed ahead!"

Today's visitors can explore vaulted corridors and peer into dark rooms of this historic fort, named in honor of Revolutionary War hero Gen. Daniel Morgan. Designed by Simon Bernard, a French engineer and former aide-de-camp to Napoleon, the five-pointed star structure pays tribute to the craftsmanship of men who labored from 1819 to 1834. As technology changed, the original fort continued to be modified and upgraded, says curator Mike Bailey. In the museum, exhibits cover military history from the fort's early days through World War II. Except for major holidays, the museum is open daily from 9:00 A.M. to 5:00 P.M., and the fort is open from 8:00 A.M. till 5:00 P.M. in winter and 6:00 P.M. during summer months. Modest admission.

After seeing Fort Morgan you may want to board the Mobile Bay Ferry for a visit to **Fort Gaines** on Dauphin Island. The ferry transports passengers and vehicles between the two forts at ninety-minute intervals. Call (334) 540–7787 for specific times and current rates.

Don't miss nearby **Bellingrath Gardens and Home** (334–973–2365 or 800–247–8420), located at Theodore about 20 miles south of Mobile. Once a veritable jungle, the sixty-five-acre wonderland lures visitors year-round. Because of south Alabama's climate, you can expect gorgeous displays of blossoms here, whatever the season. Upon arrival you'll receive a map illustrating the layout of the six gardens linked by bridges, walkways, streams, lakes, and lily-filled ponds. (Be sure to wear your walking shoes.)

After exploring the gardens you may want to tour the former home of Bessie and Walter Bellingrath (he was an early Coca-Cola executive). The house contains outstanding collections of Dresden china, Meissen figurines, and antique furnishings. The world's largest public exhibit of porcelain sculptures by Edward Marshall Boehm is on display in the visitors lounge. Separate admission fees for gardens and home. The gardens are open daily from 8:00 A.M. to dusk.

To tiptoe through the tulips or see what else might be in bloom via the Internet, click on www.Bellingrath.org.

Save plenty of time for Mobile, a city famous for its magnificent live oaks, some reputed to be more than 400 years old. Trimmed in silvery Spanish moss, the enormous trees spread their branching canopies over city streets. Always magical, Mobile is especially so during spring, when masses of azaleas explode into vibrant pinks, reds, and magentas, making the Church Street area, DeTonti Square, Oakleigh Garden, Spring Hill, and other historic districts more beautiful than ever. March is the month to view the azaleas at their vibrant peak. During the annual *Azalea Trail Festival,* you can follow the signs along a 37-mile route that winds past lovely homes ranging in style from Greek Revival and Italianate to Southern Creole. (Mobile's own "Creole cottage," adapted for the local clime, evolved from the French Colonial form).

Be sure to stop by *Fort Condé* at 150 Royal Street, a stone's throw away, for some background on Alabama's oldest city. Mobile has been governed by France, England, Spain, the Republic of Alabama, the Confederate States of America, and the United States. Built in 1711, Fort Condé was once home base for the sprawling French Louisiana territory, and a re-created version now serves as a living-history museum. Soldiers in period French uniforms greet visitors, guiding them through the com-

Indulge Your Sweet Tooth at Three Georges

*L*ong a local tradition, **Three Georges** *(334–433–6725) at 226 Dauphin Street has been tempting Mobilians and lucky visitors with luscious hand-dipped chocolates, heavenly hash, pralines, divinity, and many varieties of fudge—from buttermilk to Mardi Gras. George Pappas founded this enterprise, the city's oldest candy company, in 1917. Marble-based cases and original glass candy jars hold a rainbow assortment of jelly beans and rock candy. Current owner George— oops—Scott Gonzales shared this recipe for his ever-popular Buttermilk Fudge (my favorite).*

Buttermilk Fudge

1 cup buttermilk

¹/₂ cup margarine

3 tablespoons light corn syrup

2 cups sugar

1 teaspoon vanilla

2 cups pecans, chopped (optional)

Butter 9-inch square pan and set aside. In saucepan, combine buttermilk, margarine, corn syrup, baking soda, and sugar. Cook on medium-high heat, stirring occasionally until mixture boils. Scrape down sides of pan if sugar crystals form. Cook to 236 degrees (soft ball). Remove from heat and let stand until mixture cools to 210 degrees. Add vanilla and pecans. Stir until mixture becomes creamy. Pour into pan and refrigerate until firm (about 3 hours). Cut into squares.

plex with its thick walls and low-slung doors. A succession of exhibits and dioramas tell the city's story, and part of that story is the birth of Mardi Gras-Mobilians celebrated America's first Mardi Gras in 1703. Today's Mardi Gras festivities, which extend over a two-month period, feature twenty-two spectacular parades and magnificent balls.

Near the fort you'll see **Roussos** (334–433–3322) at 166 South Royal Street. Although celebrated for its fresh seafood, Roussos offers a variety of menu items including Greek salads, chicken, and steak. You might start with gumbo (made from a secret Creole recipe used by Mr. George when he started the business three decades ago) and then order the sautéed crabmeat. Hours are 11:00 A.M. to 10:00 P.M. Monday through Saturday.

More Mardi Gras memorabilia is displayed in the **Museum of Mobile,** located at 355 Government Street. Here you'll see a mezzanine of lavish hand-beaded gowns worn by former Mardi Gras queens. Other displays cover the area's history from prehistoric times to the present.

Only a block away you'll find the **Malaga Inn** (334–438–4701 or 800–235–1586) at 359 Church Street. A charming place to make your base, this quaint hotel started out as twin townhouses in 1862—the families of sisters shared a patio between their mirror-image houses. In 1967 the historic structures were joined by a connector and converted into a hotel.

Individually decorated rooms and suites are furnished with antiques or nostalgic reproductions. You'll enjoy relaxing in the inn's garden courtyard with its flowing fountain, umbrella-topped tables, and surrounding galleries of ornamental ironwork. *Mayme's* at the Malaga Inn offers contemporary cuisine with French flair in the courtyard or carriage house. For dinner reservations call (334) 438–9383. Rates range from standard to moderate.

Several mansions, including the **Richards-DAR House** (334–434–7320), open their doors to the public not only during spring tours but throughout the year. Located at 256 North Joachim Street in De Tonti Square, this 1860 Italianate antebellum home is noted for its "frozen lace" ironwork that decorates the facade in an elaborate pattern. Be sure to notice the etched ruby Bohemian glass framing the entrance. Other fine features include a suspended staircase, Carrara marble mantels, and striking brass and crystal chandeliers signed by Cornelius. In the rear wing you'll find a gift shop. Except for major holidays, the home, operated by the Daughters of the American Revolution, is open from 10:00 A.M. to 4:00 P.M. Tuesday through Saturday and from 1:00 to 4:00 P.M. on Sunday. The last tour starts at 3:30 P.M. Admission.

Richards-DAR House

You may also want to tour the **Oakleigh Historic Complex** in its serene oak-shaded setting at 350 Oakleigh Place. The guides dress in authentic costumes of the 1830s to conduct tours through an 1833 antebellum house-museum filled with early Victorian, Empire, and Regency furnishings.

Only a couple of blocks from Oakleigh stands another handsome historic home, *Towle House* (334–432–6440 or 800–938–6953), at 1104 Montauk Avenue. This former school makes a marvelous base for exploring and enjoying Mobile. The circa 1874 classic Italianate-style structure underwent meticulous refurbishing during its conversion to a bed-and-breakfast. With special attention to creature comforts, the home offers period antiques, spacious rooms, and more.

Owner-innkeepers Carolyn and Felix Vereen returned to their native Mobile after pursuing careers elsewhere. They welcome the travel-weary with good cheer, evening cocktails, and delicious hors d'oeuvres, a fitting prelude to a fine dinner in the Port City. Depending on your cravings, Carolyn will recommend a wonderful restaurant, make reservations, and provide directions. Guests start their day with a five-course gourmet breakfast prepared by Felix. Rates are standard to moderate. E-mail the Vereens at TOWLEBB@aol.com or log onto www.towle-house.com.

No visit to the Port City would be complete without scaling the decks of the *Battleship U.S.S. Alabama* (334–433–2703 or 800 GANGWAY), moored in Mobile Bay. This renowned vessel played the role of the U.S.S. *Missouri* in the movie *Under Siege*, starring Steven Seagal.

Now the focal point of the 155-acre park on Battleship Parkway just off the I-10 causeway, the U.S.S. *Alabama* served in every major engagement in the pacific during World War II, apparently leading a charmed life throughout her thirty-seven months of active duty. She earned not only nine battle stars but also the nickname "Lucky A" (from her crew of 2,500) because she emerged unscathed from the heat of each battle.

You can explore below and upper decks and roam through the captain's cabin, officers' staterooms, messing and berthing spaces, and crew's galley. Authentic touches include calendar girl pinups and background music, with such singers as Bing Crosby and Frank Sinatra crooning songs popular during the 1940s.

Anchored beside the battleship, the U.S.S. *Drum* gives visitors a chance to thread their way through a submarine and marvel at how a crew of seventy-two men could live, run their ship, and fire torpedoes while confined to such tight quarters. You'll also see the U.S.S. *Alabama* Battleship Memorial Park's new Aircraft Exhibit Pavilion.

Open every day except Christmas, the park can be visited from 8:00 A.M. until sunset. Admission is charged. To visit the battleship via the Internet, check out www.ussalabama.com. For more information on local attractions, call (334) 415–2006 or (800) 566–2453.

PLACES TO STAY IN SOUTHWEST ALABAMA

CAMDEN
Roland Cooper State Park
285 Deer Run Drive
(334) 682–4838

EUTAW
Kirkwood
111 Kirkwood Drive
(205) 372–9009

FAIRHOPE
Bay Breeze Guest House
742 South Mobile Street
(334) 928–8976

Church Street Inn
51 South Church Street
(334) 928–8976

GULF SHORES
Gulf State Park Resort
Hotel
365 East Beach Boulevard
(334) 948–4853 or
(800) 544–4853

The Lighthouse Resort
Motel
455 East Beach Boulevard
(334) 948–6188

MAGNOLIA SPRINGS
Magnolia Springs
Bed & Breakfast
14469 Oak Street
(334) 965–7321 or
(800) 965–7321

MARION
Myrtle Hill
303 and 305 West
Lafayette Street
(334) 683–9095

MOBILE
Adam's Mark Hotel
64 South Water Street
(334) 438–4000 or
(800) 444–ADAM

Malaga Inn
359 Church Street
(334) 438–4701 or
(800) 235–1586

Towle House
1104 Montauk Avenue
(334) 432–6440 or
(800) 938–6953

MONROEVILLE
Best Western Inn
4419 South Alabama
Avenue
(334) 575–9999 or
(800) 528–1234

ORANGE BEACH
Perdido Beach Resort
27200 Perdido Beach
Boulevard
(334) 981–9811 or
(800) 634–8001

POINT CLEAR
Marriott's Grand Hotel
1 Grand Boulevard
(334) 928–9201 or
(800) 544–9933

SELMA
Grace Hall
506 Lauderdale Street
(334) 875–5744

St. James Hotel
1200 Water Avenue
(334) 872–3234 or
(888) 264–2788

**PLACES TO EAT IN
SOUTHWEST ALABAMA**

DEMOPOLIS
The Jolly Roger
Demopolis Yacht Basin
(334) 289–8103

The Stables
Walnut Street
Demopolis
(334) 289–2967

EUTAW
The Cotton Patch
Union Road
(205) 372–4235

Main Street Eatery and Deli
208 Street
(205) 372–0209

FAUNSDALE
Ca-John's Faunsdale
Bar & Grill
Main Street
(334) 628–3240

For More Information about Southwest Alabama

Alabama Gulf Coast Convention & Visitors Bureau
23685 Perdido Beach Boulevard
Orange Beach 36561
P.O. Box 457; Gulf Shores 36547
(334) 794–1510 or (800) 982–8562
Web site: www.gulfshores.com
e-mail: hmalone@gulfshores.com

Demopolis Area County Chamber of Commerce
102 East Washington Street
P.O. Box 667
Demopolis 36732; (334) 289–0270
Web site: www.demopolis.com

Eastern Shore County Chamber of Commerce
327 Fairhope Avenue; Fairhope 36532
(334) 928–6387

Mobile Area Convention & Visitors Corporation
P.O. Box 204; Mobile 36601–0204
(334) 415–2000 or (800) 5MOBILE
Web site: www.mobile.org
e-mail: info@mobile.org

Selma/Dallas County Chamber of Commerce
513 Lauderdale Street
P.O. Drawer D; Selma 36702
(334) 875–7241 or (800) 45–SELMA
e-mail: selmaofc@zebra.net
Web site: www.olcg.com/selma/

MARION
The Gateway Inn
1615 State Route 5 South
(334) 683–2582

SELMA
Major Grumbles
1 Grumbles Alley
(334) 872–2006

Tally-Ho Restaurant
509 Mangum Avenue
(334) 872–1390

Troup House Restaurant
1200 Water Avenue
(334) 872–3234

LAVACA
Ezell's Fish Camp
near Lavaca
(205) 654–2205

CAMDEN
Gaines Ridge Dinner Club
Alabama 10
(334) 682–9707

ORANGE BEACH
Bayside Grill
27842 Canal Road
(334) 981–4899

MOBILE
Drayton Place
101 Dauphin Street
(334) 432–7438

Gus's Azalea Manor &
Courtyard
751 Dauphin Street
(334) 433–GUSS

Justine's Courtyard
& Carriageway
80 St. Michael Street
(334) 438–4535

Mayme's (at the
Malaga Inn)
359 Church Street
(334) 438–4701

The Pillars
1757 Government Street
(334) 478–6341

Port City Brewery
225 Dauphin Street
(334) 438–2739

Roussos
166 Royal Street
(334) 433–3322

Spot of Tea
310 Dauphin Street
(334) 433–9009

GULF SHORES
Fish Camp Restaurant
4297 Baldwin County
Route 6
(334) 968–CAMP

FOLEY
The Gift Horse
209 West Laurel Avenue
(334) 943–3663 or
(800) FOLEYAL

LILLIAN
Miss Kitty's Restaurant
Kit's Marina on
Perdido Bay
(334) 962–2701 or
(800) 844–2701

POINT CLEAR
The Wash House
Restaurant
U.S. Highway 98, 1 mile
south of Marriott's
Grand Hotel
(334) 928–1500

**MAINSTREAM ATTRACTIONS
WORTH SEEING IN
SOUTHWEST ALABAMA**

**The Exploreum Museum
of Science,**
*65 Government Street,
Mobile; (334) 476–6873.
This hands-on facility
features fascinating
exhibits from the world
of science.*

The Museum of Mobile,
*355 Government Street,
Mobile; (334) 208–
7569. View past Mardi
Gras costumes and dip
into Mobile's interesting
history here. Free
admission.*

Index

A

Adams' Antiques, 25
Adam's Mark Hotel, 170
Airport Restaurant, 132
Alabama Constitution Village, 4
Alabama Department of Archives
  and History, 124
Alabama Fan Club and Museum, 35
Alabama Jazz Hall of Fame, 82
Alabama Jubilee, 43
Alabama Museum of
  Natural History, 88
Alabama Music Hall of Fame, 65
Alabama Renaissance Faire, 52
Alabama Shakespeare
  Festival, 122
Alabama Sports Hall of Fame, 79
Alabama Tale Tellin' Festival, 141
Alabama Women's Hall of Fame, 143
Alamuchee Covered Bridge, 149–50
Albertville, 27
Alexander City, 98
Aliceville, 92
All Steak, The, 59
Amy's Young House, 125, 132
Animal House Zoological Park, 46
Anniston Museum of Natural
  History, 70
Arab, 26
Arlington Antebellum Home and
  Gardens, 102
Arman's at Park Lane, 101
Art on the Lake Show, 32
Ashville, 67
Athens, 39
At Home, 11
Auburn Grille, 131
Auburn Links at Mill Creek, 11
Auburn University Historic
  District, 108
Auburn University Hotel and
  Conference Center, 131
Ave Maria Grotto, 60
Azalea Trail Festival, 166

B

Baldwin County Heritage
  Museum, 160
Baldwin Museum of Art, 158
Basket Case, 31
Battle-Friedman House, 89
Battleship U.S.S. *Alabama*, 169
Bay Breeze Guest House, 157, 169
Bayou LaBatre, viii
Bayside Grill, 163, 171
Bellingrath Gardens and Home, 165
Benedikt's Restaurant, 62, 65
Berman Museum, 70
Best Western, 33, 170
Best Western Dothan Inn & Suites, 131
Betty's Bar-B-Q, Inc., 100
Bevill's Conference and Hotel, 33
Big Bob Gibson's, 41
Big Mill Antique Mall, 20
Biophilia Nature Center, 161
Birmingham Botanical Gardens, 78
Birmingham Civil Rights
  Institute, 81
Birmingham Marriott, 99
Birmingham Museum of Art, 80
Birmingham Zoo, 102
Blessing of the Shrimp Fleet, viii
Blount County Covered Bridges, 60
Bluff Hall, 146
Boaz Bed and Breakfast, 27
Boaz Shopper's Paradise, 25
Boll Weevil Monument, 118
Bombay Cafe, 100
Bon Secour, 163
Boux Rae's Four Beans Cafe, 132

INDEX

Bridgeport, 12–14
Bright Star, The, 83
Brown Chapel African Methodist
    Episcopal Church, 138
Brown's Pottery, 56
Bryant, Bear, v
Bubba's, 35
Buck's Pocket State Park, 16
Burritt Museum and Park, 6

C

Cafe Berlin, 35
Cafe DuPont, 101
Cafe LeMamas, 73, 100
Cahaba, 142
Ca-John's Faunsdale Bar
    & Grill, 144, 170
Caldwell's, 16, 35
Camden, 152
Capote, Truman, 153
Capps Cove, 63
Capstone, The, 85–91
Caroline's Gifts, 58
Carriage House, 43
Carrollton, 87
Catfish Cabin, 34
Cecil's on the Lake, 103, 131
Cedars Plantation, The, 73, 100
Center for Cultural Arts, 23
Chattahoochee Trace, 67
Cheaha State Park, 100
Cherokee, 55
Cherokee County Historical
    Museum, 22
Cherokee Pow Wow and Green
    Corn Festival, 23
Chewacla State Park, 131
Chewalla, 132
Children's Harbor, 103
China Luck, 101
Choice, The, 34
Christmas on the River, 147

Church House Inn, 34
Church of St. Michael and
    All Angels, 71
Church Street Inn, 156, 169
Civil Rights Memorial, 125
Clarkson Covered Bridge, 58
Classical Fruits, 45, 65
Claunch Cafe, 65
Claybank Church, 118
Clayton, 116
Clementine's, 35
Cliffs, The, 18–19
Cloudmont Ski and Golf
    Resort, 18
Cobb Lane Restaurant, 77, 100
Cocopelli Gourmet Cafe, 89, 101
Coleman Center, The, 151
Collinsville, 21
Columbiana, 96
Comfort Inn, 131
Comfort Suites Hotel, 63
Confederate Memorial Park, 96
Cook's Natural Science
    Museum, 41
Coon Dog Memorial
    Graveyard, 50
Cornwall Furnace Park, 22
Cotton Patch, The, 170
Country Corner, 17
Country Inn & Suites, 63
Court Street Cafe, 51
Courtland, 46
Courtyard By Marriott, 34, 100, 131
Covered Bridge Festival, 61
Covington's, 32
Cragsmere Manna
    Restaurant, 19, 35
Crawmamma's, 32
Crawdaddys, Too, 9, 35
Crenshaw House Bed
    and Breakfast, 108
Crimson Inn, 88, 100

Crow's Nest, 17
Cullman County Museum, 58
Culp, Jesse, 29
Curry's on Johnston Street, 43
Cypress Inn, 86, 101

D

DAEDALUS, 160
Dancing Rabbit, The, 151
Dancy-Polk House, 42, 63
Daphne, 156
Decatur, 41
Demopolis, 147
Deli Warehouse Cafe, 59
DePalma's, 89, 101
DeSoto Caverns Park, 75
DeSoto Falls, 19
DeSoto State Park, 19
Dessie's Kountry Chef, 17, 35
Dexter Avenue King Memorial
    Baptist Church, 124
Dismals Canyon, 54
Dixie Den, 56, 64
Dogwood Manor, 6
Dolphin Ecology Tour, 160–61
Donald E. Davis Arboretum, 108
Dothan, 116–18
Doublehead Resort & Lodge, 47, 63
Double Springs, 57
Downtown Choo-Choo
    Restaurant, 12, 35
Drayton Place, 171
Dreamland, 85, 101
Dual Destiny, 57

E

Eagle's Nest, 17
EarlyWorks, 4
Easterday Antiques, 109
Eastern Shore Art Center, 157
Econo Lodge, 33
Edmund Pettus Bridge, 135

El Camino Real, 35
El Cazador, 164
El Cazador Museum, 164
Elizabeth Alexandria, 44
Embassy Suites, 131
Emporium at Hickory
    Crossing, The, 44
Enterprise, 118
Eufaula, 114
Eunice's Country Kitchen, 5, 35
Eutaw, 147
Eva Marie's, 64
Exploreum Museum of
    Science, 171
Ezell's Fish Camp, 151, 171

F

Fagin's Thieves Market, 115
Fairfield Inn, 131
Fairhope, 156
Fant's Department Store, 31
Farmer's Exchange, 33
Fendall Hall, 115
Finishing Touches, 154
First Monday, 7
First White House of the
    Confederacy, 124
Fish Camp Restaurant, 163, 171
Five Points South, 77
FLORA–BAMA, 162
Florence, 49
Foley, 158
Food Basket, The, 28
Fort Condé, 166
Fort Gaines, 165
Fort Morgan, 164
Fort Payne Depot Museum, 20
Fort Payne Opera House, 20
Fort Toulouse–Jackson Park, 128–29
Founder's Hall, 40
Four Points Tuscaloosa-Capstone
    by Sheraton, 100

INDEX

Fox Valley, 101
Freedom Festival, 28
Friday's, 35

G

Gadsden, 23
Gaines Ridge Dinner
  Club, 152, 171
Gainesville, 149
Gaineswood, 145
Garland House, 118, 132
Gateway Inn, The, 143, 171
General Joe Wheeler Plantation
  Home, 46
George's Steak Pit, 65
Gerhart Chamber Music Festival, 32
German Sausage Festival, 160
Gift Horse, The, 159, 171
Giovanni's Pizza Italian
  Restaurant, 34
Globe, The, 90, 101
Goose Pond Colony, 9
Gorgas House, 88
Gorham's Bluff, 9
Gourdie Shop, The, 17
Grace Hall, 139, 170
Gramma's, 100
Green Bottle Grill, 1, 35
Green Hills Grille, 35
Greensboro, 143
Gulf Shores, 161
Gulf Shores' National Shrimp
  Festival, 163
Gulf State Park Resort, 163, 169
Gulf States Paper Corporation
  Headquarters, 86
Guntersville, 9
Guntersville Museum and
  Cultural Center, 32
Gus's Azalea Manor &
  Courtyard, 171

H

Hambrick Cave, 30
Hampton Inn, 33, 63, 100
Hank Williams Museum, 126
Hank Williams Sr. Boyhood Home
  'and Museum, 130
Harrison Brothers Hardware
  Store, 4
Hartselle, 44
Heart of Dixie Railroad
  Museum, 96
Heritage Hall, 74
Heritage House, The, 110, 131
Heritage Museum, 154
Highlands Bar & Grill, 77, 100
Historic Twickenham District, 3
Hitching Post, The, 17
Holiday Dreams, 89
Holiday Inn & Suites, 63
Holiday Inn Anniston/Oxford, 100
Holiday Inn East, 131
Holiday Inn Express, 33, 99
Holiday Inn Redmont, 99
Holiday Inn Resort Hotel, 33
Holiday Inn South, 131
Holmes Medical Museum, 158–59
Horseshoe Bend National
  Military Park, 99
Hot and Hot Fish Club, 101
Hotel Talisi, 103, 131, 133
House of Quilts & Antiques, 69
House of Serendipity, The, 94
Houston Memorial Library
  and Museum, 40
Hunt's Steak, Seafood, and
  Oyster Bar, 132
Huntsville, 1–7
Huntsville Depot Transportation
  Museum, 1
Huntsville Hilton, 34
Huntsville Marriott, 34
Huntsville Museum of Art, 35

Hurn-Thach-Boozer-McNiell House, 39

I

Imagination Place Children's Museum, 23
"Incident at Looney's Tavern, The," 57
Indian Mound and Museum, 49
International Motorsports Hall of Fame, 102
Inzer House, 67
Irondale Cafe, The, 79, 101
Isabel Anderson Comer Museum and Arts Center, 97
Ivy Green, 48

J

Jameson Inn, 33, 100, 131
Jasmine Hill Gardens and Outdoor Museum, 128
Jeffrey, 140–41
Jemison Inn Bed and Breakfast, The, 94
Jemison Trade Center, 95
Jesse Owens Memorial Park, 44
Jimmy's at Brookwood, 101
Joe Wheeler State Park Lodge, 63
John Looney House, 67
Jolly Roger, The, 147, 170
Jones Archaeological Museum, 91
Joseph T. Smitherman Historic Building, 138
Jubilee, 156
Justine's Courtyard & Carriageway, 171

K

KC's Coyote Cafe, 35
Keller, Helen, 48
Kendall Manor Inn, 114, 131
Kennedy–Douglass Center for the Arts, 52

Kentuck Art Center, 90
Kentuck Festival of Arts, 90
Key West Inn, 33, 63, 100
Kirkwood, 148, 169
Kozy's, 101

L

Lake Guntersville Bed and Breakfast, 31
Lake Guntersville State Park, 29
Lakepoint Resort, 112, 131, 132
Landmark, The, 62, 65
Landmark Park, 117
Landry's Seafood House, 35
Laurel Cottage, 63
Lavaca, 151
Lee County Historical Society Museum, 106
Lee, Harper, 155
Lek's Railroad Thai, 132
Leroy Brown Monument, 112–13
Liberty Restaurant, 35
Lighthouse Resort Motel, The, 169
Limestone Manor, 63
Lite Side, The, 35
Little River Cafe, 34
Little River Canyon National Preserve, 19
Little Village Shop, 27
Livingston, 149
Loachapoka Historic District, 106
Loachapoka Syrup Sop and Historical Fair, 107
Lodge at Gorham's Bluff, The, 34, 35
Loeb Center, 125
Log Cabin Restaurant and Deli, 17, 35
Log Cabin Stagecoach Stop at Cold Water, The, 47
Looney's Amphitheater and Park, 57
Los Mexicanos, 100
LOUISIANA The Restaurant, 54, 65

Lovelace Athletic Museum and Hall of Honor, 108
Lowndesboro, 129
Lucas Tavern, 125

M

Magnolia Grove, 144
Magnolia Springs Bed and Breakfast, 158, 169
Main Street Eatery and Deli, 170
Major Grumbles, 137, 171
Malaga Inn, 167, 170
Malbis Greek Orthodox Church, 155
Manci's Antique Club, 155
Mardi Gras, 167
Marengo, 129, 132
Marietta L. Johnson School of Organic Education, 157
Marion, 142
Marriott's Grand Hotel, 157, 170
Martha's Place, 132
Martin House, The, 130, 131
Mayme's, 167, 171
Mayor's Office, 111
McWane Center, 102
Mellow Mushroom, 131
Mentone, 16
Mentone Springs Hotel, 16
Mercedes-Benz Visitors Center, 85
Mezzanine, 102
Mill Street Deli, The, 34
Miss Jean's Cajun Connection Restaurant, 34
Miss Kitty's Restaurant, 160, 171
Mistletoe Bough, 98, 99
Mobile, 165–69
Monroeville, 153
Monte Sano Mountain, 6
Montevallo, 94
Montevallo Grille, 94
Montgomery, 121

Montgomery Museum of Fine Arts, 122
Montgomery Zoo, 125, 133
Mooresville, 37
Mossy Grove School House Restaurant, 119, 133
Moulton, 45
Moundville Archaeological Park, 91
Moundville Native American Festival, 91
Mountain Brook Inn, The, 99
Mountain Laurel Inn, 34
Mountain Top Flea Market, 25
Muffins 50's Cafe, 22–23
Muscle Shoals, 49
Museum of East Alabama, The, 110
Museum of Mobile, 167, 171
Myrtle Hill, 143, 169
Myrtlewood, 93, 99

N

Nabeel's Cafe, 82, 101
Natchez Trace Parkway, 55
National Peanut Festival, 117
National Voting Rights Museum, 135
Natural Bridge, 55
Nebrig–Howell House Antiques, 42
Neena's Lakeside Grille, 35
New Orleans Transfer, 65
Noccalula Falls and Park, 24
Noel-Ramsey House, 144
North Alabama Railroad Museum, 7
Northport, 90

O

Oakleigh Historic Complex, 168
Oak Mountain State Park, 100
Oakville Indian Mounds, 45
Oakwood Cemetery, 126
Octagon House, 116

Old Alabama Town, 125
Old Cahawba Archaeological
   Park, 142
Old Cahawba Festival, 142
Old Cotaco Opera House, 43
Old Depot Museum, 138
Old Harbin Hotel, 84, 100
Old Live Oak Cemetery, 141
Old Mexico, 132
Old Mill Restaurant, The, 132
Old Monroe County
   Courthouse, 153
Old Mountain State Park, 76
Old State Bank, 42
Olde Warehouse, The, 34
Ol' Heidelberg, 35
Oneonta, 60
Opelika, 109
Opp, 118–19
Orange Beach, 161
Orangevale Plantation, 74, 100
Ordeman-Shaw House, 125
Original Old Smokehouse
   Bar-B-Q, The, 100

P

Panache at Rose Hill, 122, 132
Paul W. Bryant Museum, 87
Payne's, 8, 35
Peach Park, 96
Perdido Beach Resort, 170
Performing Arts Center, 159
Petals from the Past, 95
Pickens County Courthouse, 87
Pickwick Hotel, 99
Pike Pioneer Museum, 120
Pillars, The, 171
Plantation House Restaurant, 92, 100
Pleasant Hill, 41
Poarch Creek Reservation, 154
Point Mallard Park, 65
Poke Salat Festival, 32–33

Pope's Tavern, 53
Poplar Head Mule Co. Brewpub
   & Grill, 132
Port City Brewery, 171
Potager, the , 91
Prattville, 129
Provence Market, 59
Punta Clara Kitchen, 157

R

Ramsay Conference Center, 94, 100
Rattlesnake Rodeo, 118
Raven Haven, 17
Red Bluff Cottage, 127, 131
Red's Little School House, 120, 132
Renaissance Grill, 64
Renaissance Tower, 49
Reynolds Hall, 94
Reynolds Historical Library, 81
Richards-DAR House, 167
Rikard's Mill, 153
River Heritage Museum, 154
Robert Trent Jones Golf Trail, ix
Roland Cooper State Park, 153, 169
Roses and Lace Country Inn, 67, 99
Rossi's, 101
Roussos, 167, 171
Russell Cave National
   Monument, 13–14
Russell Retail Store, 98
Ryan's Family Steak House, 34

S

Sahara Restaurant, Inc., 132
St. Andrew's Episcopal Church, 144
St. James Hotel, The, 137, 170
St. Joseph's on the Mountain, 17
St. William's Seafood Festival, 32
Salem-Shotwell Covered Bridge, 111
Sallie Howard Memorial Chapel, 19
Sand Mountain, 16, 25
Sassafras Tea Room, 127, 133

INDEX

Sawmill Days, 152
Scott and Zelda Fitzgerald
    Museum, 123
Scottsboro, 7–12
Scottsboro-Jackson Heritage
    Center, 8
secret Bed & Breakfast
    Lodge, the, 21
Selma, 135
Sequoyah Caverns, 14
Shady Grove Dude Ranch, 8
Sharlotte House, 63
Shelley's Iron Gate, 43
Sheraton Birmingham Hotel, 100
Shoals, the, 49
Shorter Mansion, 114
Siegel Gallery, 141
Silvertron Cafe, 101
Simp McGhee's, 42
Sinclair's, 133
Sippin on Ashby, 150
Sipsey Wilderness, 58
Sister Sarah's Kitchen, 58
Slick Lizard Smokehouse, 84, 101
Sloss Furnaces, 78
Smith-Harrison Museum, 96
Snead State Community College
    Museum, 25
Somewhere in Time, 26
South Port Seafoods, 163
Southern Museum of Flight, 79
Spanish House, The, 30–31
Spot of Tea, 171
Springville, 69
Stables, The, 170
Stacey Rexall Drugs, 159
Stamps Inn, 33
Stanley and Mildred Rosenbaum
    House, 50
Stevenson Railroad Depot
    Museum, 11
Studio Plus, 131

Sturdivant Hall, 140
Superior Pecan Company, 116
Surfside Water Park, 109
Sylacauga, 97

T
Talladega College, 74
Talladega Superspeedway, 102
Tally-Ho Restaurant, 141, 171
Tannehill Historical State Park, 93
Tennessee Valley Old Time Fiddlers
    Convention, 40
Terra Cotta Cafe, 109, 132
Three Georges, 166
Tom Bevill Visitor Center, 91
Tom Mann's Fish World, 112
Tony's Steak Barn, 34
Top O' the River, 34, 100
Towle House, 168, 170
Triple R Bar-B-Q, 35
Trowbridges, 52, 64
Troup House Restaurant, 137, 171
Troy, 119–20
Turkeytown, 23
Tuscaloosa, 85
Tuscumbia, 47
Tuskegee Institute, 105–6
Tutwiler, The, 78, 100
Twin House, 28
Twin Pines Resort, 76, 100

U
Unclaimed Baggage Center, 8–9
U.S. Army Aviation Museum, 133
U.S. Space & Rocket Center, 36

V
Valhalla Luxury Cottages, 34
Valley Head, 14–15
Venable's, 133
Victoria, The, 71, 99
Victorian Front Porch Christmas, 110

Village Boutique, 17
Vine and Olive Colony, 146
Vintage Year, Inc., 133
VisionLand, 102
Von Braun Civic Center, 3
Vulcan, 77–78

W

W. A. Gayle Planetarium, 125
Warehouse Bistro, 133
Wash House Restaurant, The, 158, 171
Waysider Restaurant, The, 89, 102
W. C. Handy Home and Museum, 51
W. C. Handy Music Festival, 51
Weeden House Museum, 3
Weiss Lake, 21–22
Western Sirloin Steak House, 45, 65
Wetumpka, 127–28
Wheeler Wildlife Refuge, 30
Whiskey Bottle Tombstone, 116

White Oaks Inn, 55, 64
William B. Bankhead National
   Forest, 57
Willie J's, 35
WillowBrooke, 93, 99
Wilson Dam, 49
Windham, Kathryn
   Tucker, 140
Wings Sports Grille, 102
Winston Place, 15
Wiregrass Museum of Art, 117
Wood Avenue Inn, 54, 63
Wooden Nickel Restaurant, 55
Woodhaven, 14
Wren's Nest, 73
Wynfrey Hotel, The, 100

Z

Zandy Zebra, 44
Zoettl, Joseph, 60

Recipes

Buttermilk Fudge, Three Georges, 166

Buttermilk Pie with Blackberry Sauce, Panache at Rose Hill, 123

Fresh Tomato Mango Slaw, Nancy Gross, 24

Moussaka, Nabeel's Cafe, 83

Shrimp and Corn Chowder, LOUISIANA The Restaurant, 54

Spicy Baked Shrimp with Garlic-Cheese Grits, The Landmark, 62

About the Author

Gay N. Martin, who lives in Alabama, enjoys writing about travel in the Southeast. Her articles and travel pieces have appeared in *Modern Bride,* the *Boston Herald, Kiwanis,* the *Atlanta Journal-Constitution, The London Free Press,* the *San Antonio Express-News,* the *Seattle Post-Intelligencer, Far East Traveler, The Birmingham News, The Times-Picayune,* the *Grand Rapids Press,* and other publications. She has won numerous writing awards for fiction and nonfiction in state, regional, and national competitions. She is also the author of Globe Pequot's *Louisiana: Off the Beaten Path* and *Alabama's Historic Restaurants and Their Recipes,* published by John F. Blair.

Before embarking on her writing career, Martin taught high school for eleven years, served as resource coordinator of her school's program for gifted and talented students, and sponsored the school newspaper. She and her husband, a dentist, have five children.